IDEALS AND POLITICS

IDEALS &

POLITICS

New York Intellectuals and Liberal Democracy

1820–1880

EDWARD K. SPANN

1972

STATE UNIVERSITY OF NEW YORK PRESS

ALBANY

Ideals and Politics

First Edition

Published by State University of New York Press

99 Washington Avenue, Albany, New York 12210

© 1972 State University of New York

Printed in Lebanon

Designed by Zahi N. Khuri

Library of Congress Cataloging in Publication Data

Spann, Edward K   1931–

Ideals and politics.

Bibliography: p.

1. New York (City) — Intellectual life.   2. New York
(City) — Biography. I. Title.

F128.44.S73   917.47'1'033   72–7328

ISBN 0–87395–083–6

ISBN 0–87395–183–2 (microfiche)

CONTENTS

To: Jo, L., S., B., J., Mother, and Dad, with love.

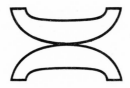

PREFACE

The best way to introduce this book probably is to indicate what it is *not* intended to be. It is not a detailed biography or a set of biographical essays. It is not a formal study of a history of ideas, politics, or aesthetics. Nor is it an attempt to apply the doctrines and principles of the social sciences to the investigation of the past. Each of these forms of historical endeavor is valid and important; to each, I acknowledge a great debt. It seems to me, however, that their virtues have often been won at the expense of one fundamental human truth: Society, whether past or present, is almost perversely varied, complex, and contradictory. What these kinds of endeavor lack is a full appreciation of the diverse and shifting relationships that draw people together—and drive them apart. As a result, such works, while perceptive in grasping the general principles of society and human nature, most often fail to convey a sense of the vital fact, central to our predicament as social beings, that every man is obstinately himself.

What I set out to do here was to write a historian's version of the novels of C. P. Snow, studies of the interplay of human personalities and the clash of attitudes within a group devoted to a common enterprise. The result is this group biography. The historian, of course, works in a discipline that differs from that of the novelist. He cannot know his subjects as intimately as can the imaginative writer, since he cannot invent personalities and must accept the direction of his sources. In one sense, this is a weakness, but it is also the source of much of the excitement and value of history; for the indeterminacies the historian must work with are the challenges all men must face and resolve.

Initially, I attempted to center this work around four major New York writers: William Cullen Bryant, James Fenimore Cooper, Walt Whitman, and Herman Melville. But it soon became obvious that they did not have sufficient characteristics in common to be considered as a group. Melville simply did not belong, while Whitman, though he suited my preconceptions of what the group should be, did not share with the remaining two writers the close and persisting ties on which to base a study of interpersonal relations. This left Bryant and Cooper. No intimate bond ever developed between them, yet their careers, different though they were, diverged like the two joined sides of a picture frame; from that relationship I built this book. Cooper was too egocentric to be the central figure, leaving Bryant to provide the necessary coherence. The poet was basically a loner who was reserved to the point of coldness, thus he superficially had no great personal magnetism to attract friends and associates. His talents, however, did draw into his sphere members of the Sedgwick family, especially Catherine, Robert, Henry Dwight, and Theodore III. Not only did the Sedgwicks strongly influence Bryant's social views but they also built a friendship with him that lasted for more than forty years. Bryant's promise as a poet also attracted the attention of Gulian C. Verplanck, who initiated an off-again, on-again friendship that survived some fifty years of political controversy. Soon I discovered that much of Bryant's pre-eminence in the group derived from his long-term work as editor of the New York *Evening Post*. It was this journalistic side that led me—and him—to William Leggett and to Bryant's editorial associate and gadfly son-in-law, Parke Godwin. And so the group completed itself.

Although in their relationships they did not always act as I would have had them do, they did furnish a rewarding opportunity to examine the interplay of attitudes among people who were very much involved in their society. On the surface, all seemingly agreed on fundamentals. All were liberal democrats in their underlying ideology. Except for Leggett and Godwin, who were too young to qualify, all came from strongly Federalist backgrounds. All initially supported Andrew Jackson, lending credence to Harriet Martineau's observation that "men of genius" joined the Jacksonian Democratic party. All built their careers in New York City. Yet, despite these broad areas of agreement, only rarely did these writers unite on the significant issues of their day. Banks, corporations government, political parties, the press, slavery, and the race question—to these matters each member responded in his own way; each became a different democrat with distinctive, though overlapping views of the nature and direction of American society.

Fortunately, the members of this group left a rich written record of editorials, novels, poems, essays, and letters, which collectively form a broad and deep source for the study of American attitudes. On the basis of this material I have attempted, following in the steps of Marvin Meyers and Robert Kelley, to determine the nature of each person's social vision in the belief that that vision was the significant point of contact between his essential character and the society he lived in. The underlying assumption here is that men are less interested in developing a philosophy to explain their world than in devising a social drama compatible with their expectations, fears, and personal values. Unlike Meyers and Kelley, I am less concerned with examining a "persuasion"—a shared vision that binds together a mass of men—than with determining the natures of the individual visions that underlie broad social attitudes.

This is a study of public as well as private and individual differences, since each member of the group, in expressing his particular vision, developed a constituency to whom and for whom he spoke. As writers and men of ideas, all the members hoped to influence the development of the American mind. Essentially, each considered himself to be working within an already established liberal democratic tradition that centered on two fundamental principles: first, equality of opportunity in its negative definition as freedom for the individual from the restraints and discriminations so characteristic of aristocratic Europe; and second, the democratic dogma that *the People*—not merely a temporary majority but Americans generally—should rule. The members of the group shared the hope of persuading the People to rid themselves of those European beliefs and practices which were antagonistic to democratic principles and, thus, to perfect their society. In sum, each of these men hoped to participate in the purification of an established social system whose very strength in tradition (European in origin) was also its weakness.

In reality, these men were forced to accept less exalted but more complex roles in the formation of American political attitudes. As

Cooper learned to his dissatisfaction, the reading public demanded to know not how to be good democrats but why the hopes raised by their apparent freedom and opportunities were often disappointed. The rapid development of the economic and political system seemed to confirm the general promise of freedom that every individual would be able to realize his talents and ambitions, but this change also acted to alter the balance of society: some men lost wealth and power while others gained and some gained less than others. Built into "progress" was frustration and anxiety—frustration because ambitions rarely could be fully achieved, anxiety because change disrupted the social and moral order on which the existing conceptions of liberal democracy were based. The most persistent question generated by this collision between the ideal and the real was not what in the system had failed but *who* had made it fail. Differences in backgrounds, temperaments, and experiences made for different answers, and so the People, as disputants, were drawn into the American political drama of conflict between the good society and its enemies.

The members of the group acted both as participants in and as narrators of this conflict. Each produced a vision differing from the others, in important details, if not in fundamentals, that won a constituency on the basis of its compatibility with the hopes and fears of a portion of the population. Thus the group shared in the formation of not one but several currents of democratic thought. Bryant and the Sedgwicks gained their widest hearing from that portion of the upward-striving middle class that wanted freedom from the restraints of government and the distractions of politics. Leggett and Godwin found the readiest reception for their ideas in the 1830s and 1840s among New Yorkers who were more radically alienated from established wealth and power than was the middle class. In contrast, both Verplanck and Cooper spoke to two increasingly disrelated portions of the established upper class: Verplanck, to the merchant–capitalists; Cooper, to the landed gentry. Collectively, the group represented the varied anxieties and aspirations of a great part of the population. Individually, the relative popularity of their visions says much about the changing nature of American society in the middle third of the nineteenth century.

All visions eventually are outrun by the society that originated them. It is significant that the views of this group developed and hardened during the period between 1828 and 1845 when the nation was preoccupied with the troublesome uncertainties of an unevenly developing political and economic system. In retrospect, it is apparent that the group spoke for the first generation of Americans to encounter seriously the problems of modern commerical–industrial society. Limited as they were by their commitment to a preindustrial past, they were unable to comprehend fully the significance of the changes that were to shape the twentieth century. Although they performed the essential service of sustaining the spirit of liberal democracy, they also served to perpetuate attitudes and policies that became decreasingly valid in a changing society. This was especially true of Bryant, to whom might be applied the rule that the greater the prestige, the more inflexible the vision. Thus the group handed on to the future a set of overlapping visions, which acted both as a bridge and as a barrier to the attainment of the democratic dream.

In essence, then, this book is a study of the life cycle of a group of Americans who attempted to find eternal answers to nineteenth century questions. As such, I hope that it will enable us to better understand both the American past and the continuing process of defining the liberal democratic tradition.

1

THE ROAD TO NEW YORK (1815-25)

Are the disappointments of the father visited upon the son? William Cullen Bryant might well have pondered that question one December day in 1815 as he walked the road in western Massachusetts from West Cummington to Plainfield. Although the journey was short, it crossed one of life's great divides, for the thin-faced young Yankee was venturing out into the world, leaving behind both home and the dreams of adolescence. The year 1815 was a promising one for the United States; two decades of domestic discord and more than two years of disturbing war had ended, opening the way for a new era of peace, power, and prosperity for the nation. But 1815 promised only further disappointments for the young man, who in his twenty-first year had been forced to suppress his fondest ambition. William Cullen Bryant was unhappy.

Both his hopes and his disappointments had been inherited from his father. An amateur poet, a self-made intellectual, and a religious liberal, Dr. Peter Bryant undoubtedly looked upon his son as a potential ally in his silent war with the rustic and Calvinist orthodoxy of the folk whose health he guarded. Although he had married into the prominent Snell family of the Cummington region, he gave his heart and mind not to these Berkshire hills but to the more sophisticated societies of Northampton and Boston. He had partial access to both societies, having acquired some of the Snell family's influence. After 1806 he often enjoyed visits to Boston as a member of the state legislature. Yet on the whole he was a country doctor, tied down in the countryside by insufficient formal education and, as his son put it, by "want of attention to the main chance." Inattention to money matters on the part of this father of eight children caused the Bryants to live for many years in the Snell family home, under the management of the doctor's prosaic but efficient wife.[1]

Peter Bryant encouraged his second son, William Cullen, whose delicate health made him unfit for farming, to aspire to a sophisticated urban life. As a child, Cullen had prayed for the gift of poetic genius and had dreamed of living as a poet and a worldly success in the distant metropolis of Boston. There was reason to hope. In 1808, when he was fourteen, Cullen had seen published in Boston his *The Embargo and Other Poems,* as revised and prepared for the press by his father. "The Embargo," a metered composite of political cliches gleaned from Federalist newspapers, had won the applause of the wealthy and cultured seaboard society.[2] But the seven years that followed taught Bryant that evanescent acclaim for a juvenile performance was no substitute for the money, experience, and education needed to enter the golden world.

Despite his many attainments, Dr. Bryant was unable to finance the ambitions he had aroused in his son. Cullen dreamed of winning educational glories at Yale as part of his triumphant march on Boston; instead, he spent only one year (1810–11) at Williams College, an experience that left him with little learning and few new friends. Although he found a substitute education in his father's extensive library and in an apprenticeship in law, this alone could not supply him with the connections, culture, and confidence needed to conquer the sophisticated society of his dreams. To his frustration, he had to take most of his training in law at the nearby village of Worthington, which he described as "consisting of a black-smith shop and a cow-stable," hardly the environment to prepare him for the great urban world.[3] His father refused to give him money to complete his law studies at Boston, saying, "You have cost me already four hundred dollars." In the summer and fall of 1814 he was able to get some legal experience in the office of Congressman William Baylies at Bridgewater, only twenty miles from Boston. Happy months, these, but they were cut short when in November a lung ailment forced Bryant to return to Cummington; not many such happy times were to follow in the next decade.[4]

His father's failure to provide a ladder to the top seemed to destine Bryant to long years on the dusty circuits of country law. Another man might have tried to make the climb, but Bryant was too shy and self-conscious to risk the competition of urban life without the advantages that he believed had been denied him. In desperation, this unwarlike man in late 1814 even had applied for a commission in the state army of Massachusetts, in hope that after a short career in the defense of his native state, "I should come into the world...with my excessive bash-fulness and rusticity rubbed off by military life." However, the state rejected his application and, before he could apply again, the end of the War of 1812 had blown his "military projects to the moon." Now in 1815, "with fearful expectations," he dolefully resigned himself to the prospect of arguing dull points of law for the amusement of rustics, whose very presence made him uncomfortable.[5]

Faced with this uninspiring future, Bryant sought comfort through faith in a benevolent deity who

> In the long way that I must tread alone,
> Will lead my steps aright.

That faith was justified, for the decade launched by the writing of "To A Waterfowl" in 1815 proved to be the most creative period of his poetic career and, as such, the essential step to the kind of life he desired. In Plainfield, a hamlet that had no post office or newspaper and almost no contact with the world outside, he set out his "gingerbread-board" as a lawyer. However, the only opportunity Plainfield afforded him was the opportunity to leave; in less than a year, he was gone, his departure hastened by the fear that the rusticity of his clients would rough away what little polish he had.[6] He escaped not to Boston but farther west, to Great Barrington in the Berkshires. While his new home was no metropolis, it was a substantial town and far less isolated than Plainfield, although its contacts significantly were not with Boston, from which it was separated by the mountains, but with Albany and, by way of the Hudson River, with New York City.[7]

In this more promising environment, Bryant resolved to subordinate his old dreams to concentration on law: Torts, not poems, were to be the staples of his new life; Coke, not Cowper, and Blackstone, not Words-worth, were to be his closest companions. From his erstwhile legal mentor, William Baylies, came a timely reminder of Swift's warning:

Not Beggar's brat on bulk begat
Not Bastard of Pedlar Scot
Are so disqualified by fate
To rise in *Church* or *Law* or *State*
As he whom Phobus [sic] in his ire[8]
Has blasted with poetic fire.

For a time both law and state occupied Bryant's attentions. Not only did he fight his client's legal battles, but he also won local elections first as tithing man and then as town clerk. In 1820 he was even persuaded to give the annual Fourth-of-July oration at neighboring Stockbridge. There Bryant expressed confidence in popular government, the fundamental goodness of the people, and the importance of agriculture to republican morals—ideas that were rapidly becoming the stock in trade of aspiring politicians throughout the United States. He had determined to take the path that has led so many literary hopefuls in America ever deeper into the pursuit of worldly success until literature is all but forgotten.[9]

The resolve to triumph over the urgings of his talents, however, helped defeat itself, for, by bringing Bryant closer to the things he loathed, it strengthened his aversion for the society in which he lived. Despite his youthful confidence in the power of the will, he could make himself neither a good lawyer nor a good politician. By nature he was much too reserved to strut on the crowded stage of public life, and as a young boy he had learned reticence from his mother: "Never talk of your religion or your love affairs," she had advised. But as a lawyer and office holder, he had—as he complained in "Green River"—"to mingle among the jostling crowd, where the sons of strife are subtle and loud," and specifically to cope with the contentiousness and low cunning of an undereducated people. To escape the abrasions of such a society, he retreated whenever he could to the calm, undemanding, and uninhabited countryside.[10]

Bryant's experiences at Great Barrington served to strengthen an important personal development. In years past his readings of some of the Greek poets and his discovery of Wordsworth in 1811 had given him a strong, though rather literary, enthusiasm for Nature.[11] Until he came to Great Barrington, however, he had identified his own personal fulfillment with the metropolis. Although his old dream survived, his life among the townsmen now gave Nature a personal and immediate

4

appeal, which made the countryside the very center of his private utopia. Great Barrington not only harbored a species of men whom the reluctant lawyer wished to avoid but also provided him with a ready means of escape. By 1820 the Berkshire region had progressed beyond its frontier stage, and civilization had established itself in the fertile valleys; but the surrounding mountains were left untamed as Bryant noted in "Monument Mountain":

> Thou who wouldst see the lovely and the wild
> Mingled in harmony on Nature's face
> Ascend our rocky mountains....

There in uncorrupted Nature he could commune with the beautiful order of a world free from human discord, and there, too, he could find himself. In the unspoiled wilderness he could associate his thoughts, his hopes, and his emotions with the receptive features of Nature, preserving them as memories ready to be revived whenever he returned; return to the familiar face of Nature, then, was a return to a better part of his earlier self. In this sense, the wilderness was for Bryant a refuge where he could protect his inner being from destruction under the ever changing, demanding mass of human society. For this man who found it so difficult to give of himself, the final beauty of Nature was that it made no demands on him.[12]

Comforting and undemanding, Nature resembled the God whom Bryant was defining for himself during these same years. Cullen derived his earliest religious views from his maternal grandfather, Ebenezer Snell, who was an ardent and outspoken disciple of the neo-Puritan revivalist, Samuel Hopkins. Hopkinsianism supplied a measure of comfort to the boy through its stress on an all-loving God, but it also held that God demanded from man a reciprocal love so absolute that it included a willingness to suffer, for the good of divine creation, the eternal anguish of Hell. The demands of such a religion were too great for Bryant to meet, and so faith in Hopkinsianism vanished with the onset of his first adolescent moves for independence.[13] For a time, he toyed with the deistic belief in a universe free from an active demanding God, but he found deism too abstract and too alien for much fulfillment; by 1820 Bryant had settled on the more satisfying doctrines of the Unitarian, William Ellery Channing. Channing also had rebelled against the all-demanding God of Hopkinsianism, but he had retained Hopkins' emphasis on divine love as the core of his creed. To Channing, God was love striving through love "to transform man into love." Love "was the harmonizing principle which reduced to unity and simplicity the vast diversity" of creation. These doctrines Bryant willingly accepted, although he overlooked or ignored much of Channing's stress on man's obligation to love man. The Unitarian God made few demands in exchange for his love, and belief in such a deity harmonized well with the young man's attitudes toward Nature. Divinity was best found not in human institutions, Unitarians assumed, but in Nature; God spoke most clearly not in the Berkshire churches, which were dominated by Calvinist orthodoxy, but in the silent woods and glades. God was on the side of those individuals who avoided the institutions of society, such as Bryant himself.[14]

At Great Barrington, then, Bryant arrived at the attitudes that were to govern his mature thoughts and emotions. The conflict between the human society in which he was obliged to live and the natural world unspoiled by man and close to God furnished the great creative tension in his life. Gladly he would have evaded the conflict, but that was impossible, for Nature could not be a permanent refuge for such a man as Bryant; to live the cultured life meant that he live and work in the cities, at least temporarily. Faced with this fact, he was beguiled by that typically American answer to such a problem: To strive for material wealth with its delusive promise of eventual leisure, power, and release from the worst features of life. Again and again, he resolved to remain a lawyer, even if his pursuit of success required that he suppress his interest in a literary career.

The Muse was a dangerous temptress, however, and devilish, too; for even before he had determined to smother her, she had prepared a delayed-action bomb, which soon blew his resolve to bits. Sometime before he left home, young Bryant had written a poem about death, a subject that was to hold his attentions until it had claimed him for its own. The young poet, still in his deistic phase, offered to his readers only the cold comfort that to die was to share the fate of all men. Nature was the tomb of Man:

> The planets, all the infinite host of heaven
> Are shining on the sad abode of death.

Bryant had left the poem in his father's desk, but Peter Bryant's frequent absences from home kept him from discovering it until his son had established himself at Great Barrington; finally, however, in May 1817 the doctor appeared at Boston to attend a session of the state senate proudly bearing the poem soon to be named "Thanatopsis" and four others written by his son. Before the end of the year, young Bryant had the pleasure of seeing these five examples of his work published in the *North American Review*, which had just begun its long career as the spark and guardian of New England culture. Soon the lawyer-poet was flattered by calls from distant Boston for more poems. In reply, he warned that by necessity law engaged most of his attention, but the fledgling *Review* was hungry for native talent and would not be put off; Bryant was informed that he labored "under a higher obligation than any American bard to do more." Shortly he began to dream of publishing "a little collection of poetry."[15]

The old dream of literary success also was encouraged by Bryant's growing friendship with the Sedgwick family of nearby Stockbridge. Theodore Sedgwick, Sr., whose old law office at Great Barrington Bryant now occupied, had been an influential Federalist leader connected by political and marital ties with the powerful "river gods" of the Connecticut Valley. Although Sedgwick had been a strong force for conservatism in western New England, when he died in 1813 he left five children who were to contribute to the liberalization of the thought, literature, and politics of the next generation. Bryant in 1818 met Charles Sedgwick, a fellow sufferer in the Berkshire legal trade and the youngest member of his family. Charles lacked the drive that had already carried his brothers out of the Berkshires west to the Hudson Valley in search of opportunity. Through Charles, Bryant soon met the others. Catherine Maria Sedgwick was a warmhearted, graceful woman whose charm outshone her rather plain features. Extremely close to her brothers, she was never to marry; her life was to be devoted to her writings and good causes. In 1821 Catherine successfully launched her career as a popular writer with her first novel, *A New England Tale,* which had grown out of a tract she had written in favor of Unitarianism. Theodore, Jr., the eldest brother, was a successful lawyer at Albany whose ill-health soon forced his "retirement" to a busy life as a writer, politician, and railroad promoter in the Berkshires and at Boston. The remaining brothers, lawyers at New York City, were shortly to become two of Bryant's closest friends: Robert and the able, dynamic Henry Dwight

(Harry) whose drive and rigid though brilliant mind were to bring him within the decade to insanity and then to a premature death.[16]

The Sedgwicks gave Bryant much needed support during his uncertain and uneasy years. Sharing his love for literature and for the Berkshires, they became his most appreciative audience; and having themselves sought opportunity outside of the Berkshires, they could understand his dissatisfaction with his situation. As fellow Unitarians who had encountered the displeasure of Christian orthodoxy, they could appreciate his sense of isolation in the strongly orthodox Berkshires: Catherine, although she had favored Unitarianism since her father's death, did not openly avow her faith until 1821 when she joined Robert and Harry in the Unitarian Society of New York. Common experiences and common tastes were to be the bases for deep friendships, which in the 1820s gave the shy and uncertain Bryant that sense of destiny denied him from the time he had begun his struggle with law. Collectively, the Sedgwicks helped fill the gap left by the death of Peter Bryant in 1821. Like the doctor, they encouraged Bryant in his old hopes, although they gave it a significant change of direction. Again, he dreamed of a literary career, but now he looked increasingly to New York rather than to Boston as his promised land.[17]

Boston, however, made one last claim on his dream in 1821. That year was a triumph for the young poet. From distant Cambridge came an invitation to deliver a poem before the Phi Beta Kappa Society of Harvard. Bryant responded enthusiastically with "The Ages," the most ambitious he had written. As in "Thanatopsis," the subject was death, but unlike that earlier excursion along the River Styx, the new poem mirrored its author's Unitarian faith and traced the upward thrust of civilization out of the endless cycles of birth and decay so evident in creation. Death, while destructive, was also creative, working throughout the ages to purge human society of its evils:

> Thus Error's monstrous shapes from earth are driven;
> They fade, they fly, but Truth survives their flight;

Truth had survived out of the wreckage of the past to take root and flourish in the "youthful paradise" of America.

> Here the free spirit of mankind at length
> Throws its last fetters off; and who shall place
> A limit to the giant's unchained strength,
> Or curb his swiftness in the forward race?

Significantly, the poet, who had considered Nature as the particular province of divine benevolence, now conceived of that same benevolence as governing human history; the God who in "To A Waterfowl" would "lead my steps aright" in "The Ages" acted to guide the eventual course of mankind aright. "The Ages" indicates that the poet had modified his pessimism as to his future in human society. This was the first of a series of efforts by Bryant to resolve, through faith in the inevitability of social progress, the inner tensions created by the conflict between his own personal needs and the demands made by society. These efforts never were totally successful, as his continued disposition to seek refuge in Nature proved, but faith in human progress based on faith in the benevolence of Nature did become the essence of Bryant's mature view of society.

In this way, "The Ages" indicated that Bryant was now emotionally prepared to venture into that sophisticated society which he had long aspired to join. His association with the *North American Review* plus his friendship with the Sedgwicks had given him confidence in himself and in his future. His journey to Cambridge strengthened that confidence, for at nearby Boston he was able to arrange for the publication of that "little collection of poetry" he had dreamed of for two years.

The slim volume, *Poems,* published late in 1821, contained in its forty-four pages most of the works that were to make Bryant the most popular poet in America.[18] They exhibited a gentle melancholy and his simple faith in the benevolence of the natural world. "Thanatopsis" emerged with a new beginning and a new ending in praise of the comforts of Nature, which deprived death of much of its dismal character; death appeared in some of the other poems but chiefly only as the corollary to life. Conspicuous in these poems was the world that Americans came to identify with Bryant: the simple, trustworthy world of Nature, friendly, familiar, and fitted to the mind and heart of man, was presented in the poems concretely and in loving detail as befitted the "garment of God." In *Poems,* too, appeared the other Bryant, the man whose faith in Nature was balanced against his suspicions of men, the poet of "Green River," who, despite his faith in the progressive character of Civilization, continued to distinguish sharply between comforting Nature and demanding unsatisfying human society.

Both the positive and the negative themes of Bryant's poetry were to have strong appeal for the increasing number of persons disquieted by the mounting pressures and uncertainties of American life after 1820. Those who were discomforted by the growing disharmony and corruption so particularly evident in the expanding cities found in Bryant's poetry assurance strife was not in the essence of life and that a gentler, more stable world remained where dreams and ideals would not be crushed under the iron wheel of change. Just as he lessened the terrors of death by reducing it to no more than a part of a benevolent system—the divine design—so did he ease the anxieties that accompanied social change by offering hope that behind the urban flux there existed a purer, more harmonious, and more natural order.[19] The need for such comfort furnished an expanding market for Bryant's poetry (and for his newspaper editorials) as well as for the paintings of his friend Thomas Cole and the novels of Catherine Sedgwick.

The response of reviewers in 1821 to *Poems,* indeed, seemed to justify the hope expressed by Catherine that the rising American demand for native works would enable a poet like Bryant to make literature his profession. At Boston, *Poems* was welcomed enthusiastically by the *North American Review* for its "strain of pure and high sentiment, that expands and lifts up the soul and brings it nearer the source of moral beauty." From New York came encouraging recognition from the littérateurs Gulian C. Verplanck and Richard Henry Dana, Jr. both of whom later became Bryant's close friends, and from Harry Sedgwick, who was beginning to take an active interest in the poet's career. In early 1822 Catherine wrote that she had never seen her friend more agreeable or happy.[20]

But the hopes were premature. Soon enough Bryant was reminded harshly of a warning he had received five years before from William Baylies: "Poetry is a *commodity* I know not suited to the American market. It will neither help a man to wealth nor office." Indeed, the general good will of the Boston and New York literati notwithstanding, during the first year after publication *Poems* sold only 270 of the 750 copies printed. Harry Sedgwick eventually was forced to remainder many copies at fifteen cents each. The total return hardly covered the costs of publication; after five years, Bryant netted $ 14.92 from his talents. Encouraged to revive his old dream, he was denied its realization by the law of supply and demand. To lift his depression, Catherine Sedgwick offered him $ 200 to write a poetic farce, but when he submitted the farce to Harry Sedgwick for criticism, Harry's response forever crushed his hopes of glory in the theater.[21]

Bryant returned to his legal work, but he could not revive his old resolve to embrace the "hag" and felt that his situation was becoming intolerable, The contentiousness in the legal arena at Great Barrington had grown so intense that some lawyers refused to speak to each other. As for clients, while they were always ready to carry their petty battles to court, they showed little zeal in paying for the lawyer's services. In addition in 1824 Bryant took a case on appeal to the Massachusetts Supreme Court, only to see the justices reverse a lower court decision that had favored his client, not on the grounds that the case was weak, but because Bryant had made a technical error in his written declaration. To add to his anger, he became involved in a public quarrel with the opposing lawyer over the costs of the case.[22] With reason, Bryant lost what little enthusiasm he had for a career in which there was no security, no peace, and, as he intimated, no justice.

When Harry Sedgwick invited him to New York for a visit in 1824, he came at the first opportunity. The city met his expectations. Earlier, he had concluded that New York was superior to Boston in its steady support of literature, and this belief grew firmer when Bryant received a warm welcome in the cultured circle of the Sedgwicks and their friends. Encouraged by this experience, he decided to leave his "beggarly profession"—if he could find an opportunity in New York. Again, he visited the city. This time he returned to the Berkshires in so happy a state that his habitual reserve almost vanished. "He kissed the children," wrote Catherine on his return, "talked much and smiled at everything." There was good reason for this extraordinary emotional display: with the help of Harry Sedgwick he had found a chance to make literature his one and only career.

Although Harry had been interested in Bryant's career since 1821, he cared even more about the literary fortunes of his sister, and when the interests of his two protégés conjoined in late 1824, he was prepared to act decisively. Earlier that year Catherine had published her second novel, *Redwood,* a moral tale in which she tried to use both an American theme and an American setting; the novel was dedicated to Bryant. Although *Redwood* was expected to appeal to the growing American interest in national literature, the *North American Review* was noticeably slow in considering it—noticeably slow, that is, for Harry, whose impatience turned to outrage when he learned that three Boston reviewers had refused to do the book. "Neglect of a native work," he wrote to Bryant, "in a periodical devoted to domestic literature and native concerns—is by many deemed equivalent to disapprobation." Bryant, though reluctant to review a work dedicated to himself, took the hint. Early in 1825 the *North American Review* published his review, which combined optimism for the promise of American literature with praise for Catherine as a writer of virtue, compassion, "great good sense and sober practical wisdom."[23]

The slow reaction at the Hub to his sister's novel strengthened Harry's aversion for the Boston literati and convinced him of the need to establish at New York a rival to the *North American Review*. Since booming New York already was challenging Boston for the literary leadership of the United States, the time seemed ripe for the venture. In January 1825 Harry was able to inform Bryant of a project to fuse two struggling periodicals into a healthy new review under the editorial direction of Henry J. Anderson, a young and well-to-do scholar. The prospective publishers, Bliss and White (Catherine's publishers), were anxious to hire Bryant as coeditor at a salary roughly equivalent to his income from his legal work—$500 per year, and more if subscriptions increased. Harry was optimistic that the new review, with Bryant as an editor, would attract many readers. The poet needed little encouragement and he set out from Great Barrington as a self-proclaimed "literary adventurer" to seek his fortune in the bustling city of gold. Few had come before him; many were to follow. After moving to New York, he wrote to Richard Henry Dana regarding his flight from Berkshire society: "I made up my mind to get out of it as soon as I could and come to this great city, where if it were my lot to starve, I might starve peacefully and quietly."[24]

2

THE PROMISED LAND

A glance at a map of the United States, James Fenimore Cooper once remarked, was proof enough that nature had intended New York to be one of the great commercial cities of the world. By 1825 New York was emerging as the commercial heart of a growing nation. Along the newly opened Erie Canal moved in ever increasing volume the grains of the expanding West; from the South came cotton to feed the hungry mills of Old and New England; and, most valuable of all, from across the Atlantic flowed the manufactures of Europe to meet the rising demands of a prosperous people. Benefiting from the shrewdness of its merchants and from its ready access to a great hinterland, New York had almost won its commercial rivalry with Boston and Philadelphia. In 1821 it handled 23 percent of national imports; by 1831 the proportion was 50 percent.[1] Along with the volume of trade grew the wealth, the influence, and the ambitions of the import merchant and his allies.

Internally, New York was undergoing a social explosion. In the five years before 1825 its population had increased by a third; what had been a modest city of 60,000 in 1800 was well on its way to becoming the metropolis of 500,000 at mid-century. Although in the 1820s buildings mushroomed amid "clouds of lime and sand, and showers of brick-bats, slates, tile, and shingles," the growing hordes of newcomers swamped all accommodations. Desperate families sometimes moved into their new homes before doors and windows had been installed in the buildings. At the same time commercial population burgeoned. Five hundred new mercantile businesses reportedly were established in 1825 alone; and in the same year city investors, often with more hopes than money, petitioned the state legislature to charter twenty-seven new banks, more than twice the number then in existence.[2] Buildings, businesses, and banks appeared—and often disappeared—with bewildering speed, as the real growth of both society and the economy was outdistanced by men's ambitions and greed.

New York attracted the ambitious from all directions, but especially from New England. They came from the commercial towns of the New England coast, discouraged by the narrow hinterlands on which they had to depend, some to found great mercantile houses: the Griswolds of Connecticut, the Fishes of Rhode Island, the Grinnells of New Bedford, the Macys of Nantucket. They came, too, from the rural areas, often lean, hard men anxious to escape from the constraints of their villages to the freedom of the metropolis where shrewdness and ruthlessness could be given full play. The Yankee invasion met resentment among the established families of New York, for it threatened both to overwhelm them personally and to obliterate the old Anglo-Dutch character of the city. For anxious "Yorkers," the Yankees appeared to be Goths rather than Gothamites, whose drive and whose "mingling of God and Mammon" endangered New York's social and moral structure.[3]

Although many Yankees in fact, had come to make their fortunes in trade, New England also sent to New York generations of its most talented thinkers, who saw in the expanding wealth of the city the chance to develop their potentials, to give as well as to take—ministers, teachers, artists, and poets whose energetic devotion to the good both countered the greed of their compatriots and transcended the often sluggish pragmatism of the Anglo-Dutch. Robert and Harry Sedgwick had come during the first decade of the century, seeking to increase their cultural opportunities as well as their wealth. Bryant also saw in the economic promise of the city something far nobler than dollars. In 1820, when his attention was turning to New York, he had asserted: "Point out, if you can, in the history of the world, the example of a free opulent and flourishing community, which had not encouragements for learning and rewards of genius." Now, in 1825, he came to put his faith to the test.[4]

The city met his expectations—at first. The growth of foreign trade had made New York more varied and cosmopolitan, and the city had begun to acquire a continental tone. Increasing numbers of New Yorkers traveled abroad, and increasing numbers of Irishmen, Frenchmen, Germans, Italians, Englishmen, and Scots, came to settle in New York. In 1825 at the Park Theatre, New Yorkers were treated to Rossini's opera "The Barber of Seville," directed by Lorenzo da Ponte, who had written the librettos for Mozart's "Figaro" and "Don Giovanni"; in the audience sat Joseph Bonaparte, once King of Spain. For those who, like Bryant, had little taste either for music or for things continental, the city offered English books and plays and ideas.[5] Little wonder that New Yorkers considered commerce the basis of civilization.

Native writers however, complained that their own work was being ignored because of a glut of foreign riches, or grumbled that local patrons favored imported tastes and ideas, if they showed any interest in tastes and ideas at all. None the less, the influx of ideas and modes of expressions from the centers of western civilization both stimulated local talent and attracted the cultured and creative from other parts of the nation. Although few rich men might favor native culture and even fewer favor with discrimination, there were some who opened their purses to a painter like Thomas Cole or a poet like Bryant. The newly elected mayor of the city when Bryant arrived in 1825 was the wealthy merchant, Philip Hone, a noted patron of the arts. Perhaps the average patron supplied greater sustenance for the artist's ego than for his stomach, but at least there was encouragement; where patronage failed, the expanding world of publishing generally provided jobs for needy artists and writers.[6]

When Bryant first settled down in his room on Chambers Street near the Unitarian Church, he discovered in New York a flourishing artistic community, which could boast of talents in nearly all orders of culture, including poetry: "Our fourteen wards contain some seven-and-twenty bards." Here in this community, Bryant soon met most of those who were to be his lifelong friends and associates. There was the shy, sensitive Thomas Cole, English born and western bred, who painted Nature with the same devotion that Bryant showed it in his poetry. There was the versatile Henry James Anderson, who after six months as Bryant's coeditor on the *New York Review* gave up the literary life to become professor of Mathematics at Columbia College. There was Robert

Sands, bachelor and free spirit, a native of New York who, like Bryant, had abandoned law for literature. And there was David Dudley Field, a fellow refugee from the Berkshires who had come to the city after graduating from Williams College in order to study law with Robert and Harry Sedgwick.[7] Bryant met other luminaries at the literary soirees given by Harry Sedgwick and his wife, Jane, but none of these new acquaintances were as important to him as two men whom he met during his first months in New York: Gulian Crommelin Verplanck and James Fenimore Cooper.

Gulian Verplanck's enthusiasm for Bryant's poetry proved to be the most constant factor in their lifelong friendship. Of mixed Dutch and English ancestry, descendent of generations of New York merchants, and grandson of a president of Columbia College, Verplanck was a New Yorker who both revered the city's past and loved the color and activity of its present.[8] In 1825 he dedicated a book

TO

HIS NATIVE CITY

TO WHICH HE IS BOUND BY EVERY TIE

OF

AFFECTION AND GRATITUDE.[9]

He had grown up with the city. One summer day in 1804 he had waited in trepidation before the house where his hero, Alexander Hamilton, lay dying from Burr's bullet. As a young Federalist politician he had founded the Washington Benevolent Society to rally public opinion against Jefferson's Embargo. Later he had held his own in a verbal duel with the politically powerful and quick-witted ex-mayor, De Witt Clinton, although Clinton had cruelly ridiculed his physical appearance: "His person is squat and clumsy, reminding one of Humpty Dumpty on the wall. A nervous tremor is concentrated at the end of each nostril from his habitual sneering and carping, with a look as wise as that of Solomon, at the dividing of the child, upon an old piece of tapestry."[10]

In spite of his trials in the nerve-racking politics of New York, Verplanck by the 1820s had acquired the geniality and tolerance of a man whose place in life was secure. Born to wealth and place and related by ties of family and friendship to part of the established wealth and influence of New York, he was intimately involved in the public life of his beloved city. Verplanck dabbled in literature and was also a scholar and moralist, a businessman, and a politician. In 1825 he had just published his *Essays on the Nature and Uses of the Various Evidences of the Christian Religion* and was preparing for the press his *Essay on the Doctrine of Contracts.* In the early 1820s this versatile Knickerbocker had been first a state assemblyman and then professor of theology at the Episcopal Seminary; now in 1825 he had begun an eight-year career as one of his city's three representatives in Congress. A warm, helpful, and influential friend, Verplanck gave Bryant a sense of belonging to New York beyond anything which even the Sedgwicks could provide.[11] These two men—one genial, the other cold—developed a relationship that was to survive for forty-five years, despite the political storms that later blew up between them.

If the New Yorker and the New Englander in personality were complements, Bryant quickly discovered that his other new "friend" was like flint to his steel. The aggressiveness of James Fenimore Cooper was stamped all over his rugged face. Although Cooper attracted many friends because of his warmth, candor, and intelligence, even they could not deny that the novelist was also a suspicious man who had resolved not to be "humbugged" by any person, a man of great ambition who resented being crossed, and a man who demanded public appreciation, on his terms, for his achievements. There was truth in a current jest that he was so egotistical that he wrote his novels in the street, leaning against a lamp post.[12]

In 1822, after the success of his second novel, *The Spy,* Cooper moved from Westchester County to New York, intent on making literature a career. Within three years he made himself the most successful American novelist of the times, a professional author who, to the envy of most writers, was able to support himself by his work. In spite of this success, however, he did not share Verplanck's clear-cut devotion to the city and its life. The son of a great landowner, related by marriage to the eminent De Lancey family, Cooper was too self-consciously the landed gentleman to feel much kinship with the commercial, rapidly growing metropolis. Although he was tied permanently to the urban world both by his career as a novelist and by his hunger for cultured society, his heart lay with the rural gentry, whose social and political dominance was being destroyed by the growth of commercial wealth and power.[13] Bound up as he was in two increasingly disparate societies, he was destined to become a belligerent critic of rapidly changing America.

But in the mid-1820s Cooper's uneasy life still lay before him. Despite

17

his faults, he had the gift of winning the attention, respect, and even the affections of many men and soon became the leading light, the "Patriarchal Highness," of a group that was sometimes called the "Cooper Club." The good cheer and good conversation of this "Lunch" or "Bread and Cheese Club" attracted military men, lawyers, physicians, and merchants as well as writers and artists. Here it was possible for Verplanck to test his latest idea or for Sands to launch a newly conceived satire. Here, too, Cooper would entertain the membership "with disputations on the French language" to the great, but secret, amusement of those who had mastered that language.

The conviviality of the club was in less genial times to be the subject of wistful recollection, but to some of the memebers, at least, the organization also had a more serious purpose. For young artists and writers, it served both as a vehicle for mutual aid and mutual admiration and as a focal point for their efforts to find places for themselves in American culture.[14] They often resented the established classes and established fashions as possible obstacles to their ambitions. In 1826 Bryant complained: "It is the fashion throughout the United States to read the tolerable English works of the day—but fashion has not made it indispensable to read the American works of the same degree of merit." To counter such discrimination, the young writers tried to find a peculiarly American justification for their works, one that would satisfy a highly practical and moralistic society that had little sympathy for the doctrine of "art for art's sake." As they saw the situation, since the American writer could neither be the guardian of a cult nor solely an entertainer, he had to be a force for the preservation and the progress of America's unique experiment in freedom. The growth of popular power in the emerging democratic society demanded a solution to the problem of establishing and sustaining general public morality, a solution that American writers announced themselves ready to provide.[15] In 1824 Verplanck urged the importance of the "secret and silent legislation" of art and literature as means "to perpetuate the liberties or animate the patriotism of the people, to purify their morals or to excite their genius," and reminded his listeners that "every swelling wave of our doubling and still doubling population, as it rolls from the Atlantic coast, inland, onward towards the Pacific, will bear upon its bosom the influence of the taste, learning, morals, freedom of their generation."[16]

Although Bryant lacked the grandeur of vision so characteristic of the temperamentally more optimistic Verplanck, he shared this faith in the secret and silent legislation of the arts. In a series of lectures at the New York Athenaeum in 1825, Bryant argued that poetry is an ideal moral force, because it works so powerfully on the passions, the "springs of moral conduct." He asserted that the passions can be moved to evil by social influences, but not by poetry, which is intrinsically pure just as nature is pure. What then can be a more powerful factor in producing human goodness than nature poetry?

> Among the most remarkable influences of poetry is the exhibition of those analogies and correspondences which it beholds between the things of the moral and the natural world. I refer to the adorning and illustrating each by the other—infusing a moral sentiment into a natural object, and bringing images of visible beauty and majesty to heighten the effects of moral sentiment. Thus it binds into one all the passages of human life with the works of creation.

Bryant suggested that poetry could aid in creating a moral landscape for America in which every prominent feature of nature prompted feelings of morality or patriotism in the hearts of the inhabitants. Such a moral atmosphere would restore Americans to "unperverted feelings," which in turn would assure correct thoughts and actions. Who, then, could better guard American purity than a native poet using native themes to clarify the moral truths particularly applicable to American life?[17]

This idea of a national literature received an even stronger endorsement from Cooper. Criticized in 1820 for the European flavor of his first novel, *Precaution,* he responded with *The Spy,* in which he appealed to feelings of national pride and patriotism, most obviously in the last chapter, which was designed to wring the last patriotic tear from every eye, and was written, paged, and printed before he had finished preceding chapters. Perhaps encouraged by the success of this novel, Cooper argued for a national literature to protect American principles and values. In defense of a proposed copyright law that favored American writers, he warned in 1826 that the foreign ideas and standards often found in imported books were particularly dangerous to a nation whose government received "its daily impulses from popular will, and consequently public opinion."[18] The novelist aimed to counter the corrupt influence of foreign ideas by supplying the values he thought were needed to give the correct direction to the popular impulse.

To the extent that they perceived literature as a moral and social force,

Bryant and Cooper were in agreement, but they differed in technique. While Bryant chose the subtle approach of poetry's silent legislation, Cooper adopted techniques so direct that in some of his later works they took on the character of the bludgeon and the blunderbuss. Cooper was increasingly prone to lecture his readers on correct principles not only in his prefaces (to which Bryant objected) but later in the novels as well. Not content to entertain his public, he offered both his principles and himself up for public approval—and was disappointed. In 1826, when he left for an extended stay in Europe, he resolved to teach Europeans the virtues of New World democracy. Out of that resolve came his two-volume *Notions of the Americans,* a thinly veiled lecture on the life and values of American society. Not unnaturally, he hoped that the book would win popular acclaim among his compatriots back home. It did not. Apparently, American readers preferred being entertained by Leatherstocking to being taught by his creator. As far as Cooper was concerned, the fault lay not in the performance but in the audience. "We shall never get to be the thoroughly manly people we ought to be," he complained, "until we cease to look to European opinions for anything except those connected with the general advancement of the race."[19] Throughout the rest of his life the melody of this complaint might change, but the basic theme remained the same: American society did not appreciate him as a defender of true principles. The popular author of novels of forest and sea was being transformed into the bitter critic of the 1830s.

Bryant suffered a disappointment of a lesser order. Like other literary men of his day, he dreamed of a symbiotic relationship between the literati and the people. In a democracy, he said, "it is the debt due from those who think to those who toil, that every citizen should be made to understand all his public and private obligations." But what if the citizen refused to accept full payment of the debt? In one sense, Bryant was more fortunate than Cooper, for his reading public accepted him for what he was and wanted to be, a poet of morality and nature. On the other hand, Cooper, no matter how great his disappointments, did command a reading public large enough to support him, whereas Bryant soon discovered that even in the apparently favorable atmosphere of New York his efforts to establish himself as a professional literary man would not be successful.

By 1826 the *New York Review*, launched with such high hopes the year before, had started to sink as financial support fell below expectations. To save the *Review,* Bryant early in April broached the idea of a merger of resources and subscribers to the Boston-based *United States Literary Gazette.* The *Gazette's* editor, James C. Carter, jumped at the chance, admitting sadly that "our reading public is not yet numerous enough to support a corps of literary gladiators." And so a two-headed gladiator was born: The new *United States Review and Literary Gazette,* edited jointly at Boston and New York, made its debut in October. Burdened by the problem of harmonizing spirits as different as those of New York and Boston and by the salaries of two editors, the journal struggled on for thirteen months and then died.

These failures convinced Bryant that New York was too preoccupied with the pursuit of trade, gain, and political office to supply much support for literature: "Nobody cares anything for literature here, and the man of genius is the man who has made himself rich."[20] Cooper and other aspiring writers could agree that the ambitions for wealth and power, encouraged among the people by the successful "geniuses" of New York society, threatened the efforts of these writers to give literature an integral place in American life.

Bryant's failure to fulfill his literary dreams rankled, but he was more moderate and modest than Cooper was and never experienced the degree of alienation from American society the novelist later felt. While Cooper was establishing a second home in Europe during his years abroad (1826–33), Bryant was developing closer ties with his adopted city. In 1827 he found some compensation for the death of the *Review* by cooperating with Verplanck and Robert Sands under the *nom de plume* "Mr. Herbert" in writing *The Talisman,* a mildly satirical and sentimental literary annual; the work was sufficiently well received by the public to encourage "Mr. Herbert" to produce two more volumes in succeeding years.[21] Moreover, by 1827 Bryant had discovered a more substantial, if less literary, channel for his talents—journalism.

His first opportunity had come in June 1826 when William Coleman, the editor of *The Evening Post,* was thrown from his gig by a runaway horse. Expecting to recover quickly from his injuries, Coleman, an oldtime Federalist from Massachusetts and an admirer of Bryant's poetry, offered his fellow New Englander a temporary position as assistant editor of the newspaper. In fact, Bryant stayed with the newspaper for fifty-two years; for, when it became evident that the accident had left Coleman crippled for life, he offered Bryant an one-eighth interest in the *Post* as well as *de facto* editorship. The offer was too attractive to reject. It was true that journalism promised to involve the poet in politics, but he thought the politicians could be kept at a greater distance from the office of the editor than from the office of the lawyer. Probably, too, Bryant saw in the job an opportunity to oblige Verplanck, who as a Congressman was happy to have a close friend in control of one of New York's most influential newspapers. In any case, the new work was more lucrative than "poetry and magazines," and seemingly would leave the poet time to pursue his literary career. "I do not like politics any better than you," he wrote to a friend, "but they get only my mornings, and you know politics and a belly-full are better than poetry."[22] Although he did not yet realize it, Bryant had found a life-role in which politics was to claim more than his mornings. It was ironic that New York bestowed the best position from which to lecture America on its manners, morals, and politics upon Bryant, the advocate of "secret and silent legislation," rather than on the more direct and pugnacious Cooper.

The full extent of this irony was yet to be discovered, and before 1832, in spite of his disappointments, Bryant had reason to be content with his situation. He had successfully escaped both the narrow social world of his youth and the strictures of his law practice. In the jovial atmosphere of the Knickerbocker circle, he found a place in a cultured society that surpassed that of his adolescent dreams. This man who considered making acquaintances one of the most irksome duties of life virtually inherited a host of friends: the Sedgwicks, Verplanck, Sands, Anderson, Cole, and, later, William Gilmore Simms, the South Carolina novelist whose long friendship with Bryant survived even the ferocious years of the Civil War. In addition, Bryant was becoming an American institution; by 1827 he could claim the dubious distinction of having some of his poems anthologized in a reader for school boys. These were sunshine years for the once lonely New Englander, years in which he grew to consider himself a New Yorker, to the point that in 1830 this lover of nature could write, in "Hymn of the City":

> Even here do I behold
> Thy steps, Almighty! — here, amid the crowd.

However as Albert F. McLean, Jr., points out, Bryant really did not come to terms with the city in this poem; with the exception of one reference to "proud piles," the poet throughout used the familiar imagery of nature.[23] Indeed, Bryant soon discovered that his position was painfully too much "amid the crowd." As a New Yorker, as a journalist, and as a friend of Verplanck and the Sedgwicks, he was drawn into an urban and political world whose growing tensions even during these successful years led him to take a more favorable look at the life he had fled. In 1829 his effusive friend, Miss Eliza Robbins, wrote: "Mr. Bryant has so often described to me the quiet of Great Barrington—all the elements in harmony—life so peaceful in all its forms—mute and material things so happily accommodated to the enjoyments of conscious beings." [24] As yet, the pressures that caused the explosive discord of the 1830s were weak, but they were strong enough to initiate the tensions that impelled Bryant to became a liberal democrat. Little did Bryant know it, but in the late 1820s the gentle shafts of the poet were being barbed for battle.

THE DYNAMIC SOCIETY

In August 1826 Bryant clipped from the *Evening Post* an account of the Columbia College commencement and, after marking "such passages as are written by me," proudly mailed this first specimen of his journalism to his wife, Fanny. Before long he was writing more important matter than comments on a college commencement, for he had to shoulder an increasing share of the editorial work. Coleman had been permanently disabled by his accident, and died three years later. Although Bryant's marriage to journalism was one of convenience rather than love, he soon discovered that journalism was not only more lucrative than poetry but that it satisfied his desire to impose simplicity and restraint on the written word; his devotion to language simple and direct was to become legendary among newspapermen.[1]

Editorial work, however, also engendered obligations that Bryant otherwise would have avoided. As an editor, he became in a sense a guardian of the immediate interests of the community; this role forced him to relate his attitudes, ideals, and ambitions to the increasingly complex society with which he had to deal. Bryant was not an enthusiastic or profound social thinker, and many of his ideas were absorbed from the times or, more usually, from his friends. However, he gave to those ideas a personal intensity that in the 1820s made him one of the most effective spokesmen for liberalism. Ironically, his very lack of enthusiasm and profundity regarding social matters contributed to his effectiveness. The 1820s were the years of apprenticeship for a master liberal.

Certainly, when Bryant arrived in New York, he had much to learn. He brought with him a view of American society that was as much a part of his Federalist past as it was a part of his Unitarian present. Like many other Americans, he considered the United States to be the heir of a benevolent historical process which had eliminated aristocracy and monarchy in favor of a new and superior system of free society, which wise and virtuous men had established in America. The American Revolution had completed the process by destroying antiquated associations and habits of mind and by calling the people to a new sense of virtue. This view of American society contained a fundamental ambiguity concerning the future. On the one hand, it strengthened faith in the doctrine of progress, for it was reasonable to assume that a nation so blessed by its past would be equally blessed by the future. In establishing their republic, said Bryant in 1820, Americans had "with cautious wisdom" prepared the nation "for a career of empire and strength and glory, such as the world never before witnessed." On the other hand, as the Federalists had illustrated, this belief could encourage anxiety, for if the ideal order and character already existed it was possible for social change to subvert them. Paradise gained could, as any Christian knew, in time become paradise lost.[2]

Before his arrival in New York, Bryant had not directly experienced rapid social change. So much greater his uneasiness, then, when in 1825 he found himself caught up in that phenomenon so familiar to nineteenth-century New York: the cycle of boom and bust. Early in 1825 New Yorkers had started to speculate heavily in cotton; new banks appeared, money flowed, and trade reached unprecedented heights. Then in the late summer cotton prices collapsed, banks fell, credit dwindled, and commerce stagnated, "leaving behind only wrecks of fortune and bankruptcy." The expectations, the speculations, the frustrations, and the apparent peculations generated by their dynamic society led some New Yorkers to examine the implications of material change. "We have some clever men to be sure," complained Bryant in 1826, "but they are mightly given to instructing the world—to elucidating the mysteries of political economy and the principles of jurisprudence."[3] The poet might yawn over the subjects of economics and jurisprudence, but he could not ignore them, particularly since some of his closest friends were striving to elucidate "the mysteries" and provide a philosophy and an ethic for the dynamic economy.

Was the spirit of enterprise in America good or bad? For Bryant and his friends, the answer was as evident as the phenomenon. Bryant, pointing to America's favorite bad example, noted that Europe stunted the character of its peoples, because its "laws chain men to the condition in which they were born.... Men spring up, and vegetate, and die." In contrast, he felt that the dynamic character of free society strengthened and enlivened character: "An intense competition calls forth and exalts the passions and faculties of men; their characters become strongly defined." Theodore Sedgwick, Jr., then beginning his career as a popular economist, gave this argument a more material focus. In his *Hints to My Countrymen,* published at New York in 1826, he argued that the striving for material things is inevitable and necessary in a free society. The acquisitive drive, stimulated by the opportunities available to Americans, strengthens the human character needed to sustain freedom by compelling men to labor; without such a drive, men become "indifferent and sleepy."[4] Regarding expenditures for dress in America, this descendant of the Puritans wrote: "Many call this extravagance. I like to see it. If the people dress better they earn more: there is more industry, thrift, skill, management. Many a man here can earn at job-work a dollar a day, and unless you make him work for shoes and stockings, a good hat on his head and a good coat on his back, what will you make of him?"[5]

The desire for goods created the need to labor and the need to labor sustained the bourgeois virtues—this was an argument that Bryant could appreciate. If his father had been indifferent to the "main chance," his mother had preached—and practiced—the practical virtues. "Never be idle," she had advised, "always be busy." But who was to deny, after having lived in New York, that the busy pursuit of wealth could also produce bourgeois vices? Greed, narrow materialism, and unhappiness— were these not, as European critics had charged, the product of American freedom? In 1827 Bryant's *United States Review* twice warned Americans that their constant "anxious exertion" to better their condition threatened to diminish the happiness and virtue "which free institutions seem at first sight fitted to afford."[6] Neither Bryant nor Sedgwick, however, held that free institutions were responsible for the destructive excesses of the spirit of enterprise. Social evils, they agreed, stemmed from the corrupting qualities of European aristocracy that continued to cling to

American society, not from any defects in the liberal-democratic system itself.

To reduce the social ideal to its basic tautology, the pure system was pure. Ideal freedom meant individual independence and responsibility, freedom from all the artificial restraints *and* protections seemingly so prevalent in aristocratic Europe. Did freedom include the freedom to do wrong? Not according to Bryant and Sedgwick, for in ideal American society equal rights and the absence of special privileges and powers put everyone equally under the watchfulness of his fellow citizens. Men were governed by a "strong natural desire to obtain the good-will and good opinions of others," wrote Bryant in 1819. "We thence learn to regulate our conduct by stricter maxims, and by watching closely over ourselves, to live not only above censure, but above suspicion." Theodore Sedgwick developed this point in more explicit social terms. Individual independence, he argued in 1826, included the "right" to fall as well as to rise in society, to suffer for one's vices as well as to reap the rewards of one's virtues; the man who preferred the fleshpots to the practice of industry, thrift, skill, and management would not prosper unless he possessed special privileges. Nor would the individual who was inclined to mistreat his fellow man long be able to practice brutality. "The *equal* condition of these people," wrote Sedgwick in reference to his fellow New Englanders, "render them *kind hearted* one to another. If kings, and law, and the rules of society, allow men to treat each other like brutes, whenever one has power and another has none, they will be brutish from age to age." Concerning the power that came with the wealth accumulated by the most successful entrepreneurs in free society, Sedgwick warned "Ye men of wealth, remember that your numbers are too few to give you power; and that your influence will be proportionate to your munificence, urbanity, and true devotion to the interests of society." Ideal free society, then, would guarantee both individual freedom and social harmony, both individual happiness and civic morality; so would the interests of the individuals and the community be reconciled.[7]

But was the ideal the real? Both Bryant and Sedgwick founded their social vision on an idealized New England village where men were close to nature and to each other; here in this ideal village society existed the equality, the stability, the harmony, and the morality so essential to true American society. It was Catherine Sedgwick who best depicted the

27

ideal environment: "I have always considered country life with its out-
lets to the great world as an essential advantage in education. Besides
all the teaching and inspiration of Nature, . . . one is brought into close
social relationship with all conditions of people. There are no barriers
between you and your neighbors. . . . There were no sacrifices of personal
dignity or purity; nor, if there was in condition or character a little
elevation above the community we lived in, was it preserved by arrogant
vigilance or jealous proscription." In *Redwood* she has a spoiled young
woman of fashion ask in reference to a New England farmer: "Of what
use is rank or fortune if it does not make you independent of such animals?"[8]

Although Bryant and Sedgwick both had experienced urban life,
neither appreciated the significance of the new conditions appearing in
the expanding cities: the rapid change, the increasing disparities in
wealth, the impersonality and anonymity of life, and the isolation from
Nature—features which plainly did not conform to the village ideal.
This failure was understandable. In the 1820s even in New York the
peculiar characteristics of metropolitan society had only begun to appear.
Moreover, though the cities expanded rapidly in the three decades after
1820, their growth was overshadowed by the development of the agricultural and rural areas as Americans brought the West under cultivation.
There were no obvious indicators for either Bryant or Sedgwick that
the United States would cease to be preponderantly a nation of farms
and villages.

There was no pressing reason, then, to abandon the favorite American
explanation for the conflict between the ideal and the urban reality: If
men were poor, if they were immoral, if they were unhappy, if they
were degraded, it was because some Americans continued to regulate
their lives and their policies by the outdated principles and prejudices of
aristocratic Europe. According to Sedgwick, Americans generally had
an instinctive understanding of the true character of their society, but
their understanding was often encrusted with the "folly, pride, old
fashions, worm-eaten superstitions" of the past. He published his *Hints
to My Countrymen* as a primer to educate Americans in correct principles
and to sweep from their "intellectual houses the dust and filth which for
ages has gathered there."[9]

Although few thinkers located their ideals in the New England village,
many American Liberals shared the belief that social reform depended

primarily on the eradication of the prejudices and practices of the European past. While the two New Englanders were formulating their vision, Verplanck was attempting to improve the legal basis for the commercial ethics of New York. As a scholar and as an intimate of several businessmen, it was natural for Verplanck to adopt—and to adapt—the Political Economy of Adam Smith and David Ricardo, which, while European in origin, seemed well suited to the American ideal. Verplanck particularly admired Ricardo as the great exponent of economic principles, which "formed a new era in the science of enlightened political administration." Although some men described Political Economy as "the dismal science" because of its assumption that population increases would eventually cancel out any economic gains to the individual, Verplanck praised it as a "science" that would, at least in prosperous America, enable men to develop and apply resources so as to diffuse the maximum comfort and happiness "among the greatest number of citizens." He hoped the science would provide the guidance —or at least the arguments—needed to free the enterprise of his beloved city from the inhibitions and the perversions of the past.

Like Sedgwick and Bryant, Verplanck identified correct economic principles with correct moral principles. This one-time professor of revealed religion and moral science observed that there was "one vast harmony and correspondence of all laws of the Creators' action and government," and that there was thus a natural harmony between moral science and economic science: sound policy was also moral policy. At Amherst College in 1834 Verplanck argued that the greater the knowledge of moral and economic principles "little less regular than those of physical being," the simpler the principles became, so that the advancement of knowledge would automatically improve man's ability to adopt sound and moral policy. Adherence to these principles would in society promote prosperity and "prevent the encroachment of fraud or force upon private rights, or the public weal."[10]

In 1826, disturbed by the cries of "fraud" raised against some New York merchants during the speculative boom, Verplanck himself attempted to define a principle that would both discourage real fraud and free legitimate business dealings from anachronistic habits and restrictions. In his *An Essay on the Doctrine of Contracts* he turned his lance against the common law doctrine of *caveat emptor*. Derived from an "uncommercial and narrow age," vague and often incompatible with current business practices, that doctrine had the double effect of justifying fraud while also discouraging "the timidly conscientious" from legitimate commercial coups, since it left businessmen uncertain of their obligations to those with whom they dealt. In place of this anachronism, he proposed that all commercial dealings be put under an existing law governing insurance contracts, which required a full statement of the facts of any transaction. Once the parties to any deal knew the exact nature of the value to be exchanged each man could bring legitimate shrewdness into play, confident that he was violating neither private honor nor public weal. Since fraud would be made obvious, such a "broad and universal principle of natural ethics" would also free trade from the capriciousness of the common law and the common law courts.[12]

Verplanck had great faith both in man's ability to discover ethical principles on which all persons could agree and in man's willingness to regulate his life by a rational system of ethics. Although he placed his greatest trust in New York's merchant class, his optimism embraced all Americans, for he believed that the energy and practicality of American life were creating the general understanding needed to conquer "moral and physical evil." Although the United States had not produced the great thinkers or the great literature of which Europe was so proud, asserted Verplanck in 1818, that the mass of the people, blessed by "the moral influence of a virtuous and intelligent ancestry," were working out the details of a new society which "before existed only in the Utopian dreams of philosophers." Even though Americans produced few profound ideas, they surpassed Europeans in the practical formulation of the simple, moral principles needed to govern a mass society. Just as Newton had reduced the complexities of physical nature to "the simple and sublime operation of one great principle of gravitation," so was America establishing the "elementary propositions" that as the basis of its social practices would guarantee it prosperity and social harmony.[13] The benevolent principles were simple and direct and the people were rational in Verplanck's America; no one in his circle could match his faith in the moral soundness of the dynamic society he saw around him.

If his friends could not equal Verplanck's optimism, they did share his distaste for the obscurities and complexities of the common law. Criticism of the legal system was as old as the Republic. In the 1780s the followers of Daniel Shays had assailed both the law and its representatives, one of whom was Judge Theodore Sedgwick, Sr., of Stockbridge.

Forty years later, the Judge's son Charles, in response to Bryant's complaints, wrote, "the law is a hag. . . . It wears the ugly drapery of forms and the principles of justice, the simple perceptions of truth, are so involved in the clouds of mystical learning and nonsense that the mind gropes in obscurity."[14] The legal situation in New York was even worse.

It was Harry Sedgwick who helped launch what in time became a full-scale assault, in the name of liberal ideals, on the existing legal system. A "professed reformer," he fought for a variety of good causes against the entrenched interests of society. In 1826–27, for instance, he vigorously—and vocally—came to the aid of Greek representatives in their battles with a New York firm that—hired to build ships to aid the Greeks in their rebellion against the Turks—had systematically squandered their funds. Earlier, Harry Sedgwick had helped fight the battles of his fellow Unitarians; later he came to the legal defense of allegedly escaped slaves.[15] Given this disposition, it was natural for Sedgwick to condemn the existing system of law as unnaturally complex, unjust, time consuming, and expensive. He soon discovered, not to his surprise, that the majority of lawyers, having learned the ways through the thickets of law, preferred the old role of guide for clients to the role of prophet of a new and simpler legal order.

In 1822, therefore, Harry Sedgwick appealed to the public in an anonymous pamphlet[16] in which he argued in favor of a more expeditious "American practice"—specifically, a more convenient and rational written code which would simplify the process of justice. In this and in later attacks he resorted to rhetoric that then and for two more decades was favored by the enemies of a wide variety of existing practices. The legal system, he charged, preserved the ignorant and aristocratic ways of the barbaric past long after independence from England had guaranteed the United States a distinctive social and political development. The different and superior nature of American society required a simpler, more precise system of laws. Sedgwick argued in 1824 that the existing system had been outmoded by the silent revolution that had occurred in free society: "The expansion of a country, the increase of its wealth, its foreign and domestic intercourse, its new acquisitions moral and physical, the new relations into which it is thrown, and the changes consequent on these all tend to produce a revolution in its jurisprudence." Failure to carry out this revolution would threaten future "human improvement."[17]

Like Verplanck, Harry accepted the progressive tendencies of the urban-industrial society that was beginning to emerge; in 1831 he expressed confidence in the social benefits resulting from the growing density of population (which would improve efficiency) and the increasing use of machinery and steam power. This dynamic society appealed to a man who had harnessed within him a nobility of vision and a strong entre-preneurial drive. Harry, having committed his own interests to the expansive tendencies of the economy, was anxious both for himself and for others to win more freedom to transact business. Even before 1820, he had started to invest his savings in likely enterprises; understandably, he classed usury laws restricting interest rates with those legal inheritances "which are alike incompatible with the present state of knowledge, and with our institutions." In a sense, the chief barrier to enterprise was the part of the legal system that had originated in the feudalistic, precapi-talistic past; the chief enemies of enterprise were the conservative portion of the landed gentry and its allies at the bar and on the bench; the friends of enterprise were all those who suffered from archaic restrictions—and not merchants alone. Although Harry died before the tumults of the 1830s began, he foreshadowed the Jacksonian coalition of petty capitalists and workers with which his friend Bryant was to be aligned, when in 1824 he coupled as anachronisms the usury laws with the "laws against the combinations of mechanics to obtain wages from their employers."[18]

Harry's views were given poignancy by the troubles he and Robert Sedgwick encountered in the 1820s. First came a dispute with James Fenimore Cooper, who, among the early friends of the Sedgwicks, was the person most closely identified with the landed gentry. In 1818–19 Cooper had tried his hand at commerce in an effort to pay off the debts he had inherited with his father's estate. Apparently in order to invest in a whaling expedition, he borrowed money from Robert Sedgwick. Robert soon learned to heed the common warning against lending money to one's friends. Not only was Cooper unable to repay the loan, but he soon began to complain that Sedgwick was cheating him by exacting 1.5 percent interest per month rather than the 1 percent that Cooper said they had agreed upon. Then in 1823 Cooper's only son died, he lost much of his property through foreclosure or fire; and he suffered a sunstroke. At the end of his resources, he turned over to Sedgwick as payment of his debt his Fenimore Farm at Cooperstown, property which had sentimental value, since it adjoined the place where he had been born. The farm did not cover the debt, because, so Cooper complained, the Sedgwicks sold off the land as a whole rather than dividing it up into more profitable parcels as he had instructed. When Robert demanded the remainder of the debt, Cooper refused to pay. In 1824–25 Robert Sedgwick sued at least three times for repayment, finally driving the harried and stubborn New Yorker to resort to what he admitted was an "odious" expedient: pleading the protection of the usury law. Early in 1826 Robert dropped the suit, but the friendship shared by Cooper and the Sedgwicks had come to an end.[19]

If Robert's loan turned out badly, Harry's major adventure in capitalism ended in personal tragedy. In 1825 he had invested both his money and his hopes in a project to mine anthracite coal in Rhode Island. "Harry is buried deep in it," wrote Catherine, "He scarcely hears you when you speak to him on any other subject." His enthusiasm even affected Bryant, who in 1825 wrote a poem in reply to those who scoffed at the quality of Rhode Island anthracite:

> Thou in those island mines didst slumber long;
> But now thou art come forth to move the earth,
> And put to shame the men that mean thee wrong:
> Thou shalt be coals of fire to those who hate thee,
> And warm the shins of all that underrate thee.

However, Rhode Island coal did not warm the shins of anyone for very long. By 1827, while shipments of anthracite had begun to reach the Boston market, there were signs that neither the capital nor the coal involved were sufficient to sustain Harry's dreams of "boundless wealth."[20]

Harry was not the kind of person to yield gracefully to defeat. Already preoccupied with his legal work for the Greeks, he drove himself to exhaustion and overused his eyes to the point of near blindness. Long days of labor with impaired eyes, followed by nights "sleepless with anxiety," did their work. Harry went insane. Catherine wrote in her journal for December 1828: "To see a mind, once so powerful, so effective, so luminous, darkened, disordered, a broken instrument—to see him stared at by the vulgar, the laugh of children—oh, it is too much." The mind was not wholly broken. Harry recovered his sanity sufficiently in 1830–31 to produce some of the more powerful defenses of his times for free trade and for abolitionism. But this brilliant mind was soon extinguished: in December 1831, at the age of forty-seven, Harry Sedgwick died.[21]

Harry's tragic end was to his friends a warning that not all was well in the dynamic society. Americans had long hoped that their unique experiment with liberty would usher in a new age of prosperity, harmony, and happiness and that material progress was in harmony with social ideals. But the years of the 1820s had indicated that even in America progress was not always compatible with paradise. Was the system wrong? The new generation of liberals ascribed America's fundamental troubles not to her system but to the presence of ideas, practices, and institutions inherited from the European past. "Here the free spirit of mankind at length," Bryant had written in "The Ages" in 1820, "throws its fetters off," but some of the fetters, he found, remained to curb "the giant's" natural strength. What champion could be found to break the fetters and release Freedom's predestined purity and strength? In 1828 Bryant and his friends believed they had found the hero who might reconcile progress and paradise.

4

THE MAKING OF JACKSONIANS

In the spring of 1823 Cooper, his curiosity prevailing over his fading Federalism, went to examine Thomas Sully's new portrait of Thomas Jefferson. The portrait was a political revelation to Cooper. To his surprise, he found not the advocate of "infidelity and political heresy," clad in the red breeches of radicalism conjured up by his Federalist mentors, but "a gentleman appearing in all republican simplicity. . . . It has really shaken my opinion of Jefferson as a man, if not as a politician." The complete conversion came in 1830 when he read a collection of Jefferson's letters published the previous year. "Have we not," he asked a friend, "had a false idea of that man? I own he begins to appear to me to be the greatest man we ever had." Further reflection led him to moderate his enthusiasm on the grounds that the Virginian had been too optimistic and too dogmatic in his views of human nature, but Cooper held to his general conclusion that the man whom Federalists had once denounced as an enemy of the social order was in fact its friend.[1]

The nature of this conversion is revealing. Cooper responded favorably when he discovered that Jefferson, far from being the dangerous "Red Breeches" of Federalist myth, was a landed gentleman. As Bryant identified his ideals with nature and with the village, Cooper—inclined to conceive of society in terms of persons rather than of systems—centered his ideals around the landed gentleman, who was as necessary for harmony and progress in Cooper's scheme of human relations as was equal opportunity in the social scheme of his Yankee friend. In 1823, the year in which his conversion began, the novelist presented in *The Pioneers,* a social ideal that in the future became the essence of his version of American society. The ideal was embodied in the person of Judge Temple. Temple, modeled after Cooper's father (and Sully's Jefferson?), is an aristocrat, the guardian of law, order, and excellence; but he is an American aristocrat, the product of freedom rather than of European class privilege. Freedom had enabled his family to win its station through talent and energy—freedom benefited by the order and excellence which he preserved.[2]

It was Cooper's hope that American society would produce a leadership elite of such natural gentlemen that formed the heart of his social views. Through their influence over the people, these men of intelligence and virtue would sustain not only the popular respect for human and moral law needed to preserve free society but also the style of living that Cooper thought essential for a superior society. Despite his real and reputed ruggedness, the novelist had a strong aesthetic quality, a respect for taste, and a dislike of vulgarity, which increased his distance from the mass of Americans. Like his friends, he believed that freedom fostered human decency, but, far more than they, he considered the people to be intellectually mediocre; the average person was inclined to imitate the fashions adopted at the top of society, even if they were bad: in *The Pioneers,* settlers build their homes in imitation of Judge Temple's great house, an architectual monstrosity concocted by ignorant builders.[3] Would the real leaders of American society be American gentlemen? Would Americans accept good leadership and good fashions? Would they accept James Fenimore Cooper?

In the 1820s the answers to these questions were generally affirmative. Cooper was the idol of the reading public, while politically his hopes were sustained both by his new image of Jefferson and by the presence of a popular leader who had won Cooper's attention by 1826, when Jefferson died. Although the novelist hardly can be ranked as one of Andrew Jackson's most enthusiastic admirers, he favored the "Old Hero" and, in a limited sense, had helped invent him as a political symbol. Jackson, in his popular character, bore a strong resemblance to the popular hero of Cooper's "Leatherstocking" novels (three of which had been published by 1827), the often cantankerous but always pure Natty

Bumppo, who possessed "little of civilization but its highest principles." But Jackson, to Cooper, was more than this simple hero of the outermost frontier; the Tennessee planter was also Judge Temple, the American aristocrat, a positive force in political society. Cooper was a strong nationalist who considered presidential leadership a necessity in American government. Jackson, he hoped, had a "formidable character for decision" which, when exercised as President, would both strengthen devotion to republican principles at home and enhance the nation's reputation abroad.[4] During his seven years in Europe after 1826, the novelist became a very self-conscious defender of national honor against European insults, and he looked for help and encouragement from home; President Jackson, at least, did not disappoint him.

Because he conceived of American politics in terms of persons rather than of parties, Cooper was able to move easily from Federalism to Jacksonianism. During his youth, he had not strongly identified himself either with the Federalist party or with the party wars that troubled the administrations of both Jefferson and Madison. In fact, as a hot-blooded young nationalist anxious to strike back at Britain's insulting treatment of the United States during these years, Cooper applied for, and received, a midshipman's commission in the Navy from the Jefferson administration. And so while other young Federalists were raging at Jefferson's Embargo, Cooper was helping to enforce that "Dambargo" on Lake Ontario. He had no strong commitments to Federalism to break and no violent antipathies toward Jeffersonian Republicans to overcome; politically, he was a free agent. Briefly in the early 1820s he did participate in partisan politics as a professed Federalist, but his political interests centered on De Witt Clinton, a gentleman of quality—and Jackson's first prominent backer in New York State.[5]

While Cooper had floated above the seething waters of politics, many of his friends had been awash in a sea of troubles. Verplanck, Bryant, and the Sedgwicks all had been devoted Federalists who, with varying degrees of intensity, had battled Jefferson and his policies. Contrary to the popular sterotype of Federalism nurtured by the victorious Republican party, these men were hostile not to Republican government but to "democracy," to demagogues who persuaded a deluded people to reach beyond their capacities. Jefferson, as they had seen him, was indeed "Red Breeches," the demagogue and ideologue who upset the fundamental harmony of the Republic. They entered politics during the stormy days of the Embargo, when it was possible to attribute all of the economic and political troubles of their day to Jefferson and his supposed leanings toward France; Jefferson, so they argued, had through duplicity and executive corruption gained the power to debase, if not destroy, the work of Washington and Hamilton—this threat was "democracy." The pronounced aim of these young Federalists was to restore the Republic to its golden days with the aid of the people; this idea was to do much service in American political rhetoric.

These attitudes were especially evident in Verplanck's early political career. The New Yorker entered politics in 1808 as a founder of the Washington Benevolent Society, a Federalist political organization created to rally public opinion against Jefferson and his Embargo.[6] Working as they were in a city that was particularly sensitive to any interference with its foreign trade, the leaders of the society soon had reason to judge their efforts successful on the local level; between 1809 and 1816 the Federalists controlled the Common Council in New York. In 1809 Verplanck analyzed for his fellow members the political situation in terms that resembled the partisan attitudes and rhetoric of the 1820s. In reference to Jefferson's policies, he noted that the American people had permitted themselves to become "the tools of the crafty and the turbulent," but in time their "cool moderation and shrewd goodness" would enable them "to distinguish their real from their pretended friends"—if their real friends would only take an active part in politics. Never fear, he told his Federalist audience in conclusion, "The people will arise in the majesty of their might, and SAVE THEMSELVES." In a footnote to the published speech he suggested another safeguard for the Republic, one which was to occupy a central place in his future thought: Because America presented "a boundless field of active enterprise" which satisfied man's ambitions for wealth and power, there was little to fear from those adventurers who, being denied political and economic opportunities in Europe, "so often throw into commotion those old and populous states."[7]

Mere political rhetoric? Certainly these arguments were to become the common stock of the politicians who came from Verplanck's generation, but behind the rhetoric was sufficient confidence in the people to lead Verplanck to reject the desperate policies that were to ruin some of his fellow Federalists. In 1811, in his "Coody Letter," he satirized the hysteria mongers of both political parties. Abimelech Coody, the innocent hero, has difficulty finding a safe place to invest his money. He considers the Bank of the United States, but is frightened off by Federalist warnings that Congress plans to blow up the Bank. He thinks of investing in a rope-walk, but the rope-walk burns down; this, warn Republicans, was part of a British plot "to burn down all the manufacturing in America," for had not the dastardly English been "found out in burning up Patterson-falls to destroy the cotton"? Coody makes no investment.[8] Partisan politics has upset the inherently smoothly functioning political and economic mechanism of republican society.

Some twenty years later a less good-humored version of this same attitude was to lead Verplanck away from Andrew Jackson, but in 1811 it helped prepare him to support "Old Hickory" in 1828. Unlike many Federalists, Verplanck backed the War of 1812—to the point that in 1814 he organized a distinct American Federalist party (the "Coodies" as its members were tagged by its enemies) in New York that both upheld the war and opposed his bete noir, De Witt Clinton. Support of the war and hostility to Clinton outlined his postwar political career. He was among those Federalists who in 1820 publicly acknowledged the political death of their party and their adherence to the Republican organization, specifically to the Republican faction in New York State headed by Martin Van Buren. (Cooper characteristically chose this time to make his strongest commitment to the Federalist party.) In 1828 Van Buren was to be the "Little Magician" who helped conjure up Jackson's victory in the presidential elections.[9]

In a real sense, Verplanck was able to adjust to the new politics that followed the War of 1812 even before the war began. Bryant was not so fortunate. After Jefferson's victory in 1800, many New England Federalists had experienced a sense of political isolation so deep that it drove some of them to desperate thoughts of secession from the Union. It was in such an atmosphere that Peter Bryant, devoted Federalist and frustrated gentleman that he was, could denounce Republicans as Jacobinical advocates of mob rule and could declare that breathing "the mephitic vapour of democracy" made him physically ill. When the Embargo troubles began, it was natural that his son should let his poetic "thunder" fly at both Jefferson and "democracy." Writing at a time when the "Dambargo" had depressed the New England economy, the young Federalist attacked Jefferson not only as an enemy of commerce but as an ally of Napoleon, the tyrant of Europe. "Throw off a weak and cunning ruler," he urged, but, perhaps thinking of the plebiscite which had made Napoleon emperor, he expressed doubt that the people would resist the specious appeal of the doctrine of human equality offered to them by knavish American demagogues:

> Men uninformed, in rage for something new
> Howe'er unprincipled, howe'er untrue,
> Suck in with greedy throat the gilded pill,
> Whose fatal sweetness pleases but to kill.

Having himself swallowed the sour pill of pessimistic Federalism, Bryant had little hope, even after a second look at the situation, that the masses would recognize the Republican leaders as the knaves he thought they were. In the second edition of his poem, "The Embargo," dated April 1808, he petitioned:

> Oh, snatch me heaven! to some sequester'd spot,
> Where Jefferson and faction are forgot;

There was one ray of hope cast by a leader ("Massachusetts' pride") who might succeed in replacing "democracy" with "Truth," but only the dimmest of rays could come from that source: Timothy Pickering, a bitter Federalist partisan associated with the seccession-minded extremists in New England.[10]

Bryant's rage against "democracy" was inflamed not only by the Embargo but by the Republican victory in the Massachusetts' elections of 1806. After 1809, with the repeal of the Embargo and the revival of Federalist dominance in the state, he exempted the people of New England from his political hostilities. Engrossed in personal concerns as he was, he said little about politics during the years between 1809 and 1814, but it is apparent that he considered the national administration to be hostile to the interest of his section, particularly when in 1812 President Madison ("His Imbecility") initiated war against the British. When in the summer of 1814 the New England economy began to suffer from the effects of the British blockade, the frustrated young man became a fire-eater prepared to fight in defense of his native state—even against the national government if necessary. But never was militancy more ill-timed; the War soon ended, and this pugnacious states' righter disappeared forever.[11]

In later years, Bryant tried to forget his youthful indiscretions, including "The Embargo," of which at times he was belligerently ashamed.

Although he never disowned Federalism itself, it is plain that his experiences did contribute to his general indifference to politics in the decade after 1815. Unlike Verplanck, he had no occasion to work with political leaders and no experience with the problems of government, except in the petty political sphere at Great Barrington. By 1820 he had became as apolitical as an American could possibly be. In his Fourth of July oration of that year, he did note how "wonderful" it was that freedom had not given birth to "dangerous and visionary doctrines," but he attributed this success to the institutions and habits of republican life, not to men or policies. During his remaining years in Massachusetts, he kept himself aloof from politics, although he did not fail to note ironically the manner of Governor Levi Lincoln when he reviewed the local militia:

> How oft he smiled and bowed to Jonathan!
> How many hands were shook and votes were won.

That he did not, like Cooper, continue to float above the miasma of politics can be attributed to the new relationships he acquired when he came to New York. The Sedgwicks, while they showed little interest in party politics, were concerned with government policy, particularly as it affected economic activity. Under their tutelage, Bryant acquired some knowledge of the free-trade principles of Adam Smith, David Ricardo, Jean Baptiste Say, and Theodore Sedgwick.[12] From Verplanck, too, Bryant gained some interest in the principles and politics of government. It is doubtful, however, that he would have abandoned his essentially apolitical stance if he had not associated himself with the *Evening Post*, where he gained not only a commitment to politics but an editorial policy that gave him specific political direction.

Twenty-five years after he joined the *Post*, the venerable editor remaked that he had set the course that the newspaper had taken. Apparently he had forgotten that as early as 1826 the general direction had already been determined by William Coleman, transplanted New Englander, Federalist, and enemy of the Embargo. In 1824 Coleman had supported Verplanck for Congress on the grounds that the New Yorker was hostile to the protective tariff, which interfered with foreign commerce. In the presidential elections of that same year, Coleman had shown a preference for Jackson over John Quincy Adams, whom he hated as an apostate from the Federalist cause; Adams had broken with Federalism in 1808 to support the Embargo. Two years later, in the wake of the panic of 1825, Coleman had published a tract blaming the debacle on excessive issues of paper money by New York banks.[13] Three main ingredients of Bryant's editorials were to be dislike for the tariff, support for Jackson, and suspicion of paper money and banks.

The Sedgwicks, Verplanck, Coleman, and the New York he observed in his role as journalist—these were Bryant's teachers in the world of politics. He learned quickly. As a newspaper editor, he was obliged to present faithfully at least one side of any controversy that might shake the commercial world, and even during the years of relative political peace, there were controversies enough to attract his attention both to economic questions and to the liberal rhetoric that frequently clad such questions. When in 1826, for instance, the panic led to a sharp drop in foreign trade, Bryant had a ringside seat for two distinct attacks launched by irate New Yorkers against two apparent sources of their woes: the auction system and the protective tariff. For years, foreign imports had been auctioned off to American merchants, a practice, that, because it promised lower prices for the goods, had strengthened New York's position as the nation's leading port of entry. But both smaller importers and native producers of goods competitive with imports were hurt by the system; and early in 1828, spurred on by poor business, they banded together to petition Congress for a discriminatory tax on auctions. The system, they argued, should be destroyed, because it was both a "monopoly" harmful to "the regular importers" and a moral evil that encouraged fraud and speculation:

> The mutual confidence that subsisted, in our better days, between the responsible importer and his customers, has long since given place to constant and well founded fears of being cheated by men who are shrouded in darkness—whose very names are unknown, and who have not any character to lose.[14]

With this cry of petty capitalists, the first of a long series against the power and anonymity of "monopoly," Bryant could sympathize. In September the *Post* condemned the system "as a monopoly exercised by a few under the sanction of law" which violated "the principles of free trade." Bryant was beginning to use the rhetoric that soon was to characterize *Post* editorials. And he was learning the panaceas, too. In October he published the proposals of Professor John McVickar of Columbia, one of the first American political economists. McVickar argued that the evil would be destroyed not by legislative restrictions such as the tax demanded by the anti-auction men, but by throwing the auction privilege open to all. If the system of special licenses protecting the auctioneers were to be abolished, "there will then be a competition of character as well as profit, and the interest of self-interest will impose a guarantee more certain and efficacious than any that the laws can devise."[15]

The fact that Bryant published these free trade arguments just two weeks before the congressional elections suggests that he was attempting to educate the public to the political virtues of Verplanck, as well as to correct principles. In 1828 Verplanck, as a member of the House Committee of Ways and Means, had voted to postpone consideration of the petition for a federal tax on auctions, because he suspected that the anti-auction movement was directed by manufacturers who wanted to diminish competition from imports. In retaliation for this decision, a meeting of "mechanics" hostile to the auction system in October nominated a candidate to oppose Verplanck for Congress. The *Post* responded by stressing the all-embracing glories of free trade, one of whose most prominent champions was the congressman. Stay with Verplanck, Bryant urged voters, because he could best help establish "the principles of free trade and unrestricted industry" so conducive to New York's prosperity. In the congressional elections, New Yorkers agreed with the *Post;* Verplanck was re-elected by a substantial majority.[16]

By stressing the virtues of free trade, Bryant apparently hoped to unite behind Verplanck the importing interests of the city, antiauction and pro auction, against the most obnoxious interference with trade, the protective tariff. Disgruntled New Yorkers had blamed the tariff of 1824 for the economic collapse in 1825; in 1828 Congress was considering an even higher tariff. To mobilize public opposition to the tariff bill, Bryant, as the editor, and Verplanck, as the anonymous Washington correspondent of the *Post,* sharpened the newspaper's already outspoken opposition to protectionism. Twenty years before, Bryant had denounced the Embargo as the

> Curse of our nation, source of countless woes
> From whose dark womb unreckon'd misery flows.

He had condemned this interference with trade, the product of corrupt and stupid politics, as ruinous to laborer, mechanic, sailor, and farmer.

Now he denounced the tariff as a conspiracy of "speculating manufacturers and bankrupt politicians. . . . to build up an artificial and short-lived industry upon the ruins of agriculture and commerce." Such efforts to force American capital into unnatural channels would further upset the economic order. The epitaph on the tomb of the prostrate economy should be:

> I was well
> I would be better,
> I took physic,
> And here I am.[17]

In the parlance of liberalism adopted by Bryant and his friends, the protective tariff was an especially dangerous example of political interference with trade in favor of the few and the expense of the many, an interference with correct and natural principles, and a return to the follies of the aristocratic past from which the United States generally had escaped. In 1828, despite the arguments, folly triumphed: Congress passed the measure that soon won just notoriety as the "Tariff of Abominations."

When President Adams signed the bill into law, he nailed one more plank in the bridge which led from Bryant's Federalist past to his Jacksonian future. Bryant remembered Adams as the archapostate from the Federalist cause during the Embargo days. Could such a man be trusted with the fate of the Republic? Hardly. Adams had been guilty of further apostasy in 1824 when, charged the *Post,* he had virtually bought the presidency, over the objections of the people, by surrendering his earlier hostility to the tariff in order to win the support of the archprotectionist, Henry Clay. Now his administration had committed itself to a "ruinous unjust and oppressive system of monopoly" which enabled a few favored capitalists to get rich at the expense of the people. In short, where once young Bryant had denounced Adams and interference with trade in the same poem in which he condemned "democracy," now the editor denounced Adams and the tariff in editorials favoring Jackson, the democratic hero.[18]

In sharp contrast to the "apostate," stood the "Old Hero." If Jackson's pronouncements in favor of a "judicious tariff" did not fully satisfy freetraders, they were at least better than Adams' outright protectionism. In any case, there were reasons for favoring Jackson other than hostility to the tariff—less tangible, perhaps, but equally as compelling. During the Embargo crisis, the boy poet had appealed for some hero to restore the harmony and virtue of the Republic:

> Oh for a WASHINGTON, whose boundless mind
> Infolds his friends, his country, and mankind;
> He might restore our happy state again.

Jackson may not have had a boundless mind, but he did appear to have the moral stature, the natural grandeur, to rally Americans to a new devotion to Republican principles. In 1828 Bryant described the frontier hero as the embodiment of the virtues resulting from the fusion of America's natural purity with the best civilized values, as a man of "strong, clear good sense and upright intentions," gifted with "that natural good breeding, that quick perception of and delicate regard to the feelings of others, which is so much superior to the politeness of forms." And President Adams? He was a mere "pedantic rhetorician."[19] For Bryant and other Federalists, Jackson had the additional appeal of offering them a way of escaping with dignity from a past they would like to forget into the democratic present, for they knew that this old Republican and hero of the War of 1812 had favored forgiveness of Federalists. And Adams? He had helped dredge up bitter memories by reviving in 1824 the old charges that Federalist extremists (such as Bryant had been) had been disloyal to the nation during its time of crisis before 1815.[20]

Jackson's presence and promise in 1828 undoubtedly made it easier for Bryant to participate in the politics of the time, not only as an editor but as a poet: He contributed a short-lived ode to the campaign, giving one Jacksonian the opportunity to claim "that the Jackson cause has all of the poetry as well as the virtue of the land." Was it possible that Bryant hoped that victory for the "Old Hero," who stood above politics, would end political discord and smother the politicians who had upset the natural harmony of the Republic? Certainly in 1827, disappointed by his failure to make literature a full-time career, he had expressed the hope that politics, which he saw as absorbing America's intellectual and aesthetic energies, would decline in the future. Some two years later, after Jackson's victory, he could exult over the inauguration of the new President: "*The long agony is over* ... and the New Administration, the strongest ever since the days of Washington, has entered upon its career." The next year he noted that at least half of

Jackson's first cabinet were "old federalists."[21]   In Jackson's triumph then, there was reason to hope for the end of that era of controversy which Bryant had experienced most intensely and painfully as a young man.   However, although the conflict between Federalists and Republicans indeed was buried, Bryant was to learn with disappointment that the anticipated era of good feelings did not begin with but, such as it was, ended with the inauguration of Andrew Jackson.

5

TARIFFS AND TURMOIL

In March 1831, during that last lucid period before his death, Harry Sedgwick, legal reformer and disappointed capitalist, wrote: "Such is the abundant provision made for man by his creator—such are the capacities with which man is endowed by his creator—that poverty and want are not entailed on man ... but are the results of war and misgovernment." On this note of hope Sedgwick opened his last crusade, writing over the name "A Friend of the Poor." He defined "the poor" as the "great majority in every community"; it is evident that he used the term in the same sense that Jacksonian Democrats were soon using "people" to include farmers, small businessmen, mechanics, and other members of the enterprising middle class.[1] Sedgwick published over the next eight months forty-seven letters in the Philadelphia *Banner of the Constitution* attacking the protective tariff as a particularly gross act of misgovernment. It damaged "every trade and occupation," violated property rights and the Constitution, shortened human life, deterred railroad construction, depressed land values, discouraged immigration, caused the substitution of "poisonous for genuine liquors," and (Harry bowed to the rhetoric of the day) corrupted the public morals needed to maintain "our republican institutions."[2]

Above all, however, this "friend of the poor" spoke for that commerce in European imports and American agricultural exports which New

York had developed with its expanding hinterlands. The tariff, he charged, had damaged not only the import trade but the whole fruitful union of agriculture and commerce as well, depressing "the mercantile cities in general, and the country which received its supplies and the stimulus to its industry, in great part, from the mercantile cities."[3] Agriculture and commerce—traditional though this union appeared, it was not the old Jeffersonian relationship in which agriculture reigned and commerce served, but a dynamic, progressive economy in which the capitalist and the city played the vital roles. Harry had identified himself with the age of Steam and Money, which was introducing America to the Industrial Revolution. In his articles he condemned the tariff for checking such essentials of a capitalistic economy as the accumulation of wealth, the use and improvement of machinery, the division of labor, and the creation of efficient transportation in the form of railroads, which he considered superior to canals in moving masses of freight; many New Yorkers, dazzled by the success of the Erie Canal, would not recognize the superiority of railroads for at least another decade.[4]

Harry's ideas were scattered and undeveloped. Perhaps, if he had lived longer, this most brilliant of the Sedgwicks would have learned to grapple with the great problem, so important to the 1830s, of reconciling the new capitalistic reality with republican ideals. But Sedgwick died, and part of the responsibility fell to his part-time protégé, Bryant, whose enthusiasm for the capitalistic reality was considerably less than his love for the harmonies of nature. This bias was particularly evident in the editor's attacks on the protective tariff during the late 1820s. Although he most often denounced the tariff for depressing the commerce of New York, he also expressed concern that it would stimulate industrial progress disruptive of the existing social order, particularly of that strongly individualistic society that was his ideal.[5]

In 1827 and 1828 the *Evening Post* had cautioned its readers that the tariff, by encouraging factory manufacturing, would bring the worst features of the Industrial Revolution to America. In November 1829 Bryant warned that industrial England had purchased its prosperity and power at the expense of thousands of English lives, the exploitation and degradation of factory workers, industrial turmoil, and the concentration of wealth in the hands of the relative few. He closed his editorial with a quote from the *Southern Review:*

The period will approach rapidly when no small capitalist can enter into competition with a great one. It will no longer be the trial of skill, industry or economy, but the contest of machinery, which no small capital can acquire or maintain—and no laborer will find employment who will not work for the lowest wages on which life can possibly be supported.[6]

The factory system, then, would weaken the class of small entrepreneurs in favor of a mass of dependent, degenerate, and desperate proletarians. The result would be a breakdown of morality, freedom, and social order. In 1828 the *Post* warned that a strike and rumored riot at Paterson, New Jersey, omened what the tariff would bring: "When instead of manufacturing villages, we shall have manufacturing cities, and when turning out and frame-breaking shall become the common incidents of the day."[7]

In 1829 New York politics threw up more tangible and immediate evidence of the dangers of industrialism. In April economic troubles drove some workingmen to unite politically against efforts to lengthen their workday or otherwise damage their interests. Before the year was out, the Working Men's party apparently fell under the influence of Thomas Skidmore and the English feminist and gadfly, Frances Wright, both of whom Bryant identified with the alien notions of class conflict, abolition of private property, and atheism. The editor's first response was to ridicule "the petticoat Gammaliel" (sic) and her "atheistical fanaticism," but he was less amused when prior to the city election in November the "Fanny Wright" party seemingly won much worker support for its radical program.[8]

At election time the *Post* earnestly urged "all the sober, respectable mechanics" of the city to vote against "persons who scoff at morality, and propose a system of public robbery." When the workingmen showed considerable strength in the local elections, Bryant lectured then on the virtues and necessity of the existing system of petty capitalism. The "agrarian" doctrines (for the equal division of property) of the radicals, warned the *Post*, would lead to "the abolition of all social relations" and thence to the disintegration of society itself. Private property was essential to civilization; to destroy every man's right to possess what he acquires by his own labor would remove "all incentive to industry, and all deference to public opinion," and so lead men into a state of idleness, poverty, and violence. There was no need for industrious workers to adopt the agrarian scheme, because New York was "an active and industrious community" in which men of all ranks could rise. Indeed, there were "multitudes of young men" who expressed satisfaction with the existing system: "They want no re-partition of property, no abolition of the right of inheritance. Every day they see the laws of society effecting this re-partition without other aid. The wealth of the luxurious and idle leaves their coffers to replenish those of the industrious and the frugal." How simple and effective was the ideal economy![9]

Although in November 1830 Bryant repeated his warning against the radicals and their "wild, Jack Cade scheme of legislation," he had begun to recognize that the mass of politically conscious workingmen, far from being "agrarian-minded" proletarians, were actually small enterprisers struggling to preserve the very system he had outlined. Bryant, both as editor and poet, showed little compassion for the poor and the helpless. In the winter of 1831, the *Post* both condemned, on constitutional grounds, federal allotments of wood to the poor in the District of Columbia and suggested (seriously) that those unable to afford adequate blankets should use a single blanket covered with snow—although it could suggest no way of preventing the snow from melting during the night.[10] But Bryant could sympathize with the "plainer part of the community, respectable mechanics and trades people," the class of enterprisers with whom he was to join in the mid-1830s battle against the monied capitalists of New York.[11] The workingmen, then, hardly threatened to disorganize society; however, the pervasive menace of the protective tariff remained. In fact, by 1831 the monster had begun to breathe its disorganizing fire not only on New York but on the nation as well.

The center of the danger was South Carolina. That State had staked its fortunes on cotton planting, and so suffered even more severely than New York from the collapse of cotton prices in the mid-1820s. In 1826 Bryant's brother, Cyrus, who tended store in Columbia, had warned his brothers Peter and John to stay away from South Carolina because "the general depression in the cotton market has made business very dull in this part of the country." Dull business made for sharp tempers. By 1828, convinced that the protective tariff had caused their plight, some South Carolinians vowed resistance to protectionism "no matter to what it leads." Initially, both Bryant and Verplanck had welcomed the rumblings from the South as a convenient illustration of the evils of the tariff, but, as South Carolina began seriously to threaten to nullify the tariff within its borders, the two men realized that the nation faced a crisis.[12]

Although they sympathized with the state, neither the editor nor the congressman would countenance the doctrine of nullification. In December 1830 the *Post* warned that to apply the doctrine would disrupt the Union and advised South Carolinians that they had two choices: To secede from the nation (which Bryant did not anticipate) or patiently to appeal "to the natural equity in the people and the legislators." Bryant apparently had forgotten his own militant mistrust of national majorities during his Federalist youth. In the summer of 1832 Congress exhausted the meager patience of the Nullifiers by enacting a protective tariff less obnoxious than that of 1828. Moderate freetraders considered the new tariff to be a step toward the end of protectionism; radical South Carolinians feared that its acceptability to the moderates would make it the basis for a permanent policy of protection. Soon after President Jackson signed the bill, the Nullifiers won control in South Carolina and prepared to put their doctrine into effect. The crisis had come.[13]

Who was responsible for disturbing that "profound quiet and repose" in the nation of which Bryant had boasted less than two years before? The crisis, as Bryant defined it, stemmed not from any deep-seated conflict between interest groups, whether between Northerners and Southerners or between manufacturers and planters, but from the machinations of selfish politicians, particularly of those "bold politicians of the West and South," Henry Clay and John C. Calhoun. Calhoun, whom Bryant had described earlier as looking "as if the fever of political ambition had dried up all the juice ... of his constitution," had fired the burning discontent in the South. Henry Clay was the arch villain, since he was responsible not only for the extremism of northern tariff supporters but also for the protectionism that had caused most of the trouble. On the eve of the presidential elections in 1832, the *Post* warned that Clay's election "would be the signal of the dissolution of the States." Bryant was formulating that strongly partisan style that was to make the *Post* one of the most hated journals of his day. Rarely did he treat issues as arising from differences of principles and interests, for he preferred to attribute any disharmony to the selfishness and unreason of individuals.[14]

If there were villains, there was also a hero, in this case the "Old Hero" himself. Jackson had disappointed the freetraders during his first two years in office, for he had failed even to modify the "Tariff of Abominations" and then had added apparent insult to injury by appointing two protectionists (Samuel Ingham and Louis McLane) as his first secretaries of the treasury. Even in 1831 when he advocated tariff reform, he still offended the *Post* by defending the government's right to provide tariff protection for selected industries. By 1832, however, he had begun to live up to his promise of 1828 as a defender of the Republic against disorganizing politicians. During the presidential campaign, Bryant was able to predict that Jackson's firmness and wisdom would triumph over the twin enemies, the tariff and sectionalism. He was right. The President's re-election weakened anti-tariff extremism in most of the South, thereby isolating South Carolina and dampening the ardor of the Nullifiers. It was true that in late 1832 the South Carolinians made good their threat to nullify the tariffs of 1828 and 1832, but Jackson's forceful use of a carrot-and-stick policy both compelled the extremists to hesitate and helped reverse the protectionist tendencies of the previous decade.[15]

It was here that Verplanck narrowly missed achieving glory. Moralist though he was, the congressman also took pride in his role as a practical man. He believed that it was in the market place of human affairs rather than in the library of the theorist that men learned to understand and to apply the principles needed to manage society. Temperamentally a compromiser, he did not share Bryant's tendency to view controversies as conflicts between a fixed social good and perverse men. The tariff to him was simply poor policy, to be corrected gradually by exploring the possibilities for improvement, particularly those possibilities that benefited the merchants and shippers of New York. Such was his attitude in 1831 when he became convinced that the Nullifers were prepared to trigger their explosive doctrine.[16] On the one hand, he denounced protectionism as a "hazardous interference with the natural and spontaneous direction of labor and enterprise." On the other, he rejected as a dangerous error the southern contention that any protective tariff was unconstitutional, and he warned that such a contention, by threatening the immediate end of the protective system, precluded compromise. Verplanck felt that, wrong though it was, the system must be dismantled gradually, for total repeal would damage protected industries, upset the economy, and drive protectionists to a last-ditch defense of their interests.[17]

Early in 1833, with South Carolina teetering on the verge of armed resistance to federal authority, Verplanck followed his own advice; he introduced a bill for a step-by-step reduction of tariff duties over a two-year period to the mildly protective levels of 1816, under which (said the bill's defenders) manufacturing had flourished. Although it was condemned by South Carolina extremists for retaining the principle of protection, Verplanck's measure promised to end the crisis. But then Henry Clay shouldered Verplanck out of the spotlight by submitting a similar yet less drastic proposal that was more pleasing to protectionists. Congress, including Verplanck, voted Clay's bill through. Offered a substantial concession, and faced with Jackson's resolve to meet force with force, South Carolina drew back.

Ignoring the irony that Clay, the archprotectionist, received the credit for ending the crisis, Bryant applauded the compromise of 1833 as a major victory for Jackson, free trade, and sound morals. On the day of Jackson's second inauguration, the editor declared that the principle of free trade had prevailed over the opposition of corrupt men who "swarmed" in both houses of Congress. "A system founded on the most short-sighted selfishness has received its death blow. . . . The experiment has been fully—almost fatally—tried; and it will be recorded in our history only to avoid it."[18]

Seemingly, then, Verplanck and Bryant had good reason to congratulate each other; but the congratulations were few, for by the opening of Jackson's second term their partnership in literature and politics had broken down. The two friends, in the midst of their common triumph over the tariff, found themselves on opposite sides of what proved to be a permanent political fence. So long as the tariff issue dominated politics, the distinctive qualities of their approaches to public affairs were obscured by their general agreement that protectionism was hostile to the principles and promise of a free economy. But what were the principles? What was the nature of the promise? Indeed, what was a free economy? These were questions that both Bryant and Verplanck had to answer in the context of another explosive issue that in its effects on the two men revealed new dimensions of the liberal democratic mind.

6

BANKS—AND *THE* BANK

One April day in 1831, William Cullen Bryant, senior editor of the *Evening Post,* publicly avenged an attack on his character in the *Commercial Advertiser* by striking the editor of that newspaper, William L. Stone, vigorously over the head with a whip: "After a few blows the men closed," wrote an observer, "and the whip was wrested from Bryant and carried off by Stone." The peace-loving Bryant in the future carefully avoided any kind of physical brawl, but this incident did mark the beginning of a long series of violent verbal battles with his fellow journalists.[1]

The belligerent attitudes so ubiquitous in New York journalism during the 1830s in part grew out of the mounting tensions in American life. In these years, Bryant and other politically minded encountered head-on a perplexing problem that was inherent in the republican experiment. They had learned to conceive of the Republic in utopian terms, as an ideal society of stability, happiness, morality and, particularly, opportunity. To a degree, the reality matched the ideal. Opportunities had grown after 1815 with the rapid expansion of agriculture, commerce, and manufacturing. Americans seemingly had reason to dream noble dreams for themselves and for the nation. But hopes were accompanied by anxieties and dissatisfactions. The apparently limitless opportunities raised expectations that could not be fulfilled. Unlimited opportunities threatened to unleash limitless greeds, which would weaken the moral foundations of the Republic. How could all of the promises of the Republic, the promises of stability, happiness, and virtue as well as those of individual aggrandizement, be realized?

Americans may have disputed over the answer to this question, but they did agree that the problem somehow involved money. Gold, the traditional moral corrupter, did not concern them, however, for during these years they accepted almost without question the intrinsic virtue of gold. Rather, the issue centered on the less tangible kinds of mony demanded by an increasingly sophisticated commercial economy—bank notes and bank credit. Technically, bank notes were not money, because they were not legal tender, and yet by the 1820s they formed a great part of the currency used by Americans. Borrowers received their loans from a bank in the form of the bank's notes (promises to pay), used the notes to make purchases, and so added to the existing supply of paper currency. Banks, then, governed not only the credit system but much of the money supply. Having as they did the power to affect the lives of individual Americans for good or ill, the banks were natural issues in a society possessed by material ambitions.[2]

Were banks good or bad? Were city banks good? Country banks? Big banks? Small banks? These were important questions. Some Americans favored banks, because they appeared to stimulate progress. Harry Sedgwick, for instance, applauded his brother Theodore's efforts in 1824 to get a charter for a bank at Stockbridge. He felt it would energize the sluggish rural economy of the Berkshires by supplying much-needed currency for the area and by encouraging ambitions. True, there was the often-repeated objection that rural banks led farmers into debt, but Harry throught this was an advantage, since indebtedness taught farmers "punctuality" and forced them to give up "the shiftless way" in which they normally tilled their fields.[3]

Other Americans, however, had not outgrown "the common prejudice against country banks," or, in many cases, a prejudice against all banks. If currency and debts promised to promote economic progress, might they not also engender degrading dependence and destructive change? By late 1825 many New Yorkers had grown concerned about both city and country banks. Bryant's *New York Review* at this time quoted a contemporary comparison of the banking system to a monster: "It has no heart, no sympathy; all within its bosom is as cold as death. . . .

It never rests, until it gets everything within its bed, and what it cannot devour, it destroys by filth." The monster, indeed was active. Although the boom which had begun earlier in 1825 was beginning to falter, there were numerous projects to establish banks; when the state legislature met in January 1826, it received twenty-seven applications for bank charters from New York City, and some one hundred more from the rest of the state. Ambitions outran the state of affairs. When the speculative bubble broke, some of the newer banks broke too, taking with them the money of hundreds of luckless New Yorkers.[4]

The causes of the financial panic were complex, but many persons put the blame on "the new-fashioned money-making establishments." In November 1825 William Coleman, writing in Bryant's *United States Review*, attributed the trouble to the excessive issue of bank notes, which had engendered the "spirit of speculation," which in turn had brought the collapse. Governor De Witt Clinton made the same charge in his annual message for 1826.[5] Resentful New Yorkers thought they saw the hands of shady manipulators at work when the failure of some of the new banks revealed that their earlier enthusiasm in issuing their notes had not been matched by resources to pay off the issues. The failures left innocent note holders, depositors, stock owners, and, more generally, the people holding the bag. What, asked the *Evening Post* of the bankrupt Franklin bank, was "the secret of the magic by which the property of the bank, which no longer than last January made so fair appearance on paper, has been silently and swiftly made to disappear so as not to leave enough to pay notes and deposits?"[6]

Panics, bankruptcies—how could the public be protected from the abuses of the mysterious banking power? In the late 1820s the *Post* proposed an easy solution: Let the legislature confer charters only on those banks "in whose solidity and safety the public can confide, especially on those which have stood the test of experience. Let all the solid old Banks be rechartered." But this conservative solution ran counter to the explosive ambitions of Americans. Who could resist the temptation to back a new bank when he learned, as did the *Post's* readers, that one Albany institution had declared a dividend of 50 per cent? Moreover, the "ardor of competition and improvement," the excess of which had already troubled Bryant, proved too strong for Americans to resist. Richard Cooper summed up the situation when he wrote to his brother: "Every little village that can boast of its bar room and its store seeks to elevate itself from obscurity into commercial importance by the establishment of a bank, and it is hard to tell whether the importunity of the people in asking, or the liberality of the legislature in granting, is the greater."[7]

Prior to 1832 the *Post* was inclined to speak in favor of the established banks of New York City. In 1830 it urged that the "Safety Fund System," recently established by the state to protect noteholders, be modified so as to make it acceptable to the sound city banks, which had objected that the new system made them indirectly responsible for the notes of the far-from-sound "country" banks. But in 1832 a new issue exploded in national politics that soon drove Bryant to attack not only the shaky banks but "the solid old banks" as well.[8]

The Second Bank of the United States was a natural issue in a society concerned with matters of money and credit. On the one hand, as the only nationally chartered banking institution, as a power over the monetary system of the entire nation, it won widespread support among those who saw it as the most effective check on the free-wheeling propensities of state banks. On the other, because of its great power, it was a natural target both for those men who mistrusted all banks and for those bankers who resented its restraints, particularly for New Yorkers, since the headquarters of this great institution was in Philadelphia, New York's chief rival for commercial supremacy. Ears twitched and eyes widened, therefore, when in December 1829 President Jackson announced that he would oppose any effort to recharter the Bank.

Since the Bank's original charter did not expire until 1836, the announcement (contained in a short paragraph in the president's annual message to Congress) had little effect in diverting attention from the issues of the tariff and the state-banks. The *Post* restricted itself to praising Jackson "for giving early warning so that there would be ample time for free discussion." Bryant did not expect that the free discussion would turn into public controversy, at least for several more years. The issue, however, was too tempting and too important for political leaders to ignore. In April 1830 the majority of the House Committee of Ways and Means undertook to refute Jackson's charges that the Bank was of questionable constitutionality and expediency. Verplanck was one of the majority. A year later, majorities in both houses of the New York legislature approved resolutions against rechartering the bank, an action perhaps motivated by a desire to deflect public interest from the state's controversial banking system. Late in 1831 some of Jackson's political opponents decided to make the question an issue in the presidential election of 1832. In the summer of 1832, four years before the Bank's old charter would expire, Congress passed a bill rechartering the institution; Jackson responded with a stinging veto, and the "Bank War" was on.[9]

The controversy politically embarrassed both Bryant and Verplanck. So long as the tariff issue dominated the public mind, they could carry on their joint war against protectionism, confident that they were defending the true interests of New York, whether the interests were those of merchants, bankers, artisans, or consumers. But the Bank issue split New York society into special interest groups, even splintering the interest groups themselves, separating banker from banker, merchant from merchant, enterpriser from enterpriser. Before it was over, the controversy forced a reshuffling of the political cards in New York. It was soon apparent that Bryant and Verplanck had drawn different hands.

No one had been surprised when in 1832 Verplanck voted to recharter the Bank, for he was one of its natural supporters. The very house on Wall Street in which he had been born had been purchased in 1822 by the Bank as the site for its New York branch, a purchase that had substantially increased his father's holdings of stock in the institution. In 1829 Verplanck had joined with John Jacob Astor and other prominent New York businessmen to borrow $ 200,000 from that branch in order to establish the New York Life Insurance Company.[10] But he did not have to be a direct beneficiary to recognize the usefulness of the Bank. In years past he had concerned himself with the problem of maintaining the soundness of bank notes and other forms of credit that served as media of exchange in the business world. Although he opposed any interference with traffic in goods, particularly with the import trade, Verplanck believed that some regulation of the money supply was necessary for sound economic progress. The New York commercial community, he assumed, could manage its own financial affairs; established bankers and merchants knew their business and knew each other and could police transactions among themselves without supervision from the outside. However, because of New York's extensive dealing with its hinterlands, it was deluged daily with bank notes and bills of exchange issued by men who lived beyond the direct control and oversight of the business community. How was the city to protect itself from unsound notes and bills? The natural answer was a national bank. With its national influence and apparent devotion to sound finance, the Bank acted to facilitate honest transactions and at the same time served as a dike protecting commercial New York from a flood-tide of questionable notes and bills issued by unreliable "country" banks and merchants.[11]

The fact that to a considerable extent the Bank was owned by established businessmen such as his father undoubtedly disposed Verplanck to assume that it worked for the public good. He had great confidence in the ability of the commercial community, experienced as it was in financial matters, to determine correct monetary policy. Financial questions, he told the Mercantile Association of New York in 1831, require "the assistance of a long-continued and a broad experience, and of the reasoning of good and wise men, so that he who presumes to decide upon them from his own first impressions without consulting those aids, is in his way but a rash theorist. On all subjects, quackery under the disguise of plain common-sense, self-interest masked as philanthropy. ... are constantly at work."[12] In one sense, this kind of argument is impeccable. Experts do know more about their fields than other men do. But do the interests of the experts necessarily harmonize with the interests of society? Bryant was inclined to think that they did not. Unlike Verplanck, his disposition, background, experience, and profession left him psychologically outside the business community. Whereas Verplanck was able to visualize the Bank in human terms, as identified with friends and fellow businessmen, Bryant saw it chiefly as a distant institution, a grander version of the questionable banking institutions of New York. In contrast to the Bank, President Jackson was very much a flesh-and-blood representative of a society of individuals. It was natural that Bryant followed the "Old Hero" into every battle in his war against the Bank.

Initially, the editor expressed no more than mild annoyance that the supporters of the Bank had, by introducing the recharter bill, diverted public attention from the tariff issue, which in his mind, still had priority. In the midst of the congressional debates over the recharter bill, however, a new controversy virtually exploded on his doorstep. Beginning on 16 April, the *Post* day by day reported the charges made by opponents of recharter that the Bank had made loans to key newspapers in order to buy their favor; day by day, Bryant showed a growing disposition to believe that the charges were true. Verplanck, perturbed by the accusations, considered refuting them; but, if he tried, his efforts had no influence on his friend. On 24 April the editor added his own personal accusation that "an individual" had visited his office in order to offer him "certain pecuniary advantages for certain services to be rendered the United States Bank." What had first been an annoying issue now became a personal insult and challenge to his character as a journalist.[13] Bryant's sense of personal involvement undoubtedly was strengthened by a nearly thirty percent decline in the *Post's* earnings in 1832. In October 1832 he rather anxiously applied to the Jackson Administration for a government printing contract.[14]

When Jackson's veto of the recharter bill made the Bank a party issue, Bryant was ready to stand with the president. The picture of the Bank War created on the editorial page of the *Post* was essentially a moral one: Jackson was the supreme individual who, "following the dictates of his frank native honesty," had accepted the challenge posed by the corrupting power of "a mighty pecuniary institution." Some of Jackson's political enemies warned that his forceful individualism—particularly his defiance of a congressional majority—marked him as a potential dictator who was preparing to establish tyranny with the irrational support of the adoring masses. As a young Federalist critic of "democracy," Bryant himself had once made similar charges against Thomas Jefferson. Now, however, he argued that the competitive nature of American life made the people "too wary, too distrustful" ever to yield up their liberties to any individual. Far more dangerous than Jackson's forceful drive was the subtle corrupting power of money as exercised by "a combination" of venal men. When late in 1833 the Bank helped precipitate an economic recession by calling in many of its loans, Bryant condemned it for putting to "wicked use" its power over the monetary system and over a corrupted press so as "to destroy confidence, ruin credit, and overwhelm individual fortunes." Although his warnings varied to meet the situation, they were consistent on one main point: That the Bank War was being fought for the individual and against a bloodless institution controlled by anonymous but obviously corrupt men. In Bryant's intensely individualistic vision of society there was no place for bloodless institutions—of any sort, as the near future would show.[15]

The Bank issue not only caused social discord; it also destroyed friendships—in Bryant's case his friendship with Verplanck. Prior to 1832 the two men had written together and voted together. With the Bank War, they began to drift apart, despite Bryant's efforts to preserve their literary partnership. In April 1832 Verplanck was virtually compelled to choose between the Bank and his party by the stirrings of a movement among anti-Bank Jacksonians in New York to block his renomination in October. He chose the Bank. As he had done in the past, Bryant tried to head off opposition to his friend by stressing the continued importance of the fight against the tariff. Politicians thought differently; Verplanck was not renominated. In subsequent weeks, the *Post* again came to his defense. He had, so it argued, voted for the Bank before the efforts to bribe the press had made the Bank a moral question and before Jackson's veto had made it a party issue. Since then, "Mr. Verplanck has freely determined to be governed by the will of his constituents, and his belief that his constituents were generally opposed to the United States Bank." Had Verplanck made such a promise? Was Bryant mistaken?[16] (Thirty-eight years later, Bryant said that Verplanck had been refused the nomination only because he had refused to pledge not to oppose Jackson on the Bank question.)[17]

Whatever the answer, Bryant soon learned to his sorrow that his friend was also very much a friend of the Bank. When in November 1833 Verplanck ran unsuccessfully for the state assembly on an anti-Jackson ticket, Bryant denounced the ticket for its association with "an odious monied monopoly," although he emphasized his warm regard for Verplanck as an individual. This regard showed signs of wearing thin, however, when in the spring of 1834 Verplanck ran for mayor of New York. Nominated by the newly formed Whig party because of his close identification with the City as well as with the Bank, he was too strong a candidate to be taken lightly. In March the *Post* declared that he had "deserted his party" and hinted that he was supported secretly by "convicted knaves and rogues." In June after Verplanck had lost the election by fewer than 200 votes, it praised him as a scholar but then asserted that "he has deserted the democratic principles which he so long professed." In September, when he was being considered as possible Whig candidate for governor, the *Post* attacked him—without qualifying praise—as a renegade, an apostate, and a turncoat. [18]

Verplanck did not hold Bryant responsible for this last attack, since early in June the editor had left the management of the *Post* in the hands of his young assistant, William Leggett, and had fled from the political turmoil. With the waning of the Knickerbocker circle, Bryant had become increasingly restless in New York. Because of mounting political pressures, the cooling of old friendships, and increasing anxieties, by the end of 1833 Bryant found himself in an urban equivalent of the frustrating atmosphere of Great Barrington. Again, he had to face the "sons of strife." Again, they stole an increasing amount of time away from his literary pursuits: between 1830 and 1832 he had written little poetry and in 1833, apparently, none at all.[19]

Late in 1833 Bryant decided to shake off his political concerns by taking a trip to Europe, but before he could depart he ran into financial frustrations. In order to increase his share of the *Post* to a full one-third, he had stretched his resources, and so was in no position to pay when Mrs. Coleman, the widow of the former proprietor, suddenly demanded in cash the $2,000 that Bryant still owed for the shares he had bought from the Coleman family. Anxious to "get out of the power of those people who hamper my movements," he met the demand by mortgaging his share of the *Post*. Free once more, he sailed in June for Europe, after announcing to a friend that "I am sick of the strife of politics." He did not plan to resume an active role on the newspaper.[20]

Bryant found relief in the color and tradition of the Old World, but his experiences strengthened his faith in the moral superiority of American society. "Italy is a beautiful woman no better than she should be," he wrote to a friend, "and her suitors must feel the alternative admiration and disgust usual in such cases." In Italy he noted how man's long history had done more to deform than to embellish nature—and human nature as well. The people of Florence, he thought, were "as indolent and effeminate as their ancestors of the Republic were hardy and enterprising —a degeneracy, owing I have no doubt to the want of political liberty." In Europe he renewed his appreciation of American society, even of its "party spirit and political ambition." In Europe's corrupted society he again was thankful for America's good fortune in escaping the mistakes and misdeeds of the past.[21]

Would that good fortune last? Some fourteen years of life and eight years of involvement in politics had passed since his youthful expression of optimism in "The Ages." With Europe before him, and with the Bank War behind him, Bryant set down in 1834 a new version of his old hope. In his poem "Earth," written at Pisa, he asked:

My Native Land of groves! a newer page
In the great record of the world is thine;
Shall it be fairer? Fear and friendly Hope,
And Envy, watch the issue, while the lines,
By which thou shalt be judged, are written down.

"THE WORLD IS GOVERNED TOO MUCH"

In April 1833, almost two years after Bryant's attack on Stone, New Yorkers were treated to another sidewalk spectacle by an editor of the *Evening Post*. Seething with rage, William Leggett avenged himself for an insult in the *Courier and Enquirer* by spitting into the face of its editor, James Watson Webb. In front of a gathering audience on Wall Street, Webb struck back with his cane, then tried to flee. But Leggett caught him on the opposite sidewalk, seized his cane, returned the blows, and brought down the curtain on this little drama by again spitting into the offender's face.[1] Fourteen months later, when Bryant sailed for Europe, Leggett assumed control of the *Post*. Within a month, the newspaper began to breathe fire on a mounting host of prominent and influential enemies. A local popular hero, a local Andrew Jackson, was beginning to appear.

Unlike his prototype, Leggett was a born loser. His father, a once respected merchant, had gone bankrupt during the Panic of 1819, which embittered him and drove him to seek a new life in Illinois. The collapse of the family fortunes compelled the seventeen-year-old Leggett to abandon permanently his college education. (In contrast, his cousin, Samuel Leggett, acquired prominence in New York as a founder of the first gas company in the city and then as the president of the Franklin Bank. This apparently was the Franklin Bank denounced by the *Post*

in 1828.)² To regain his footing, he joined the Navy as a midshipman—
a job that would be the stepping stone, so he thought, "to profit and
glory." He found only disgrace and humiliation. In 1825, while on a
cruise in the Mediterranean on the ship *Cyane,* he was court-martialed.
Leggett was accused of "disorderly and seditious conduct," particularly
of quoting "several passages of poetry of a highly inflamatory, rancor-
ous, and threatening import" against his commander, Captain John
Orde Creighton. He was also charged with leaving his station—to
attempt a duel with a fellow midshipman. A third charge was "conduct
tending to the destruction of morals": Leggett had tried to commit
suicide while awaiting trial for his part in the abortive duel. The court-
martial ordered Leggett dismissed from the Navy. When he made
countercharges against Captain Creighton to the Adams administration,
President Adams remitted the penalty, but he also rebuked the young
midshipman for the "tone and character" of his protest. Disgraced, his
career ruined, Leggett resigned from the service. In a letter to the hated
Creighton, he asked bitterly: "Am I in the onset of my enterprise to
be prostrated in the dust, and then told that it is the privilege of power
to tread upon the hearts of the weak?"³ He was not to forget.

He returned in 1825 to New York as a virtual outcast, seeking redemp-
tion. During the next five years he tried to find his way to profit and
glory through literature—not the literature of protest but that of the most
banal kind acceptable to the reading public. In 1825 he published a
collection of poetry, *Leisure Hours at Sea ... By a Midshipman of the United
States Navy.* There was little in the poems to indicate that they had been
written by a flesh-and-blood Navy man, for they were pale imitations
of sentimental poetry, full of bathos, adolescent gush, and moonshine.
Four years later he tried again with his *Tales and Sketches By a Country
Schoolmaster,* ten feeble imitations of the Knickerbocker school. His luck
was no better with a weekly literary journal, *The Critic,* which appeared
in 1828 and soon disappeared, despite Leggett's desperate efforts to save
it. Lacking both money and patronage, he wrote the last issues himself,
put them into type with his own hands, and personally delivered them
to his subscribers.

Frustrated but still hopeful, in 1829 he joined the *Evening Post* as an
assistant editor, stipulating that he be excused from writing on political
topics so that he might concentrate on literary matters. Like Bryant,
however, he soon found himself caught up in the controversies of the

time; unlike Bryant, he responded almost joyfully to the challenge. Leggett's concept of an editor was as simple and direct as his ideas: To be, like the "Old Hero" himself, as "bold as a lion; a sure friend and irreconcilable enemy." Seated at a desk in the *Post's* printing plant, surrounded by the noise of the presses and by the conversations of "political loungers," he poured out in 1834 and 1835 a stream of long editorials written with an acid pen, a rich harvest of dogma that made Bryant's writings seem tame by comparison.[4]

The Bank War was undoubtedly a major factor in this explosive emergence of the crusader from his literary cocoon. The controversy was a grim reminder of his father's banckruptcy and of the train of frustrations that followed, for the Bank had been widely condemned in 1819-20 as the cause of the Panic. Leggett had not forgotten what failure had done to his father. In his story "The Rifle" he gave a brief but revealing description of "a gentleman who had formerly been a wealthy merchant in the city of New York; but whom misfortune had suddenly befallen, and stripped of all his possessions. While surrounded by affluence, he had been considered remarkably meek and affable, but he became proud and unsociable in adversity; and not caring to remain among scenes that continually brought to mind the sad change in condition, he had emigrated with his whole family to the wilderness of Illinois." As if to strengthen the memory, 1832—the year in which the Bank issue burst on the political scene—brought Leggett financial hardships that drove him to thoughts of suicide. To save himself, he finally borrowed $6,000 from his actor friend Edwin Forrest. No wonder that Leggett launched a violent attack on the Bank as the Great Monster in American society.[5]

When he took control of the *Post* in 1834, however, Leggett had occasion to crusade against a number of monsters, of which the Bank seemed only the chief representative. He soon became the champion of disappointed workers, businessmen, and others who had suffered from the economic vicissitudes of an expanding metropolis. These people often were the ones who had felt the full weight of the recession precipitated when the Bank sharply curtailed credit in late 1833; these were also the ones who were hurt when in 1834 the Bank partially surrendered by reversing its deflationary contraction of credit. The next years saw the creation of new banks, speculation, growing economic activity, and rising prices. Some New Yorkers were able to ride the crest of the wave, but expansion and inflation damaged the interests of many more: People on fixed incomes, men whose wages lagged behind prices, mechanics and small businessmen who suffered from the competition of bigger and better-equipped rivals. Some of the consequent discontent found an outlet in the renewal of the workingmen's movement and in the creation of an energetic trades union movement. Much more found release in a violent attack on the state banks.[6]

Through his editorials in the *Post*, Leggett supplied some of the ammunition used in the war against the banks. (Most of his arguments were borrowed either from his friends or from William Gouge, whose *Short History of Money and Banking in the United States* was published in serial form by the *Post* in September 1834.) Mounting prices? Economic uncertainties? Leggett thought both were caused by the increasing number of bank notes issued by an increasing number of banks. In this, his reasoning paralleled the arguments of his friends during the late 1820s but, while they had distinguished between trustworthy old banks and fly-by-night manufacturers of bank notes, he proceeded to attack banks and bankers generally as the source of the trouble. He argued that bankers, who were able to govern money, "the measure of value," through their note-issuing powers, had adopted policies that favored a speculative rather than a stable economy, thereby producing "seasons of preternatural prosperity and severe distress, shaking public faith, exciting a spirit of wild speculation, and demoralizing and vitiating the whole tone of popular sentiment and character." And this was only part of the banker's capacity to harm. Bank notes, warned Leggett, were instruments used by a few to rob the helpless and the unwary: since many of the notes quickly depreciated in real value, people who accepted all notes at face value soon discovered to their sorrow that one dollar in paper was frequently worth far less than one dollar in gold. Let workers remember, Leggett urged, "when paid in small uncurrent notes that the longer they retain possession of these notes the greater is the profit to the banks that issued them."[7]

For Leggett, the banks were not the only danger; behind them loomed a growing web of corporations, of which banks were only a part. For those men who, like Bryant and Leggett, conceived of ideal American society in terms of individuals, the corporation was a disturbing anomaly. "Having neither souls nor bodies," said Leggett, expressing a common attitude, "corporations cannot be brought to a sense of shame by exposure nor a sense of justice by the fear of punishment. . . . They belong to no genus of animals; are subject to none of the laws of nature and society; and when justice seeks to lay hold of them, it finds that it has grasped a shadow." Although corporations lacked the substance of individuals, they were far more powerful. In October 1834 the *Post* expressed fear of "vast manufacturing enterprises . . . whose overwhelming capitals and corporate privileges enable them to paralyze or destroy individual competition." As concentrations of capital and power, corporations threatened a day when individual enterprisers, model Americans, would be reduced to dependent workers in organizations that would "gradually monopolize the whole of that particular business in which they are engaged."[8]

Having learned to visualize ideal free society in terms of independent individuals, Americans such as Leggett now encountered in the city the beginnings of that urban-industrial future where bigness, dependence, and corporatism increasingly were to prevail as they already prevailed in some New England textile towns. Leggett, however, viewed the existing corporation not as part of the democratic future but as part of a system of age-old evil, not as a source of strength to be incorporated into American society but as a corrosive element to be expelled. Like Bryant, he assumed that the United States already had the essentials of the good society; since corporations particularly banks, threatened to change that society, they appeared to endanger the political and moral as well as economic foundations of American life.

Like many other Jacksonians, the young editor conceptualized the bank dispute in terms of the European past rather than of the urban-industrial age. The conflict, as he pictured it, was one between an "Aristocracy," the selfish and unproductive privileged class, and the "People," the legitimate producers, the farmers, mechanics, businessmen, and others who were willing to stand as productive individuals. This class warfare was not natural to American society: neither was the class of "aristocrats"; both were artificially induced by government interference with the natural laws of society. Leggett assumed that in a totally free society, there would be only individuals, no concentrations of power, no monopolies, and no corporations. No man or group of men would have the power to damage the interests of the people.[9]

Society, however, was not wholly free, for government had granted special favors and privileges (such as those provided by corporation charters) to the few. By doing so, government had upset the balance that in a free society would naturally exist between "the social feeling in a community" and "the selfish feeling which, in its proper exercise, is the parent of all wordly good, and, in its excesses, the root of all evil." In ideal society the restraining hand of the community and the natural drive of the individual worked in harmony to produce both stability and progress, just as in the Newtonian universe centrifugal force and gravity harmonized to prevent the two evils, stasis and chaos. Government had encouraged selfishness by giving some men privileges that freed them from the supervision both of their neighbors and of the laws. Protected from punishment for their excesses and given special powers, the favored few could accumulate wealth far out of proportion to their labor, talent, and devotion to society; the result was social disharmony and "artificial inequality in human condition." Since privilege stimulated the appetite for more privilege, "partial legislation" threatened permanently to elevate the few at the expense of the many, in the end creating "a powerful aristocracy," which would overthrow the liberal experiment.[10]

What was the antidote for the poison of aristocracy? Leggett summed it up in two words: Equal Rights. Government should restrict itself to its only true function in the liberal system, the equal protection of every man's rights, particularly the fundamental right of acquiring and holding property. In a state of freedom where all men enjoyed no more nor less than equal rights, no man would get more than he deserved, which to Leggett meant that there would be a general diffusion of property and happiness among the people.

Leggett neither expected nor wanted equal rights to produce equality in wealth, for he held to the common assumption of this "democratic age" that men were unequal in character and talent. He did, however, argue that the general opportunities available in free society would act constantly to keep human inequality, in character and condition, within manageable limits. Because the average man, the farmer or mechanic, was encouraged by opportunity to participate actively in political and economic life, he acquired "the common sense and common experience" necessary for him to manage his own affairs and to help manage the affairs of the community. In contrast, the leisured class, so idolized by conservatives as superior to the people, was in fact inferior in character and sense, since its members did not participate in the workaday world.

In a society free of privilege, then, there was little danger that the rich would get richer to the point that they were able to dominate the community. In the United States "the progress of knowledge and intelligence among the laboring classes has been for years upward; while that of the class which derives its information from books has been rapidly downward." Wealth required knowledge and intelligence to survive—in a society of equal rights.[11]

Leggett's arguments were hardly novel. Nearly every American liberal accepted as dogma the assumption that free society, by encouraging men to participate in the practical affairs of life, strengthened human character and intellect. When it came to the application of this dogma to policy, however, there were wide differences of opinion. Verplanck, for instance, reasoned that the practical experience of commercial and political leaders made them ideal policy makers; familiar as he was with established authority, he believed that knowledgeable men could use power, public and private, for benevolent ends. On the other hand, Leggett, ever suspicious of authority, assumed that the positive use of power, even for the most benevolent ends, would do harm. To legislate against sin was futile: "If it cannot be suppressed by the force of the moral sense of the community, it cannot be suppressed by statutes and edicts." Such legislation would defeat its own ends, because, by lulling individuals into a false sense of security, it would weaken the only effective restraint on sin, the watchful oversight of the community. Government efforts to stimulate economic progress would also be self-defeating, for they would only create a "hot-bed system" less healthy than "the system of nature and reason." In the end, political interference would have just one general result: The establishment of privilege, which in turn would upset the natural mechanisms by which men solve their problems.[12]

> The maxim of *Let us alone* will be acknowledged to be infinitely better than all the political quackery of ignorant legislators, instigated by the grasping monopolizing spirit of rapacious capitalists. This country, we hope, ... is destined to prove to mankind the truth of the saying that *the world is governed too much*.[13]

This was Leggett's answer to the National Bank and to Captain Creighton. But it was hardly a final answer; in fact, in a social sense, it was no answer at all. Leggett dreamed of a society in which all men were individuals only, without any power to affect the lives of other individuals, but even he had to recognize that in the real-life situation of the 1830s power could not simply be obliterated without damaging the interests of those for whom he spoke—the "people," the workers and petty enterprisers of the city. In the face of rising prices and the growing power of employers, workers in New York and elsewhere had turned to collective action, to trade unions, to protect themselves. As an idealist, Leggett considered all combinations of men to be based on wrong principles, but as a realist, he defended the right of laboring men to unite for protection against the power of monopoly. If the rich enjoyed the power of unity then so should the real producers of society. Because he thought that all combinations were wrong, the best Leggett could hope was that once the unions had served their purpose of enabling the worker to achieve his true individuality, they would dissolve in the natural individualism of free society.[14]

In a more general sense, Leggett recognized that individuals might have to combine to solve problems beyond their own capabilities; that they might need to pool their capital if they were ever to construct such agencies of economic progress as the railroads, which had made their smoky debut in the late 1820s. Corporations menaced the interests of Leggett's ideal individual, the petty enterpriser; but if petty enterprisers needed at least some corporate powers to achieve their goals, then what? Reluctantly, he had to come to terms with the enemy—but only by convincing himself that it was no enemy at all. As he saw it the existing corporations provided the most egregious example of government-granted favors to the few. It had special legal rights and powers: eminent domain, limited liability, and, in the case of banks, the privilege of issuing notes. Were these powers open to all men on an equal basis? Not in New York State in the 1830s. Prior to 1838 the state granted corporation charters only by special act of the legislature, a procedure that appeared to restrict corporation privileges to those people who had the time, money, and influence needed to win the favor of the majority in the legislature.[15]

In 1834 Leggett proposed that the state replace the old system with a "general law of partnerships" that would give every individual who met certain simple requirements applicable to all the powers needed to carry on enterprises "which are now exclusively performed by incorporated companies." No longer would individuals have to apply for a special act of the legislature. Leggett was able to convince himself that these partnerships were not corporations, because "the very nature of a corporation is to be endowed with special privileges," whereas the partnerships would be denied the special rights of perpetuity, eminent domain, and, perhaps (he was undecided), of limited liability. Banking partnerships, moreover, would not have the privilege of issuing notes that would pass as currency. On the other hand, the partnerships would have the right to sell stock (hence Leggett's indecision in regard to limited liability) and so accumulate the capital required for enterprises beyond the powers of the individual. Leggett hoped that by avoiding the institutional character of corporations, the plan would restore the ideal society of free and independent men, and at the same time give individuals the power to achieve the ambitions excited by a dynamic economy.[16]

The principle of equal rights, then, would be the magic bridge between individualism and economic progress. If Americans would adhere to the principle, "we shall present to the admiration of the world a nation founded as the hills, free as the air, and prosperous as a fruitful soil, a genial climate, and industry, enterprise and intelligence can render us." But the "if" was a gigantic one, for Leggett's paradise could be saved only by a Puritan's devotion to principle. Salvation required that all Americans be faithful to the idea of negative government by abandoning public postal systems, poor houses, and insane asylums. It required ending all efforts to regulate trade or morals. It required that individuals refrain from getting into debt, for debts reduced independence: the debtor "cannot look out on his fields of grain and grass with the calm satisfied consciousness of independence, but, like the first parent of mankind, he views them as the paradise from which himself and his posterity are about to be banished forever." And above all, salvation required that all men suppress their selfish strivings for special privileges and for a special place above their fellow men.[17]

The demands were too great. Leggett's ideal American was the petty enterpriser, the one-man operator; but what enterpriser, excited by the opportunities of a dynamic economy, wants to remain a one-man operation? To Leggett, equal rights meant individualism; to others, equal rights meant the opportunity to acquire the new powers of emergent capitalism. To Leggett, banking corporations represented the dangerous power of credit, the power to disrupt the economy, the power to turn independent producers into dependent debtors. To many enterprisers, the banking system was bad only because it denied them access to the power of credit, particularly to the credit they needed to expand their operations. Disappointed and frustrated New Yorkers might cheer Leggett as their champion in their war against dangerous power; but this did not mean they were prepared to follow him across the deserts to the promised land.[18]

Late in 1834 Leggett's outcry against power was joined in the *Evening Post* by a voice more pleasing to the ears of aspiring capitalists. Another Sedgwick had made his debut on the American political scene. Although he was ten years younger than Leggett, Theodore Sedgwick III had a more mature sense of American society. Born in Albany in 1811, bred in the Berkshires, educated at Columbia College and Cambridge Law School, young Theodore had almost all that Sedgwick money and Sedgwick intelligence could provide; but shrewd, self-confident, and politically aware though he was, he lacked the idealism necessary to rise to the heroic level possible to Leggett and even to Bryant.[19]

Sedgwick's political experience was more varied than that of either of his two older friends. As a precocious adolescent, he went through a period of what he later called "early aristocratic follies," probably an elitist contempt for the bumbling democracy of the 1820s. Whatever doubts he had as to the American experiment vanished, however, when in 1833 he went to Europe to finish his law studies. Like Bryant, he noted the atmosphere of decay in the Old World: "It makes one formidably national to see this old Europe which has gone to seed. . .& to compare her with our young flourishing sprouts." In early 1834, while serving as an attaché in the American legation at Paris, he helped the French aristocrat Alexis de Tocqueville prepare his great book, *Democracy in America*.* Disappointed in his law studies and apparently disappointed in love (he was engaged briefly to a granddaughter of General Lafayette), in July 1834 he cut short his stay in Europe. Anxious to practice law on his return to America, he hoped that "politics will be calm when I come home, for I wish to keep clear of them and attend to my business. I am sure that if there be a fray, I must be in it."[20]

There was a fray. And Sedgwick soon discovered that, "as an attorney without clients," he had ample time for politics. Even before he left Europe, he had grown concerned about the social effects of the bank controversy. Having abandoned his "aristocratic follies," Sedgwick

*He had first met Tocqueville in 1831 when the Frenchman had visited the Sedgwick home at Stockbridge. It is possible that Sedgwick ideas influenced Tocqueville's analysis of American society.

accepted democracy as the best way of easing class tensions in society as "the most elevating for the masses and the most humanizing for the educated." Leggett might, out of his pugnacious individualism, dream of a society without human authority; Theodore, scion of an established family, thought in terms of a harmonious class system based on man's natural inequality in "morality and industry." Distinctions in society "must always subsist. It is the holy object of Republicanism and of Democracy to reconcile all men to their condition, and by removing every barrier of birth, rank, and monopoly, to leave those who suffer, nothing to inveigh against but hard fortune or their own imbecility." The rub was, however, that American society was not harmonious, because Americans faced a system of privilege, which, by their "inattention," they had permitted to rise during the presidencies of Monroe and John Quincy Adams.[21] As an example of privileged monopoly, Sedgwick singled out the New York Insurance Company (of which Verplanck was a major stockholder), whose immunity to competition, he charged, had enabled it to realize profits since 1830 of $1,500,000 on a $2,000,000 investment. He attributed the tumultuous state of Jacksonian politics to the efforts of the producing classes to reedem the rights and opportunities necessary for them to advance to their proper station in life.[22]

Although he ascribed most of the disharmony to the privilege-seeking opponents of free trade and Jackson, Sedgwick was also disturbed by what he considered to be the irrational character of much of the anti-bank crusade. He admired Leggett's sincerity but disliked the editor's tendency to fire shotgun blasts of indiscriminate criticism at all banks and corporations. In September 1834, therefore, he began to contribute articles on the corporation issue to the *Evening Post* under the *nom de guerre,* "Veto." In these articles and in his short book, *What Is A Monopoly?*, he tried to wean Leggett and Leggett's followers from some of their hostility to commercial capitalism.[23]

Unlike the fanatically individualistic Leggett, "Veto" had the entrepreneur's appreciation of organization. Believing that human progress depended on "Union—united action—associated exertions," he saw nothing objectionable in corporate rights such as perpetuity and limited liability. While Leggett tinkered with his partnership plan, Sedgwick argued for a general incorporation act that would enable all interested persons to acquire the corporate powers then possessed only by the special charter companies. "Corporations will then have no advantage over the public at large, because any individual can become a corporator, when and for what purpose he pleases." Within fifty years this kind of argument began to look rather absurd in the face of the growing power of such corporate goliaths as the Standard Oil Company.[24]

In the 1830s, however, it was still possible to assume that even the fullfledged corporation, once its restricted character had vanished, could be assimilated into a system of free competition among individuals. This assumption applied to banking as well as manufacturing corporations.[25] Although he followed Leggett in denouncing the existing bank note system, Sedgwick appeared more concerned with freeing banking of its restrictive character, so as to afford "needy and industrious borrowers" access to bank credit. Unlike his friend, he appreciated the value of paper money to aspiring entrepreneurs in a sophisticated economy. One of his objectives was to dispel the fears of those hostile to bank notes that a system of "free" banking corporations would add to the inflation and instability of the times. He argued that it was only the privileged position enjoyed by the existing chartered banks that encouraged them to pour out notes in disregard for the real needs of the economy. If everyone could get banking powers under a general incorporation act, he predicted, the currency system would regulate itself to the benefit of all. The reform, by increasing the number of banks, would give them "a more local character and credit, and their issues a more local character than they have now." Stripped of their privileges, forced to deal in localities where they were known and faced with competitive pressures from their rivals, bankers would exercise more caution in their note issues; bank notes would be as good as gold.[26] Sedgwick was not opposed to some public regulation of the currency such as the prohibition of small bills and limitations on bank issues, though he did consider such public control wrong in principle. His free-banking arguments, however, were borrowed wholly and without qualification by Bryant in the late 1830s. (See chapter 9.)

Whatever their differences over the questions of corporate power and the currency, Sedgwick and Leggett shared a faith in the magic of general incorporation. In October 1834 they launched a strongly partisan attack in the *Post* on both the system of special charters and the Whig party. In the rhetoric that prevailed among New York Jacksonian Democrats, the Whigs championed privilege and aristocracy. Hence, Leggett could rage against Verplanck as an apostate from democratic principles and as the tool "of an infamous faction." Hence, too, the *Post* could hail the victory in the city elections of all eleven Democratic candidates for the state assembly as a defeat of monopoly and a triumph of the producers over the "consumer, the rich, the proud, the privileged." Unfortunately for this simple partisan interpretation, however, Democratic politicians proved just as likely to grind out special charters in the old legislative mill as the Whigs were. The Democratic-controlled legislature remained deaf to the demands for general incorporation.[27]

Politicians!—what could be done with them? Sedgwick, aware of the advantages of party organization, hoped that time and public pressure would eventually persuade Democratic leaders such as his political friend, Martin Van Buren, to commit themselves against the existing system. Not so his aggressive and hot-tempered comrade. Early in 1835, Leggett blasted some of the politicians of his own party as "a set of creeping, designing, dissembling creatures, who had grown fat on the drippings of unclean bank legislation," his own version of the common charge that the old system encouraged bribery of legislators. Never having learned the art of compromise, the editor was soon locked in violent combat with much of the Democratic press, particularly with the Albany *Argus,* the mouthpiece of the "Albany Regency," which controlled the state party. By the fall of 1835 Leggett found himself reviled by both Whigs and Democrats as a dangerous radical, an "agrarian," and "a Jack Cade, Jacobin, Utopian, disorganizer, lunatic." But he was not alone, for his zeal won him the support of a small but militant band of workers, enterprisers, and professional men in New York City who called themselves the Equal Rights party. These "Methodists of Democracy" hailed Leggett as their champion in the struggle to renew "those heaven-born principles which had been so long trodden under the foot of monopoly."[28]

In the eyes of Democratic regulars, the protesters were "Locofocos," dangerous schismatics who jeopardized party unity. The politicians could not have foreseen that the appearance of the Locofoco movement would mark the beginning of two decades of intraparty conflict, which was to have a great influence on state and national politics, but they did sense that the zealots meant trouble in the next election. As the spokesman for this faction, Leggett endangered the shaky alliance that the politicians had created among diverse groups during the bank wars.

Worse, in 1835 the editor stormed into a dispute that threatened the unity of the national party: That year the Jackson administration, in order to soothe southern anxieties, had closed the Federal mails to abolitionist literature addressed to the South. With his usual disregard for the niceties of political management, Leggett had editorialized in favor of freedom of opinion for the abolitionists. This stand was rank treason in the eyes of party regulars. In mid-September, the Washington *Globe*, the official journal of the national Democratic organization, "excommunicated" the *Evening Post* because of its "Utopian temper." When he learned that the leaders of New York's Tammany Hall were considering a similar step, Leggett reaffirmed his support for the abolitionists; in October, Tammany cast its anathema down on his head.[29]

By this time, Leggett had learned one of the journalistic facts of life in this heyday of the partisan press: many newspapers depended to some degree on government printing contracts—and politicians controlled the contracts. The *Post* soon lost such valuable perquisites as the contracts to publish the advertisements of the Navy, Post Office, and Treasury departments. Conservative business advertisers had been alienated by his crusade against the banks, and Leggett found himself in severe financial trouble. Then came the final blow. In pouring out his many long editorials, Leggett had pushed his body to the limit; in late October he was laid low by an attack of "bilious fever of a high grade." And so the *Post* drifted, under the command of such interim editors as young Theodore Sedgwick.[30]

News of this dangerous state brought the senior editor hurrying back from Europe. Although he did not share Leggett's warlike disposition, Bryant had agreed with the general editorial stance his partner had taken. Anxious to remain in Europe as long as possible, he had continued to trust Leggett's judgment, despite warning hints from the business manager of the *Post*, Michael Burnham: "I could and want to say a whole book to you, but must wait until I can blow it into your ear like thunder." In January 1836 some of the "thunder" reached Bryant's ears in the form of news that his anticipated dividends from the *Post* would not be forthcoming. He departed for the United States posthaste, leaving his wife and children behind. Francis Bryant noted in her diary on January 25: "Mr. Bryant has gone. He left me at four o'clock this morning and no one knows what I suffer at his departure. I am sure he does not, or he would not leave me."[31]

After his arrival in New York, Bryant soon discovered that he had waited too long to return home. Not only had the newspaper lost advertisers, but its affairs had been mismanaged by "a drunken and saucy clerk." Even worse, Leggett had shown himself not only inept but less than honest in financial matters. In November 1835, driven to desperation by his mounting troubles, he had paid operating expenses with dividend money that should have gone to one of the owners, Mrs. Coleman. Bryant joined Mrs. Coleman in forcing Leggett to give up his share in the newspaper. The former partner was retained as an editor, but even under the best of circumstances Leggett resented a state of dependence. Early in November, he moved on to form a new weekly, *The Plaindealer,* leaving Bryant to struggle for four agonizing years to keep the *Post* afloat.[32]

And so ended the formal partnership between two men who, because of their high-strung moralism, were called by their enemies "the chanting cherubs." It ended without bitterness. The *Post* sent its ex-editor off with the highest praise as a "worthy and efficient coadjutor in the cause of Equal Rights, in the warfare against corruption, in the great work of rescuing the pure principles of democracy from the interpolations which selfish men have labored to darken and debase them." In the future, Bryant kept the *Post* on the course that Leggett had taken, with little regard for political consequences. He, too, adopted as his guide the principle that "the world is governed too much." Thus, burdened by debts but heartened by Leggett's examples, Bryant faced the mounting pressures of rapidly changing, chaotic times.[33]

THE VORTEX

In November 1833 James Fenimore Cooper arrived in New York harbor from Europe. As his ship approached land, he remembered the words spoken by some of the friends he was leaving behind when in 1826 he sailed out of this same harbor: "You will never come back." He came ashore on 5 November with his wife, their two daughters, and four Swiss servants. Cooper indeed had come back physically, but the return was no more than the beginning of a life-long quest for a spiritual place in American society. Psychologically, he had come home to exile.

The seven years Cooper spent abroad had altered both his own character and that of New York. He returned as a consciously self-confident man of the world. As an outspoken defender of American principles, he had, in his own eyes, successfully countered the traps and snares of aristocratic Europe; indeed, he had dined with the lions in their dens and had survived as a man and as an American. But if his stay among the Europeans had strengthened his confidence in himself, it had weakened his confidence in his native land. For seven years he had fought to defend what he considered to be the true image of the Republic; but for the last three years he had with increasing conviction believed that he was being attacked from the rear, not by Americans generally but by those who influenced American opinion.[1]

Like many of his countrymen, Cooper had great faith in the power of the printed word. Books, he had written in 1820, were "the instruments of controlling the opinions of a nation like ours. They are an engine alike powerful to save or to destroy." In his works written abroad, most notably in *Notions of the Americans* and *The Bravo,* he tried to "save" American principles. With what rewards? None, so far as Cooper was concerned, for neither book was received enthusiastically by the reading public. Cooper never quite could understand that, as America's premier novelist, he had become a public possession who was expected to provide what the public wanted: plots, actions, descriptions of American scenery, and the Leatherstocking; lectures on political principles readers expected to find in their newspapers. When Americans appeared indifferent to his efforts to inculcate his principles, he concluded that they were indifferent to the principles themselves and that they were still mentally dependent on European conventions. But Cooper refused to yield his belief, as stated in *Notions of the Americans,* that American "polity" and manners were deeply rooted in the character of the people. The fault, therefore, lay not with the public but with those who presumed to mold public opinion. Such was his reaction when in 1832 he learned that some newspaper critics in America had condemned him for betraying his obligations to his readers by writing, in the opinion of the critics, dull novels that touched on controversial political issues. Cooper's response was characteristic: in November he complained from Paris that he was the victim of "foul play" on the part of a set of "quasi litterateurs at home . . . who have no sympathy for the real opinion of the country"—i.e., that the critics were really attacking him for championing American principles in Europe.[2] Having been stung by a gnat, he reacted as though he had been stomped by an elephant.

He returned to New York with the attitude of a hunter about to set off into the wilderness with his gun primed to blast the first enemy who should appear. What he found in New York only made him more wary, for the city was moving rapidly away from the old Gotham he had known in the mid-1820s. He arrived just in time to experience the "bank recession" of 1833-34; he stayed long enough to observe the worst features of that tumultuous period of expansion, inflation, and speculation that gave birth to the Locofoco movement. Society was in rapid motion, powered by the optimism and the passion for wealth unleashed by the apparently limitless opportunities of American life. It was not what Cooper wanted.

The novelist himself was hardly indifferent to the lure of the dollar. In December 1831 he had written to a relative: "I tell you *in confidence* that I have the prospect of receiving this year near or quite twenty thousand dollars." As a professional writer, he exploited every publishing trick he could find in order to maximize the returns from his novels. But, if he shared the common American interest in money, he decidedly did not share the all-too-common tendency to set the dollar above everything else. He was a man of taste and integrity, vitally concerned with the "tone" of society, who measured both things and persons by well-established standards.[3] And New York? While he was still in Europe, New Yorkers had occasion to view the statue group "The Cherubs," sculptured by his friend, Horatio Greenough. Cooper expressed the hope that such art works would improve the tastes of his countrymen, but he received this report from another friend:

> Our literal folks actually suppose that they were to sing, and when the man turned them around in order to exhibit them in a different position, they exclaimed, "Ah he is going to wind them up; we shall hear them now." I wish the scene of this story lay anywhere but in New York, but it cannot be helped, and I must continue to consider my townsmen as a race of cheating, lying, money getting blockheads.[4]

On his return, Cooper himself noted that New Yorkers honored quantities rather than qualities, possessions rather than culture and character. Every man, "brains or no brains, taste or no taste," presumed to judge everything and everybody. "In short," Cooper wrote Greenough, "expect your own matured and classical thought will be estimated by the same rules as they estimate pork, and rum, and cotton." In his eyes, this was something more than simple vulgarity; for New Yorkers who lauded Broadway as the longest and therefore the best street in the world and praised Americans things, also ignored or even deprecated American principles, the vital principles of the Republic. In *Notions,* he had expressed the common American view that the United States, if it had not achieved the cultural level of Europe, excelled all nations "in the truths of human excellence." Now, however, he felt that society seemed to have entered a great "moral eclipse" in which devotion to the truths had yielded to selfishness, and in which half the language was compressed into one word, "Dollar." Wealth had become the standard of virtue; the wealthy were able to claim for themselves, on the basis of their material success, "taste, judgment, honesty, and wisdom." Selfishness had achieved such dominion that a man who acted on principle rather than self-interest was considered to be either a hypocrite or a fool. Ominously, the eclipse threatened to obscure the "immutable truths" that should have been "so many moral guides in the management" of American affairs.[5]

Why had this apparent breakdown occurred? Although he lacked the gift of systematic analysis, Cooper did recognize one source of trouble that his free-trade friends might well have considered: the social and geographic mobility encouraged by the expanding opportunities of American life. Material prosperity, he noted, had enabled the "dross" —the vulgar profit-seeker and his values—to rise to a position of social influence. Drawn to New York City in their search for wealth, they had turned the city into a "bivouac," an ever changing agglomeration of transients who had no established relationships with others and measured men not by their intrinsic worth but by their net worth. As money became the rule and measure of life, New York had begun to drift under the influence of "foreigners"—American "merchants and others a degree below them who are to a man hostile in feeling to the country." Here in the restless, dollar-conscious life of the city had appeared the beginnings of a "vulgar aristocracy," which looked for its values and fashions to the corrupt and privileged society of England.

What could be done to stem this drift away from the Republic? Confident that his European experiences enabled him to see dangers ignored by those "who live in the vortex," Cooper set out to warn his countrymen against the mounting power of the enemy. The new Paul Revere might better have stayed in bed, for the vortex-dwellers were too busy, if not too hostile, to listen. His *A Letter To His Countrymen* published in 1834 provoked widespread criticism; his effort to satirize the vulgar aristocracy of the times in *The Monikins* was generally ignored. He concluded from this experience that in America "men *follow* out their facts to results, instead of reasoning them out." In New York the blinding force of the vortex drew men on to results which in the end could only be disastrous. Fact dominated principle. And so the dollar dominated the city—and much of the rest of the country, too, for "the accumulated vulgarity and ignorance" of the urban centers had great influence in the rural areas.[6]

Disgusted with his countrymen, pained but not humbled by their response to his well-intended advice, Cooper thought of fleeing to Italy, the sunny though corrupted land that had caught his imagination while he was in Europe. "Bad as many Italians are," he wrote, "they are no worse than our own people have got to be. All my family agree that the lies, frauds, and meanness that used to disgust us, at Florence, have been enacted here before our eyes. Of the two I prefer the *dolce far niente* to go-aheadism. The first may be gentlemanly, commonly is; the last is almost always vulgar." But Cooper's roots were anchored too deeply in America for him to take the road later traveled by American expatriates. Instead, in 1836 he moved his family from New York to Otsego Hall, his boyhood home at Cooperstown, which he had purchased two years before. And there the family remained.[7]

Cooper was too intimately identified with society for him to go into seclusion at Otsego Hall; the move was intended as a dignified—and partial—retirement to the traditions and stability of a beloved region rather than a headlong retreat from the city. Yet, although he later spent many months in New York and Philadelphia, his move to the country was as much a psychological flight from urban America as if he had fled to Italy. Intellectually and emotionally he returned permanently to "Templeton," to a way of life that was disappearing from American society. The social ideal he had sketched out in *The Pioneers* more than a decade before he now sought to define and to defend in many of the novels which he wrote during the prolific last fifteen years of his life (particularly in *Home as Found,* in his "anti-rent trilogy" *Satanstoe, The Chainbearer,* and in *Redskins*—all written in the mid-1840s; and in *The Ways of the Hour,* written in 1850). Cooper's ideal world was a true community (not a bivouac) where values were clearly defined and each man's intrinsic worth was known to his neighbors. Here was the ideal republican society, which would elevate to positions of influence not money but character and talent, where gentlemen would govern with taste, humanity, and devotion to high principles. Gentlemen were the natural protectors of the Republic, for they were the true beneficiaries of the ideal republican system.[8]

The ideal social order was founded on the possession of land. If the drive for money powered the urban vortex, landed wealth provided the basis for the preservation of the moral and physical resources of America. Judge Temple in *The Pioneers* not only breathes life into the moral and legal order but also assures sound progress by restraining the money-hungry who would raid and destroy the material blessings that nature has bestowed on all generations of men. When he returned to "Templeton" in his novels *Homeward Bound* and *Home as Found,* Cooper took care to contrast the influences of property in land and property in money by describing two men of the same stock. Edward and John Effingham are cousins. Edward is a landed gentleman, who, while he is neither as keen "in the exposition of subleties" nor as "imposing with the mass" as hundreds of others, is a model 'of good breeding, unselfishness, and virtue. John, the wealthier of the two, has invested all his wealth in, as he put it, "corporations, that were as soulless as himself." Although he is more cultivated and more intellectually vigorous than his cousin, "he also possessed passions less under control, a will more stubborn, and prejudices that often neutralized his reason." If the possession of money could flaw the character of the talented John Effingham, then what could the raw drive for money do to the mass of Americans?[9]

Cooper tried to convince himself that the landed gentlemen, the Edward Effinghams, would survive and flourish in America, and that the destructive energy of the dollar-seeker was simply a passing phase in the progress of society toward civilization. In the 1830s he continued to hope that the vortex would eventually vanish, that the cities would in time become what he thought they should be—neither centers of monied wealth nor human hives but cultural and political capitals for landed gentlemen. But could the Edward Effinghams successfully counter the raw energies of the cities as they were? Ironically, Cooper's hopes depended on how well his social views were received in the urban world, for he recognized that the concentrated influence of the cities had the advantage over the "intelligence and breeding and taste" of the gentlemen who were "scattered" throughout the countryside of America.[10]

The novelist had influential friends in the city, including such men as Bryant and Leggett who opened the columns of the *Evening Post* to him, but his efforts to propagate his views in his novels ran into a barrage of criticism and abuse from literary journals and newspapers. His outspoken support of Jackson, his denunciation of merchants, nonpolitical though they seemed to him, enraged the Whigs, who repaid his apparent partisanship with partisan attacks on Cooper and his novels. Cooper became a favorite target of the Whig press; he fought back, and so began in the late 1830s a battle that he never wi couldn, though he won most of the skirmishes, In the end, as a novelist, we has figuratively driven out of the urban world, relegated by the critics to the world of sailors, frontiersmen, and Indians, the popular stuff of his novels.[11]

Much of the criticism, professional and partisan, was directed at Cooper's most sensitive spot, his position as a gentleman. Some critics condemned him for his "aristocratic" pretensions. Others denied that he was a gentleman at all. In answer to Cooper's attacks on the fashionable classes of the cities, the *North American Review* charged that he did not know, or care to know, "the tone of good society," because he preferred to escape "into the back-wood settlement, or still further into the wilderness." As a contrast, the *Review* referred to Catherine Sedgwick, whose novels proved that she was at home "in the polished scenes of the drawing room."[12] The assertion that Cooper was not familiar with polite society was as unfair as it was infuriating to the sensitive novelist, for with some reason he took pride in his qualifications as a cosmopolitan gentleman; but the contrast itself was by no means inaccurate. In his novels he made no effort to depict the virtues of the urban drawing room or even to deal with urban society in general. Catherine Sedgwick, on the other hand, did attempt to come to terms with the city in her works.

Like Cooper, she accepted the vision of republican society as essentially rural and agricultural, although in her mind it was founded on the village rather than on a landed class. If Cooper found his ideal at Cooperstown, the Sedgwicks centered theirs around Stockbridge. As Catherine saw it, this New England town was a true community, a close-knit society where "the intrinsic claims of each individual are known and admitted." Here was a society sufficiently stable to preserve those "associations" that sustained virtue and humane feelings: "Human virtues partake of the human constitution—they are weak and need external aid and support." Here, too, men were close to Nature, to her beloved Berkshires whose beauty, the physical expression of the divine intelligence and benevolence, appealed "to our moral and intellectual principles." And for Catherine, here was her home and her family, where during her youth she had enjoyed a life of security and culture, where talk then was not "of making money; that now universal passion had not entered into men and possessed them as it does now." Entranced by Stockbridge, she might have married and settled down there, but she gave her life to her brothers—three of whom pursued their ambitions into the city.[13]

The city threatened her vision of life. It was artificiality, where life was cut loose from the beneficent order of Nature. It was anonymity, where the individual, freed from the oversight of his neighbors, was at liberty to trample on the rights and persons of his fellow man. It was Sodom, where men were tempted to worship the golden calf. It was the relentless vortex, which swallowed human lives—which destroyed her beloved brother, Harry. And yet the city was too compelling and too necessary to be either rejected or ignored, for it was "the theatre of great men" whose energy and light made the countryside by comparison seem, if more virtuous, also mediocre. The city summed up the dangers and the promises of American life. Equality of opportunity had unleashed a tremendous zeal for human improvement, which was carrying America above any other society in the world. But the mobility, the change, the drive for the new that accompanied the emergence of the enterprising society seemed to be, as Cooper and Leggett could agree, dissolving the bonds of the liberal social order to the detriment of excellence, purity, and happiness.[14]

In her own gentle and modest way, Catherine tried to bridge the gap between the village ideal and urban reality. By the late 1820s, resigned to the single life, she had resolved to avoid that bane of the spinster, a sense of uselessness. She found something worthy to do in the city. In her first novel with an urban setting, *Clarence* (published in 1829 shortly after Harry's breakdown), the heroine, Gertrude Clarence, invades New York, protected against the vortex by the character she has acquired in a rural atmosphere. Gertrude is "a fit heroine for the nineteenth century, practical, efficient, direct, and decided—a rational woman— that beau-ideal of all devotees to the ruling spirit of the age—utility." But this woman of reason is also a woman of sensibility who, enriched in imagination by her exposure to Nature, gives "her faith to the poetry of life." While the less fortunate are destroyed morally and physically by the temptations of the city, she not only survives uncorrupted but also becomes a part of a circle of friends "of the most elevated and attractive character."[15]

Gertrude was very much like Catherine herself. Armored not only by her association with Stockbridge but also by her strong Unitarian faith in the benevolence of the divine order, the novelist tried to tame the demon at the center of the vortex. Like other Americans of her day, she attributed social troubles to the tendency of city dwellers to imitate "the artificial and vicious society of Europe," particularly the life of high fashion with its "false gentility," ostentation, and fundamental emptiness.

Out of such imitative attempts came failure, crime, brutality, and moral death. In 1836 Catherine's brother Theodore, Jr., published the first volume of his *Public and Private Economy,* intended to teach Americans the value of political economy. He warned that "fashion" was the chief obstacle to prosperity and happiness, because it led men to misapply their resources in money and labor in the quest for the things that, if not useless to begin with, soon became useless as prevailing fashions changed. Not only did fashion encourage waste; it also was the chief instrument used by those Americans who tried to establish artificial, as opposed to natural, class distinctions.[16]

In Catherine's novel *Home* (1835) John Norton dooms himself by marrying "a poor stylish girl" who is fatally attracted to the glitter of fashionable life. Desperate for money to support his wife's expensive tastes, he plunges "deeply into that species of gambling called speculation," loses what money he has, perpetrates fraud, and, as ruin closes in, commits "self-murder" on Christmas Eve.[17]

Faced with the speculative boom of the mid-1830s with its prospect of an increasing number of John Nortons, Catherine tried in a string of homiletic novels to arm her readers against the temptations of urban life (*The Lindwoods,* 1835; *Home,* 1835; *The Poor Rich Man and the Rich Poor Man* 1836; *Live and Let Live,* 1837; and *Means and Ends,* 1839). As a counter to the status seeker and the speculator, she offered the example of the Christian gentleman—or, more frequently, of the Christian lady, for she was particularly anxious to reach the homemakers with their powers over the habits and attitudes of future generations. Her ideal woman was to be the source of those virtues and values that the city, unlike the country, could not provide for itself: contentment, humanity, humility, common sense, and piety. In the family environment, insulated from the urban vortex, women could implant in their children the inner checks on that lusting after empty status, which perverted the healthy ambitions of Americans into forces of destruction.

Catherine's ideal woman literally was not the world shaker, but the homemaker who was protected from the contaminations of the real world of politics and capitalism: "What, then dear girls, does it signify if you are shut out from the halls of legislation?"—nothing. But Catherine herself could hardly avoid the real world. By placing her source of moral authority in an urban setting, she could not, as Cooper was doing, ignore the city and its problems, particularly that great problem that increasingly disturbed nineteenth-century America: the widening gulf between the rich and the poor. Like most Americans, her attitude toward wealth was ambivalent. On the one hand, she considered the possession of and the striving for money as possible moral dangers, for riches could corrupt by strengthening the taste for high fashion. On the other hand, she had too much of the Sedgwick confidence in the spirit of enterprise for her simply to condemn wealth. In *Clarence,* the hero argues that "mediocrity of fortune is most favorable to virtue, and of course happiness"; yet he cannot bring himself to turn his back on material riches, for "money is the representative of power—of the most enviable of all power, that of doing good."[18]

In the hands of men who are armored against the temptations of fashion, money was a positive boon to free society, for private wealth could be used to enable the truly unfortunate to stand on their own feet, to create the "institutions where the dumb are taught to speak, the blind to read, and the insane are restored to reason." It could be also used to educate the growing host of foreign immigrants, corrupted by European aristocracy and by Roman Catholicism, to the republican and Protestant values of American society. There were even times when the rich philanthropists might try to improve the miserable living conditions of the urban poor, since "the want of comfort and convenience" was a cause of intemperance and other evils of society.

The wealthy, then, had an obligation to the unfortunate poor. But identifying the unfortunate poor has long perplexed Americans. The physically and mentally incapable plainly belong in that category; even the foreign immigrants might be included. But what of those who are neither foreign born nor obviously incapacitated? Here, indeed, was *the* question? It is notable that in Catherine's novels poverty is mentioned chiefly as a challenge to the rich, for she appears to stress the "habit of giving" less for what it can do for the poor than for what it would do to counter the corrupting power of wealth. Otherwise, she keeps the poor in a state of limbo, outside society; for underlying her novels is the common American supposition that in free society there should be, with the exception of the truly unfortunate, no poor. She wrote in *The Poor Rich Man and the Rich Poor Man:*

> In all our widespread country there is very little necessary poverty. In New England none that is not the result of vice or disease. If the moral and physical laws of the Creator were obeyed, the first of these

causes would be at an end, and the second would scarcely exist. Industry and frugality are wonderful multipliers of small means.

Her "rich poor man" in the book is not really poor at all but the possessor
of that "mediocrity of fortune" so productive of character and happiness,
the true "riches" of human existence.[19]

If some men failed to possess the happy "mediocrity of fortune," then,
the reason for their failure lay not in life itself but in their approach to
life. Particularly, men fell into true poverty when they permitted themselves to be dominated by the lust for false gentility. It was this lust that
led many to sacrifice their chances for health, happiness , and mediocrity
of fortune in a futile quest for wealth and status. If only the average
man could be taught to recognize his good fortune under the existing
system—could be taught to be content with his natural lot in life—there
would be poverty neither of purse nor of spirit.

In effect, Catherine offered her readers a remedy for social ills that
involved not the reorganization of society but the education of the
individual in the correct approach to republican life. If the talented and
the rich could only be taught a sense of brotherhood with the rest of
men, and if the mediocre could only be taught not to envy the rich, then
urban life would be as stable and harmonious as ideal village society,
"the rich would no longer look with fear upon the poor man, nor the
poor man with envy upon the rich." In a real sense, what Catherine
placed before Americans as the social ideal was not only the village but
also what she supposed her own family to have been during her youth.
Here was an orderly life in which the more talented and mature watched
benevolently over the other members; where all enjoyed a place of
security and light; where, instead of embittering envy and destructive
selfishness, literally there was brotherhood.[20]

If by the 1830s Catherine had become the spinster in her family, as a
novelist in society she was accepted as everybody's maiden aunt, as the
source of apparently inexhaustible advice as to how to end family quarrels
and soothe family feelings. "Possessing a heart softened with the love of
human kind," a reviewer for New York's *Knickerbocker Magazine* wrote
regarding her place as a writer, "she will enjoy the reputation of having
been, pre-eminently, the moral benefactress of the first nation of freemen
on the globe; having sown broadcast, in the hearts of the youth of the
republic, the seeds of humble domestic virtue, which shall yield in the
future a hundred fold." Everyone loves a maiden aunt, provided he does

not have to take her seriously. Catherine became the first (and probably the best) of that line of female authors who were to dominate the popular literary tastes during the middle years of the century. *Home* ran through twelve editions, while *Poor Rich Man* sold well enough for its author to declare that "like bread-stuff" it was "suited to the market, the thing wanted."[21]

She was right, for her books did meet a variety of needs arising out of the uneasiness of the times. Cooper, by condemning urban wealth, placed himself in the withering cross fire of partisan politics. But Catherine offered something to all. To those who anchored their hopes in the rural villages, she offered assurances that the rural life was still the essential life of the country. To those who had committed themselves to the cities, she offered a comforting model of urban family life. To those disturbed by the urban flux, she offered the hope of stability; to those disturbed by urban conflict, the hope of harmony. Capitalist and farmer, Democrat and Whig, could find comfort in her books.

But her strength was also her weakness, for this broad appeal, viewed from another angle, was simply ambiguity in regard to the problem of wealth and poverty. Some might love her for her obvious faith in the basic integrity of individuals and her equally evident devotion to the cause of human brotherhood. Others, however, appeared to love her chiefly because, in a sense, she helped to keep the children quiet, for one of the effects of her books was to rob the real poor of a strong basis for protest. By making individual improvement the basis for social progress, she placed much of the responsibility for social evils on the very persons most afflicted by the evils. If poverty were usually produced by vice or at least by an incorrect approach to life, then were not the poor to be blamed for their poverty? If reform was to be effected through the reformation of individual characters, then was not reform the responsibility chiefly of the poor? As for the rich, was it not comforting for them to learn that, except in the case of speculators, "property is a sign of good morals?" It was true that the rich had responsibilities to their less fortunate brethren, but their chief obligation was to improve the character of the poor, in part by exemplifying the bourgeois virtues, in part by supplying direct education, and in part by making certain that the poor learned not only the rewards of virtue but the penalties of vice as well: "Infinite harm is done by alms-giving," Catherine warned young readers; "habits of lying, laziness, and dependence, are kept in the parents, and generated in the children, by encouraging them to live upon the supplies of charity, instead of working for the rewards of industry." All in all, was it not possible to reason that in the Republic wealth and poverty were rather exact rewards for the moral state of their respective recipients?[22]

Catherine did not intend to justify indifference to the plight of the poor any more than she intended to justify the worship of wealth. In search of something worthy to do, she committed her whole life to improving the physical and moral condition of individual Americans, her efforts sustained by her Unitarian faith in the regenerative powers of the individual and her liberal faith in the soundness of free society. Encouraged by the hope that any inherent defect in urban life would be negated by the pervasive purity of a nation essentially agricultural, she dreamed that through her books Americans could be brought into correct relationship with the blessed system the United States had inherited from the past. Nonetheless, by stressing the moral attributes of success and failure and by assuming the reality of the liberal democratic ideal, this warm-hearted woman did help prepare the way for smug Victorian optimism, which too often in the future would ease the conscience of a nation faced with the urban degradation Catherine so much abhorred.

Cooper and Catherine Sedgwick differed in their responses to the city, but they did share a common uneasiness over the boom, which set them both apart from their old friend, Verplanck. While many of his literary friends drew back from the turbulent vortex, Verplanck's natural cautiousness was dominated by his equally natural optimism, and he rushed headlong into the turmoil. Devoted to the city, closely identified with the business community, he thrilled to the boom-induced enthusiasms of the men at the center of economic life, "their hearts throbbing with hopes, envies, sorrows or fierce desires, and angers." Though he was not a man of fierce desires himself, he shared the hopes generated by the boom, at least by the time it reached its peak in 1836. Two years before, when his father died, he had become the guardian of the family fortune, only to see part of it almost literally go up in smoke as a result of the strains put on the insurance companies by the great New York fire of late 1835. Commercial New York had risen from its ashes to a more vigorous life than before, offering Verplanck, landowner and investor that he was, a golden opportunity to recoup his losses. The high interest rates and high prices of the boom hurt those who formed the Locofoco movement, but they often benefited the man with money at the center of commercial life. Verplanck became a boomer.[23]

In July 1836 in his commencement address at Union College, *The Advantages and Dangers of the American Scholar,* he defended the commercial world against its critics in general and, perhaps, Cooper in particular. The critics reacted uneasily to the dynamic thrust of the urban economy, but Verplanck plunged right in:

> We are pressing and hastening forward to some better future. No single mind can well resist the general impulse. The momentum of the whole mass of society, composed of myriads of living forces, is upon the whole individual, and he flies forward with the accelerating velocity, without any power over his own motion than that of the direction of its course.

Verplanck was not indifferent to the dangers of the dynamic society. Like Catherine Sedgwick, he recognized that the "gambling speculation" so common to the times was a possible menace to individuals and to society. Like Cooper, he saw that in America the pursuit of "the practical and profitable" might possibly degenerate "into selfish materialism" to the death of taste and the paralysis of reason. But after conceding the possibilities, he argued that the dynamic society provided its own antidotes to the poisons.

While his friends were trying to determine why there was disharmony between American fact and liberal theory, Verplanck asserted that there was no serious disharmony, that the experiment in freedom was a great success that not only confounded its critics but surprised its warmest friends. At the root of this optimism was his belief that the energetic competition unleashed by America's open society stimulated the mind and thereby strengthened the morals of the individual:

> The mind is not suffered to brood undisturbed over its little stock of favorite thoughts, treading the same unceasing round of habitual associations until ... its whole existence is but a dull, drowsy dream. On the contrary, it is forced to sympathize with the living world around, to enter into the concerns of others, and of the public, and to partake, more or less, of the hopes and cares of men."

So much for the stable village environment favored by the Sedgwicks, Bryant, and Cooper. Art, taste, and manners, perhaps, were lost in "the railroad noise and rapidity of the workaday world of America," admitted Verplanck, but the loss was more than balanced by the gain "in the healthful development of understanding, the more equable poise of the judgement, richness, variety, and originality of the materials for reflection, combination, or invention thus stored in the memory." Thus the energy of the dynamic society, by pervading all corners of human nature and human institutions, promised moral and material progress.[24]

If participation in American enterprise was the way to human improvement, then was it not logical to assume that the man of business would be a better man than "the mere man of books," and the pragmatic man of action would be superior to the theorist? Fundamentally, this was the same kind of argument that Leggett was making in favor of the Locofocos, except (and a most important exception it was) that Verplanck included the wealthy businessman in his beneficent system of forces—in fact, by inference placed him at the very center of the system. Cooper warned that the position near the vortex made men blind to the moral eclipse that darkened overhead. Verplanck warned the graduating scholars at Union to avoid the epic plans of professional writers who were not also men of affairs. Adherence to "grand plans of intellectual exploit," led only to disgust and disillusionment with a society that by its very nature was bound to go its own practical way. Believing that their talents had been spurned by society, seeing "duller schoolfellows outstrip them in worldly success," these writers were tempted to attribute their failures to American life and so become rebels "in heart to our glorious institutions." How well the hat seemed to fit the vexed and quivering brow of America's premier novelist.[25]

Verplanck's warning was also a prophecy of those future days when American intellectuals were to flee in disgust from the realities of their practical minded homeland to Greenwich Village, Europe, or foreign ideologies. In a sense his speech also gives us a glimpse of why the intellectuals were to flee. Verplanck was more successful than his friends in incorporating the liberal ideology into the world of urban capitalism, but at the cost of making practical, dollar-conscious capitalism and the capitalist the basis for social progress. Cooper, the Sedgwicks, Leggett, and Bryant all in varying degrees built their social vision on the individual and on interpersonal relations. Verplanck came very close to building his vision around the business community, around the successful managers of materially oriented enterprise.

And so this scholar, this genial man of affairs, this New Yorker who year by year, pound by pound, grew to look like Father Knickerbocker himself, became in his defense of the boom not only one of the first theorists of pragmatism but also, in a limited sense, one of the first of the modern American philistines. Himself in the vortex, he staked his reputation in 1836 on its assumed beneficence. It was a mistake, for the immediate future was to prove that Cooper, not Verplanck, had divined the direction of the boom.

THE NATURAL WAY

Although Verplanck smiled on the boom in 1836, his old friend Bryant found it odious. Wrenched from his European tour by Leggett's illness, the editor was plunged back abruptly into the turbulent atmosphere that had so repelled him two years before. He found the strife, the change. the noise, the lust for the dollar more disagreeable than ever. And now he had to face the vortex almost alone, for time, politics, and the boom had conspired virtually to destroy the circle of friends who had comforted him in the 1820s. His two walking companions, Thomas Cole and William Gilmore Simms, had gone—Cole up the Hudson to Catskill, Simms back to his native South Carolina. Cooper was moving north to Cooperstown. Harry Sedgwick and Robert Sands were dead, and Theodore Sedgwick, III soon departed for Europe. The old New York was gone.

On occasion Bryant still had recourse to his favorite comfort, the countryside. Stuffing some biscuits or apples in his pockets, he would set off on a walking tour of the Catskills or the Berkshires, there to immerse himself in nature and to enjoy the conversations of rural folk. He could even continue to dream of that day when, like Cooper, he would abandon the city almost entirely. In 1836, however, the day seemed far away, for he had now to toil to save his debt-ridden newspaper from bankruptcy—and with little help except for the occasional journalistic contributions of some of his friends.[1]   Between 1836 and 1840 James K. Paulding (before he became Van Buren's Secretary of the Navy), Henry J. Anderson, Theodore Sedgwick, III (when he returned from Europe in 1837), and Parke Godwin (soon to become Bryant's son-in-law) supplied articles or editorial assistance, but most of the burden was Bryant's.

Bryant tried to meet the challenge by making the newspaper more attractive to both readers and advertisers, continuing Leggett's Locofoco principles while leavening his young friend's monomaniacal devotion to equal rights with touches of Bryant humor. But though he succeeded in improving the *Post,* he found that not even a year's intensive effort could immediately restore the prosperous past. In 1836 net income fell to less than 60 percent of what it had been in 1832 and in the next year income collapsed to one-third of the 1832 figure—by far the poorest financial return since Bryant had joined the *Post* ten years before. Bryant soon thought he knew what was wrong. The prospect of losing his newspaper and of having to "go out in the world again loaded with a debt too large to leave me any hope of discharging" turned this man who had no taste for financial matters into a dedicated critic of the nation's monetary system.[2]

He blamed the speculative boom, though like Cooper, he was not adverse to making money. During the 1830s he invested what cash he could spare in Illinois, where his mother and three brothers were discovering that, as she phrased it, those "who have any industry at all gain property fast." He had started in 1833 by lending money, but in the face of a state usury law that limited interest rates to 12 percent, he soon began buying land, anticipating a return of 25 percent or better.[3] What disturbed him in New York was the high cost of simple survival for those enterprisers, such as himself, who did not have direct access to the boom world of the speculators. Workers, mechanics, persons on fixed incomes, all those who were denied the quick gains of speculation, were hurt by skyrocketing prices in 1836 and early 1837: flour, which had sold wholesale at $6.00 per barrel in October 1835, went for $9.00 in October 1836 and for as much as $12.25 in January 1837. "People of small fixed incomes complain that they cannot live as formerly," Bryant wrote to his wife in 1836, "and some talk of going abroad to find a cheaper country." If persons on fixed incomes complained, what then of the man whose income was declining in terms of dollars as well as purchasing power?

As a consumer, Bryant was brought face to face with one of the problems of urban life: the greater subjection to price fluctuations than in the countryside, where one could be more self-sufficient.[4] As a journalistic entrepreneur, he also had to face the problem of credit. The great paradox of the boom was that, while high prices indicated a plentiful supply of money for purposes of consumption and speculation, equally high interest rates indicated that there was not enough credit to meet all the legitimate demands. In early 1836, for instance, Cooper applied for a $10,000 loan, offering as collateral "some of the best paper in town;" he was told that he might get $1,500 at from 9 to 12 percent. And this was only the beginning, for by the end of 1836 interest rates, which had been 7 percent in 1834, rose to over 18 percent, twice the average in New York for the period 1831-60. For men such as Bryant who needed credit simply to finance their existing operations, simply to avoid sliding backwards, the situation appeared desperate. What was the cause? Like many other Americans, Bryant blamed speculation for having drawn off credit from productive enterprise into the get-rich, inflationary schemes of the boomers. Those who had access to the gilded world of high finance prospered; the rest were left with a few crumbs from the credit table. How was it that the few enjoyed their privileged position, while the mass of legitimate producers, the workers and small business-men such as Bryant, suffered?[5]

In 1836 Bryant opened fire from his newspaper office on what he considered to be two obvious pillars of this credit "monopoly." One was the "Restraining Act," first enacted in 1804, which restricted the rights of discounting and of issuing notes to banks incorporated by the state legislature. The other was the Usury Law, which limited interest rates on loans to a maximum of 7 percent. It is easy to see why a borrower should protest an act that limited the sources of loans to a relatively small number of institutions incorporated by the state, but why should he also condemn a law intended to restrict interest rates? The Usury Law, Bryant argued, illustrated how government interference with free trade injured not only the community but even the interests of the very persons it was intended to protect. Credit, he asserted, was a commodity like coal or flour, a matter of private transaction, whose price should be governed only by the law of supply and demand. By attempting to regulate interest rates, government interfered with the natural flow of credit. If the demand for loans drove interest rates above the legal limit, the law discouraged honest lenders from meeting the needs of legitimate borrowers, since no one could expect the man with the money to "turn philanthropist...out of mere love of his fellow man." Interference served only to divert loans from legitimate enterprise into the shadow world of speculation where both lenders and borrowers were willing to agree on interest charges far above the legal rate. Hence the paradox of a shortage of credit for producers and an overabundance for the speculators. Because of the laws, "credit is a captive in chains, the strong-limbed slave of a few hundred men, who make huge profits by letting out his services."

When the anti-monopoly drive provoked shrill accusations that it endangered the whole credit system, Bryant wryly compared the persons who believed the charges to "a superannuated old gentlemen, living...on top of a hill, who was thrown into a paroxysm of alarm by a stout young fellow, armed with a pickaxe, who threatened to dig up the well, and roll it downhill, water and all." The "stout young fellow," Bryant might have added, merely wanted a well of his own, for the main objective of the anti-monopoly drive was to make credit, the vital fluid of the economy, available to all enterprisers. The editor himself wanted credit not only to salvage his newspaper but also perhaps to increase his land purchases in Illinois with the thought of building up another source of income. In 1836 he did invest at least $200 in western lands, which he hoped would rapidly appreciate in value; he apparently never considered the possibility that such investments were a form of speculation as threatening to land-hungry westerners as urban speculation was to him.[6]

Like many of his compatriots, Bryant wanted both to eat his cake and to have it—that is, to share in the rapidly expanding wealth of America and also to preserve the simple, stable, moral, republican world that was his ideal. At the same time that he was demanding greater opportunities for himself and for others, he was denouncing the feverish "clamour about money, money, money" of the boomers as a moral disease that endangered the health of the Republic. A society that substituted "arithmatic" and selfishness for "honest feeling and virtuous impulses," he warned, was on "the high road to despotism." And also on the high road to ruin, for Bryant, like Cooper and Leggett, believed that the violation of principle and of the natural order would soon be punished by economic collapse.

The laws of trade as well as of moral law would have their way. In

April 1836 Bryant warned that the boom had encouraged dangerous "overtrading" in European imports. Indeed American imports had jumped from more than 126 million in 1834 to nearly 190 million in 1836. New York import merchants flourished, but at the expense of exhausting American credits in Europe. Since the boom not only stimulated imports but also acted to price some American exports out of existing foreign markets, the dread day would soon come when the United States, in order to redress its unfavorable balance of trade, would have to export part of the specie needed to maintain a sound monetary system: "the banks must break, or at least cease to discount. Debts must remain unpaid ... bankruptcy prevail, and one scene of wide ruin cover the land."[7]

As Bryant had predicted, in the spring of 1837 the golden bubble burst; banks broke, or ceased to make loans, businesses failed, imports dwindled, and prices fell; the abnormal activity of 1836 gave way to deathlike stillness. Bryant joined in the general moralizing on the ruins. The panic, he wrote, had purged New York of its extravagant habits and of the notion that it was possible to prosper without work; now men had to abandon their fixation on speculative "castles in the air" in favor of the cultivation of the earth where the real wealth lay. Society and the economy both, brought by disease to the point of crisis, were being restored to moral and physical health; the crisis had passed.

Unfortunately, recuperation was a long, painful process not completed for at least six years. Bryant's pleasure in gloating over the prostrate body of speculation soon lost its zest when he discovered that his friends and allies as well as the speculators had been caught in the collapse. Both Verplanck and the Sedgwicks had lost money. When he first learned of the Sedgwick losses, Charles, the one brother who had stayed at home in the Berkshires, wrote to his sister, Catherine, with perhaps more irony than he intended: "Only think what luck it is; instead of owning twenty thousand and owing a million, you owe nothing and own the half of what you have ... I have read an excellent manual upon the subject which I will show you when you come up, which tells how to make a dollar go a great way. It is called the 'Poor Rich Man.'" But there was nothing humorous about the situation. Before the depression ended, Robert and Theodore, Jr., would die from strokes, and Leggett would lose his newspaper, *The Plaindealer,* as a result of the failure of his publisher during the Panic.[8]

As for Bryant himself, his plight was worse than ever. During the boom, he had at least been able to dream of eventually selling the *Post* and of moving to Illinois to share in the prosperity of the rest of his family, but the Panic had punctured the dream as effectively as it had the boom; neither his western lands nor his newspaper now could be sold at any profit. Finding himself trapped in an unpleasant environment, he wrote wistfully to a friend in 1838 that he was willing to settle for far less than he would have accepted before. "If I had the means of retiring, I would go into the country where I could follow a simple mode of living." But it was too late for the simple life. Instead, the collapse compelled him to be "a draft horse harnessed to . . . a daily paper; I have so much to do with my legs and hoofs, struggling and pulling and kicking that if there is any thing of the Pegasus in me I am much too exhausted to use my wings."[9] For the first time in his career, he began to worry about the survival of his poetic talents. In one of the few poems he wrote during this dark period, "The Future Life," he lamented:

> For me, the sordid cares in which I dwell
> Shrink and consume my heart, as heat the scroll;
> And wrath has left its scar—that fire of hell
> Has left its frightful scar upon my soul.

More biting than ever, here before him during these years was the contrast between the rural paradise and the urban hell.

No ambitious man likes to feel himself the helpless victim of fate. What had gone wrong? It was tempting to blame speculators and merchants, but what had encouraged these men to do ill rather than good? Speculation and "overtrading," as Bryant analyzed the situation, were only the surface causes of the Panic; the fundamental flaw lay not in the economy but in the realm of politics and government. The unhealthy features of the boom were products "of our bad monetary system—a system that offers the most dangerous commercial temptations." Men by themselves would not resist the lure of easy money; they had to be kept from temptation. But the existing monetary system, far from discouraging avarice, both excited it and removed the avaricious from effective social restraint. Like Leggett before, Bryant found the source of evil in the system of special charters for banking corporations, which he thought enabled the favored few not only to monopolize credit but also to run riot with the money supply. Since the system restricted to the few incorporated banks the right to issue bank notes, it protected bankers from the most effective check on their actions, competition. Encouraged to overissue by their privileged position, bankers had swollen the currency supply, thereby feeding speculation and driving up prices. The profusion of currency had excited the abnormal growth of 1836, which had led straight to the Panic of 1837. The profusion itself was caused by faulty laws.[10]

What could be done to regulate the money supply in the interests of economic health? Bryant thought that men should not try to regulate the supply at all. Building on the ideas of Leggett and young Theodore Sedgwick, Bryant crusaded in the *Post* for total freedom in banking from either government aid or interference. The magic solution was rigid adherence to the principle of equal rights, which in this case meant replacing the system of special charters with a general incorporation system giving everyone an equal chance to acquire banking powers. Free banking would form the basis for a "natural system" where credit and money would be governed by powers far wiser than politicians—namely by competition among the greatly increased numbers of bankers and by the watchful oversight of the community. Stripped of their special privileges, bankers (and banks) would become individuals in a society of individuals. Free banking would in this way restore the financial system to the simplicity and stability of the village community, where all men were known by their reputations, where each man's credit depended on his known property, honesty, and ability. Here was the basis for "natural credit" based on the lender's soundness and on the borrower's needs and worth—credit that would automatically adjust itself to the real needs of the community. In this ideal system, there would be no worthless paper money, no overtrading, no speculation, no unhealthy booms or depressions. Here was the way to re-establish the stability that Bryant emotionally identified with his native Berkshires: here was the way of re-creating the old communal helpfulness and honesty in the face of the impersonal, moral chaos of the city.[11]

In his pursuit of the "natural way," the editor joined the Locofoco movement, which grew during the depression years from a faction in city politics to a statewide reform movement within the Democratic party. He became a powerful spokesman for the growing number of Democrats who, for a variety of reasons, denounced banking "monopolies" and the dominance of the party by "bank" politicians. Fighting at his side were those two stalwart opponents of monopoly, William

Leggett and Theodore Sedgwick, III. Though weakened by illness, Leggett had in 1837 intensified his efforts to "dissolve the affairs of politics from that of trade." There could be no compromise with the politicians who favored any kind of state aid or regulation. The dispute over the monetary system, as he saw it, was a case of all or nothing: If state interference with the laws of trade could not be ended, then "we must go back to the system of federal supervision. We must either have no chartered bank, or we must have a national bank. We must either leave trade wholly free, or place it under effective control." Leggett believed that federal control was the horrible alternative to complete individualism; he could hardly have recognized that vaguely he was prophesying the evolution of modern liberalism. This dedicated crusader soon lost his last public voice, *The Plaindealer,* but not before he had consolidated his position in New York as the patron saint of Locofoco democracy.[12]

Leggett's war against government interference and against the politicians was carried on by his friend, young Theodore Sedgwick, III, who in October 1837, after his return from England, won a Democratic nomination for the New York State Assembly. More than either Leggett or Bryant, Theodore spoke for the entrepreneur, for the man anxious to escape from the restraints and influence of government. In September at Tammany Hall he repeated his proposal for the general incorporation of banks, "which shall enable capitalists to combine their property for whatever objects they please, and on whatever terms they choose, and under wholesome uniform regulations to become private bankers." The new system, he argued, would not only aid the honest capitalist but also disarm the dishonest politician: "So long as the idea is kept up that government whether local or central, is to repair every private calamity, or foster every private speculation, so long will all politics be but a low scramble for office and power—so long will the great mass of the people be imposed upon by the knaves who have the means and the leisure to make trade of politics." This coupling of free trade with honest government was to be a favorite theme of liberal reformers such as Bryant for the next fifty years. Sedgwick's nomination under the banner of "Freedom in Trade—Freedom in Banking—Freedom in Everything" marked the triumph of the liberal wing of the Democratic party in New York City over the "Bank Democrats" identified with the system of special charters. Fate, however, denied the Liberal Democrats a major role in winning the victory they most desired.[13]

Ironically, the laurels went to the hated Whigs, some of whom had launched their own anti-monopoly drive against special charters in an effort to oust the Jacksonian Democrats from control of the state legislature. In 1837, to counter the anti-monopoly slate of the local Democrats, city Whigs nominated a ticket headed by Bryant's old friend and defender of the boom, Verplanck, who ran for the state senate. Although he had no sympathy for the extreme free trade views of the Locofocos, Verplanck's attitudes were not, as it proved, too different from Sedgwick's. In 1819, just before his first venture into state government, he had denounced the "lobby tribe," which, drawn to Albany by the system of special charters, had been chiefly responsible for "the scenes of corruption which for years past have disgraced the state." In the 1830s, as a Whig faced with a Democrat-controlled legislature, he had additional reasons for resentment of a system that seemed better suited to the needs of political partisans than of businessmen.

Despite the presence of his old friend on the Whig ticket. Bryant condemned the Whig candidates as the worst enemies of the "natural way," as "narrow minded politicians from our own camp, speculators in lithographic cities and fog lots"—in other words, those chiefly responsible for the boom and depression. The people thought otherwise. Acting on the characteristic American assumption that the party in power was responsible for their troubles, the voters gave the Whigs control of the lower house of the legislature by a landslide. Buried in the general Democrat debacle, Theodore Sedgwick never ran for elective office again.[14]

It was Verplanck, newly elected to the state senate, rather than Sedgwick or Bryant, who helped shape the nature of the anti-monopoly victory, although with his usual political luck he was deprived of a significant role in legislation by the fact that the Democrats continued to control the senate. Early in 1838 the new senator submitted a bill for the general incorporation of banks and also for government regulation of bank note issues. When, as he must have anticipated, his bill bogged down in the senate, he threw his weight behind a similar bill from the Whig-controlled assembly. In April the senate approved this bill providing for a new system of "free" banks, which soon rivaled and ultimately supplanted the special charter system. Monopoly had been defeated—but how decisive was the defeat?[15]

The Free Banking Act produced a variety of reactions among the

Locofocos. All applauded the general incorporation principle as a victory over privilege, since it enabled men to get bank charters without going to the legislature. From that point on, however, they disagreed among themselves as to how much of a victory it was. Most expressed the hope that now the many would acquire the banking powers previously held by the few. On the other hand, the *Denmocratic Review*, which often expressed the Locofoco viewpoint, denounced one provision of the act, which required that all banks have a paid-up capital of no less than $100,000, as a cunning device to concentrate the banking business "in the hands of the great monied corporations," a disquieting prospect for those who had formed their ideals in the individualistic mold. For his part, Theodore Sedgwick III praised the act as fulfilling the need for banks "of large capital at the principal emporia" to facilitate financial transactions, particularly to regulate the transfer of funds from one part of the country to another.[16]

Sedgwick was less pleased with the provisions of the act requiring banks to back their notes, dollar for dollar, with government bonds and mortgages to be deposited with the state controller. He called this provision "fundamentally incorrect in principle," but then dismissed the requirement as "a very minor matter" in comparison with the problem of creating and governing credit. His friend, Bryant, however, denounced the requirement as one more pernicious interference with natural principles. Although he was no monetary expert, the editor threw himself into the debate over the nature of money that raged beneath the surface of the bank controversy. Verplanck, as a representative of city merchants, wanted to protect them from unsound bank notes issued in other parts of the state. Experience, as a member of a commercial community that lived by the exchange of goods, had convinced him that money as the medium of exchange had to be distinguished from the goods exchanged; free trade in goods benefited New York; an unregulated, fluctuating currency did not. On the other hand, Bryant believed that money was a commodity whose value, like that of any other commodity, should be regulated solely by the laws of trade. Like Sedgwick before him, he argued that the only true safeguard for the currency was the local and highly competitive character of wholly free banking. The banknote requirement, as he saw it, gave bank notes a privileged position, because attempted government regulation would in fact simply be government sanction of paper money. Deluded by the false belief that regulation could actually maintain the value of bank notes, the public would give to them a greater value than they actually had in terms of other commodities. Government interference could have only one effect, to upset the natural relationships between goods and so again disrupt the economy as such interference had done in 1836 and 1837.[17]

In the end, Bryant accepted the Free Banking Act on the grounds that "a bad general banking law" was better than none at all, but he never abandoned his opinion that the efforts to supervise the monetary system were foolish and dangerous tamperings with the natural order. Throughout his career, he reserved a special resentment for the meddlers, for those who believed themselves "wiser than the laws of trade—persons, who, if they could only get at the stars in their course, would amend the solar system." Above all, he looked with suspicion on the class of political and economic specialists, the would-be managers of other people's lives, who found their reason for being in the growing complexities and interdependence of the times. These "visionaries and theorists," these men who "are so much wiser than providence as a quack doctor is wiser than nature," had introduced the "pernicious novelties" from which all the evils had risen: political quarrels, corruption of the press and of the legislature, speculation, poverty, exploitation, and economic disturbances. The chief villains were, of course, the politicians, for they had opened the Pandora's box of law. Here, in fact, were the great specialists, the political technicians, who in their management of government took the specialist's delight in trying "to complicate or mystify it, with a view to place it above, or hide it from the scrutiny of persons of good common sense."[18]

Bryant, like Leggett, spoke for those unnumbered Americans who felt a sense of frustration and impotence before political and economic events beyond their control. As individuals, they saw themselves threatened by the appearance of faceless, impersonal, amoral corporate power. In defense, they attacked government as the ultimate source of the power. "Individuals are only the image of their Maker," said Bryant sarcastically, "but corporations are the image of the legislature, and therefore entitled to a higher and more reverential regard." To destroy corporate power, to frustrate the politicians, Bryant proposed that government be brought as close to the individual level as possible. It was not enough to reduce federal powers to their narrowest possible scope; the same should be done to the states. Even public works projects such as roads and railroads, he argued, should be made the responsibility of county and local government where "the power is kept nearer the people, where they can watch, check, control, or resume it at pleasure."

Without the corporate power derived from government, there could be no monopolies, no encouragement to violate the laws of nature, no privileged protection from the will of the community. In a society composed exclusively of individuals, no man or no group of men could with impunity interfere with the laws of trade or violate the interests of the people. The result would be a truly republican society in which all men would get what their talents, labor and character deserved; in which the best would be at the top but no man would be at the mud bottom except for those who violated moral and physical laws: "Personal dignity, domestic comfort, social order, and happiness may be proved to be the inevitable results of the removal of the restraints imposed upon the free actions of men." In destruction of government interference, then, lay the natural way to re-create the spirit of the Berkshire paradise in the inferno of the city.[19]

During these years, Bryant became, like Leggett, a prophet. This retiring and rather passive man, no instinctive reformer, threw himself into a crusade not for the new but for the old. Emerson later criticized Bryant as one of those "historical democrats who are interested in dead or organized liberty, but not in organizing liberty.[20] What was dead for the Sage of Concord, however, was very much alive for the poet of nature. Emerson might think in terms of organizing liberty; Bryant believed that all men should reject the "pernicious novelties" of the times in favor of a renewed devotion to a fixed, eternal order that had been and always would be the one and only true system for human betterment; a return to the "good old paths" of republican society was the only way to achieve healthy progress, moral and material progress, toward a better life for all

In his defense of the natural way, Bryant strengthened a social vision that had an almost archetypal quality in the nineteenth-century American mind. Even well into the twentieth century, Americans continued to visualize the ideal democratic society in terms not of an abstract system of moral and economic law but of some version of the village community. The happy virtuous independent individual, the petty enterpriser, the neighborly community, the harmonious countryside—these were the basic constituents of the American dream, particularly as it was dreamed by the middle class. In a real sense, the idealized village community was symbolically a place where God and man, divine kingdom and earthy republic, met.

In 1839 a reviewer of Catherine Sedgwick's *Means and Ends,* writing in the *Democratic Review,* pointed to Stockbridge as proof that there was no incompatibility between a true democratic social order and "the highest degree of social refinement." In this "little society" located "in the midst of a fertile and smiling valley," men had found happiness and harmony: "A general spirit of mutual kindness appears to pervade the whole village, with a perfect deference, on the part of all, for the rights and feelings of others. The poorer and richer classes mutually respect and esteem each other, according to individual character and desert." Surrounding the village is "a moral influence as healthful as that of its bracing and pleasant mountain breezes upon the physical constitution." The reviewer noted that Stockbridge was not "a manufacturing place."[21]

If the true role of the prophet is to replenish the image of paradise, then Bryant, the most popular poet and one of the most influential journalists of his times, was successful. If that role is also to restore popular adherence to the principles of paradise, however, then Bryant was no more successful than the long line of major and minor prophets who came before him. He urged Americans to reject the temptations of modern life in favor of a modest place in a stable social order; few men could resist present temptations out of hopes for future happiness. He urged men to accept the beneficent oversight of the community; many sought to escape the petty restrictions of real village life for the growing anonymity of the city, where there were no watchful neighbors. He urged them to forego the dream of quick and easy wealth in favor of a happy mediocrity of fortune; many tried to get their share, and more, of the rapidly increasing wealth so evident in the cities. Bryant himself had fled to New York from the petty squables and restrictions of Great Barrington; despite his preference for the life of the countryside, he was to stay with his newspaper until it had made him the richest poet in America. If in Bryant's own person the poet and the prophet could not overcome the money-maker, what then of the millions of Americans whose ambitions were largely entrepreneurial in scope?

Nowhere was the prophet more disappointed than in his hopes that Americans would be content with individual status, for few ambitious men could resist the temptation to acquire corporate power in the face of the growing opportunities and complexities of urban-commercial life. Bryant hoped that general incorporation would give men all the advantages of the old corporations except the power to affect the lives of others, but the end result was simply to give a relatively few more men the power he wanted destroyed. Encouraged by the passage of the Free Banking Act, for instance, Verplanck joined with other prominent New Yorkers in an effort to establish the American Exchange Bank to be capitalized at $50 million, part of which was to come from New York City and New York State; the bank was undoubtedly intended as a check on the banks in the city's rapidly expanding hinterlands. The project fell through, but such men of standing in New York as John Jacob Astor and Albert Gallatin did establish the Bank of Commerce which, while considerably smaller, was created for much the same purpose. By 1850 some 136 banks were operating under the new act, along with seventy-three more that had received their powers under the old system of special charters.[22]

As Bray Hammond has pointed out, the results of the crusade for equal rights benefited not the average individual but the relatively few shrewd and energetic enterprisers who wanted all the power they could get. In the end, the chief result of "free banking" was to give more capitalists access to, and control over, the credit and money supply, while at the same time weakening any systematic public control of their affairs. The capitalists won; the average individual person lost. By the end of the century, the war against the monopoly of money and credit had become a war against the influence of New York bankers and for government intervention to protect the people. So in a broader sense did the system of general incorporation serve eventually to multiply the numbers of private corporate powers at the expense of the individual. Forty years later, Parke Godwin, Bryant's son-in-law and biographer, added this sobering footnote to his discussion of the editor's role in the free trade movement: "Incorporations have conferred prodigious material benefits upon the nation; but are they not masters of the nation?—the modern Frankensteins [sic] which have got the better of their creators?"[23]

But the Locofoco movement had positive results as well. The efforts of Bryant and other free traders inadvertently helped pave the way for corporate capitalism, but their work also served to strengthen the American liberal tradition. Just as Verplanck's pragmatic outlook was needed to balance the dogmatism of Bryant and Leggett, so was their devotion to principles and to individualism required to balance Verplanck's excessive confidence in the benevolence and skill of the business community. Equal rights, free but responsible individualism, the archetypal community—these became the chief ideological and emotional counters in the struggle to shape an urban commercial society that would meet the needs not only of the capitalists but of the people. The nineteenth century liberal tradition, which Bryant helped create, often failed to supply realistic answers to social problems; but, on the other hand, it was *the* liberal tradition. From the disparity between the liberal dream and the social reality came much of the creative tension (if not the direction) that motivated efforts to reform American life in the next century.

Many Americans criticized Bryant's position as utopian, even in the 1830s when his social vision still approximated American reality. In 1837 his old friend Richard Henry Dana advised him: "As to reforming the world give all that up. It is not to be done in a day, nor, on your plan, through all time. Human nature is not fitted for such a social condition as your fancy is pleased with." Human nature, indeed, was hardly fitted for such a social ideal; yet was not there the possibility of continuous progress toward; if not the attainment of, the ideal? In 1848, on the outbreak of the French Revolution and in the year of the *Communist Manifesto,* a chastened but still optimistic Bryant gave what in effect was a belated reply to his friend's warning: "That the earth is to become a paradise in consequence of any political changes that may be made, I do not believe; but I believe it to be the order of Providence that republican institutions will come in with a higher and more general civilization, and that their effect is good and wholesome."[24] Although the end of the troubled 1830s was to diminish his prophet's zeal, Bryant was in future years to continue the fight to protect and extend republican institutions—and to preserve the natural way.

PRESS, POLITICS, AND PUBLIC OPINION (1837-45)

By the 1840s Americans could conclude that Liberty had triumphed over
the more obvious forms of tyranny, but who would doubt that the old
enemy still worked in subtler ways to subvert the Republic? "He shall
send," Bryant warned in "The Antiquity of Freedom" (1842):

> Quaint maskers, wearing fair and gallant forms
> To catch thy gaze, and uttering graceful words
> To charm thy ears, while his sly imps, by stealth
> Twine round thee threads of steel, light thread on thread,
> That grow to fetters.

The uneasiness was old yet also new, for political events had convinced
Bryant that Freedom's guardians, the people, indeed could be lulled
into inattention by maskers, quaint and not so quaint.

Bryant, Cooper, and other liberals believed that their ideal republican
society answered the age-old problem of reconciling order and excellence
with individual freedom. Europe had tried to solve the problem by
establishing a privileged elite, but Americans had rejected this solution
as inimical to the Republic. Such ex-Federalists as Catherine Sedgwick
and Cooper attributed the demise of Federalism to their fathers' outspoken elitism. There was no need for a privileged elite, the liberals
believed, because the Republic offered a superior governing power, the
will of the community. They embodied their hopes in an idealized

community in which all men were equally free and equally subject to the supervision of their neighbors. Since in this ideal society all men shared the same fundamental republican beliefs, the community will promised always to sustain correct principles. Although the will was essentially that of the people, it would be carried into effect by the most talented and virtuous men, a local elite raised to influence not by privilege but by popular respect for its moral and intellectual excellence. This natural relationship between the leaders and the led would render men free from institutionalized power but subject, nonetheless, to a pervasive and benevolent authority.[1]

The dream of the community is one of the noblest and oldest in the history of man, but could it be realized even in a nation as favored as the United States? In the 1830s some Americans saw reasons for doubt. The ideal community depended on stable relationships among men and on popular agreement in matters of principle. In contrast, America, the land of horizontal and vertical mobility, encouraged men to change their places and their roles; society was in motion. There was apparently little agreement among the people. And there were few leaders who could legitimately claim power as the natural representatives of the community.

What, then, was the will of the community? Was it an election majority? Was it so-called "public opinion"? William Leggett doubted both definitions. In 1834 this ardent individualist had gone to the defense of abolitionists and Negroes persecuted by New York mobs. By 1837, faced with widespread hostility to himself as well as to the abolitionists, Leggett thought the public had deserted him. Could it be denied, he asked in *The Plaindealer,* that not only abolitionism but also "a thousand matters of less startling moment" had been scarred by the "marks of the iron heel of despotism, as expressed by the majority"? Here was "the most cruel of despots—a despotic majority." In June he lamented that in America rational concern for the "naked dignity of abstract propositions" had fallen before the selfishness of demagogues and "the passions of the multitudes." Such was one of the last public utterances made by this hero of equal-rights democracy.[2]

Few Liberals equalled Leggett's passionate devotion to individualism and to abstract rights, but many shared some of his concern over public opinion. In most cases, their concern varied with the election returns; often they were able to find comfort in the rationalization that the people had been misled or mismanaged this time, but they would speak more truly at the next election. Even this rationalization, however, could not always quiet the uneasiness. Why had the people not united in favor of republican principles? Why had they apparently threatened the true interests of the individual? Why, in other words, was public opinion not an accurate expression of the will of the community?

There was one disturbing answer to these questions. Bryant and Cooper, each in his own way, dreamed of a stable political society governed by gentlemen, by gifted amateurs; but as early as the 1820s the reign of the amateur, if it ever existed, was yielding to the influence of politicians, journalists, and other professional opinion-makers. Ironically, the very individualism for which the liberals were fighting contributed to this development, since professional organizers were required in order to form the mass of individuals into that force needed for effective popular government. Here was the paradox of individualism in republic: effective government demanded organized efforts, yet such efforts brought into being technicians who specialized in manipulating people in defiance of the ideal of free individualism.

Liberals such as Bryant condemned the technicians for their alleged tendency to pervert the real will of the community. In 1828 the *Evening Post* had expressed the hope that Jackson's victory would "teach political managers that they shall not again divide the country into factions in order to take the elections from the people." The political managers, however, were not easily downed. In 1838 Bryant complained that Whig politicians and publicists had stopped discussing the real issues, although they contributed "plenty of prattle" about such matters as a Democratic plot to marry one of President Van Buren's sons to Queen Victoria. This was only a prelude. In 1840 Van Buren, the archmanipulator of the Democratic party, himself became a victim of mass politics, as he was systematically smeared by the Whigs. Bryant condemned the Whig "Tippecanoe and Tyler, Too" campaign as an attempt to substitute emotion for reason. Noting the widespread use of campaign songs, he commented wryly: "The plan is to exterminate us chromatically, to cut us to pieces with A sharp and to lay us prostrate with G flat, to hunt us down with fugues, overrun us with choruses and bring in Harrison by a grand diapason." But there was little humor to the situation. "We can meet the Whigs on the field of battle and beat them without effort," Bryant complained, "but when they down their weapons of argument and attack us with musical notes, what can we do?" The Whigs won the national election, a victory that Bryant attributed to the "foul arts" of professional politicians.[3]

Democrats were not the only victims of political managers, as Verplanck could attest. The New Yorker accepted political disputes both as natural to a society of diverse opinion and as beneficial stimulants to public awareness. But his experience during the Bank wars left him with a distaste for "active professional partisan politicians," whom he accused of being more interested in party discipline and party victories than in the public good. It was the politicians who called on "popular prejudice . . to put down the innovator," who in the name of party unity were prepared to sacrifice the independence of thought and action so necessary for good government. In 1836 Verplanck warned the graduates at Union College of the great hazard faced by the scholar in politics: "His soul is not his own."

Verplanck rediscovered the truth of this assertion in 1841 when his old-fashioned refusal to bow to popular prejudice ended his political career. As a member of the state senate, he had backed Governor Seward's proposal to use state funds for Roman Catholic parochial schools, and so provoked the enmity of the growing numbers of anti-Catholic nativists within the Whig party. When he stood for renomination in 1841, the hostility to his stand was so intense that he withdrew his bid and retired to work on a scholarly edition of Shakespeare's works. He never ran for elective office again.[4]

Both Bryant and Verplanck, then, had to recognize that public opinion, far from being the dependable force they hoped it would be, was in fact an uncertain force that seemingly was being shaped and reshaped, directed and redirected, by a complex of opinion-makers. But neither man abandoned the hope that in the long run public opinion would approximate the will of the community. Verplanck, naturally buoyant and experienced in politics, viewed the politicians with relative equanimity. Bryant, though more suspicious of the political manager, took comfort in the thought that as an editor he exercised a power over opinion that could counter that of the politicians.

By the 1830s newspapers had become the first of the mass media. Like most news media, they were credited with more influence over the public mind than they actually possessed. "A newspaper can send more souls to Heaven and save more from Hell," boasted James Gordon

Bennett of the *Herald,* "than all the churches or chapels in New York."
More modestly, Bryant called the press a powerful weapon for good or
evil, depending on its direction. Bryant once expressed the hope that
journalism, because of its power and importance, would "attract men
of the first talents and the most exalted virtues." By the 1830s, however,
the press seemed more cesspool than kingdom of virtue. The period was
the zenith of partisan newspapers, whose dependence on party patronage
drew them full-tilt into the mud hole of politics. No matter how un-
enthusiastic his devotion to journalism was, Bryant did have a strong pride
of profession easily disgusted by the below-the-belt attacks of other editors. In 1830 he placed his rival on the *Commercial Advertiser* among

> ...the coarse, licentious tribe
> Of fifth-rate typemen, gaping for a bribe,
> That reptile race with all that's good at strife.
> Who trail their slime through every walk of life.

The "reptile race" replied in kind, though few went so far in impugning
Bryant's integrity as Horace Greeley, who at a later time screeched: "You
lie, you villain, you sinfully, wickedly, basely lie!" Political patronage
and the strongly competitive nature of journalism at the time, mixed
with a large dose of freewheeling, if not irresponsible, individualism
resulted in a press that lacked either the means or the inclination to find
much good in the position of the other side.[5]

If, as Bryant complained, newspapers "by an artful mixture of truth
and falsehood" transmuted the most innocent acts into apparent crimes,
how reliable was the press? Bryant himself remained stubbornly confident that journalism would ultimately become the independent, objective
medium he claimed it was when in 1829 he urged the elimination of
electioneering because "the merits of every candidate reach every individual in the community thro' the medium of the press." Throughout,
he could believe that he was shaping public opinion in conformity with
the will of the community, that he was effectively countering the perversions of politicians and partisan pressmen. But what if one did not
have Bryant's apparent access to power?[6]

In 1840 James Fenimore Cooper wrote to his son, Paul: "Depend on it,
my son, we live in bad times, and times that threaten a thousand serious
consequences, through the corruption of the nation. If public virtue be
truly necessary to a republic, we cannot be one, but, unknown to ourselves, must be something else." It was this pessimism that made Cooper

one of the most incisive and also one of the most ineffective critics of his times. More than either Bryant or Verplanck, Cooper centered his ideal republican society around gentlemen such as himself. Prior to his return to the United States in 1833, he had been able to believe that American society came close to being the ideal community where the people are wise enough to choose their natural leaders. All in all, he had seen conditions as favorable to the gentleman and amateur opinion-maker. Perhaps if he had remained in Europe and in happy isolation from social realities in America, he might have continued to believe that the real approximated the ideal. But this was not to be. Return he did—to fight first a skirmish and then a war both with the American press and with public opinion.

In his *Notions of the Americans,* written during the first year of his European tour, Cooper had a good word for American newspapers, which "compared with the rest of the world . . . are models of propriety—bad as I confess we are." The superiority of these newspapers, he wrote, stemmed from the greater "respect for private feelings" and the greater liberty for "fearless discussion" in free society. Given his tendency to evaluate social matters in personal terms, it is very likely that he was influenced to these conclusions by his friendship with Charles King, the editor of the *New York American.* If so, this same tendency acted to reverse his favorable view when in 1832 he began to receive evidence of newspaper attacks on his personal character, the most offensive of which were printed in the *American.*[7]

Such attacks were common at this time. Bryant had learned to live with them after his abortive and humiliating effort to chastise William L. Stone in 1831. From then on, he heeded the moral in the story of two young men: One, approached by a barking dog, ignored the animal and it slunk off. The second young man, however, decided to teach the cur a lesson with a kick; before long, he was surrounded by a pack of snarling beasts which forced him to slink off, fortunate to escape, if not with his pride, at least with half his clothes. Cooper never did learn the moral; he kicked. When in 1834 he published his *A Letter to Americans* in reply to the newspaper attacks, he put himself right in the middle of the political wars of the times. The *United States Gazette* of Philadelphia, observing a notice of *A Letter* in the *Evening Post,* warned him that if he "has entered the troubled waters of politics, and performed to win the applause of the *Post,* then, we suspect that we have seen the last of the

'Mohegans'." Cooper was as stubborn as he was sensitive. The first threats, far from silencing him, merely spurred him on; the "mohegan" had only begun to fight.[8]

While in Europe, Cooper had promised that "if these attacks on my character should be kept up five years after my return, I shall resort to the New York courts for protection." In less than five years, he was in the courts—in response, significantly, not to the attacks of the urban press, at least in the beginning, but to the combined hostility of people and press in his beloved Cooperstown. Characteristically, the conflict started over an apparently trivial affair. In 1837 some of the residents of Cooperstown had chopped down a tree and made other "improvements" of Cooper family property at Three Mile Point on Lake Otsego. Since the point had long been used by the townsmen as a picnic ground, they treated it as if it were public property. Cooper saw the act as an invasion of property rights, doubly sacred because by will he was obliged to hold the Point in trust for a younger member of the Cooper family. He responded with a blunt warning against trespassing that categorically denied the public any right to use the property.

Local leaders, assuming that the right had been established, answered with a blast of their own. A public meeting denounced both Cooper and anyone who would dare uphold his side of the controversy, and then, to twist the dagger, recommended that all his books be removed from the town library. Soon a local newspaper, *The Chenango Telegraph,* entered the fray by asserting that "this gentleman, not satisfied with having drawn down upon his head universal contempt from abroad, has done the same thing for himself at Cooperstown." Cooper sued for libel. And so this warm and generous—and stubborn and irascible—man found himself at war with the very people whom he so much wanted to lead. In contrast to *The Pioneers,* in which Judge Temple was accepted as the deciding voice in local disputes, real life saw the public turn hostile. To make matters worse, the Three Mile Point "Affair" was given publicity by hostile newspapers throughout the state. The curs had gathered.[9]

Angered and hurt, Cooper tried to explain in a series of books why the gentleman, the crown of republican society, had been repudiated by the people. In 1838 he devoted more than a quarter of *The American Democrat* to the press and public opinion, expressing the ideal of "opinion being the fountain whence justice, honors, and the laws equally flow." In reality, from this same opinion flowed the corruption of principles, morals, manners, and almost everything else he held dear. He even complained of the "popular abuses" of the English language arising out of efforts to substitute general linguistic rules for "the usages of polite society," one abuse being such "uncouth innovations" as the pronunciation of "clerk" as the word was spelled instead of as "clark."

Cooper put much of the blame on the newspapers. By 1838 he had turned his earlier optimistic appraisal of the American press inside out. Now he concluded that native journalism was inferior to that of Europe, in part because of the opportunities of American life. So many men had been able to establish newspapers, he argued, that the average editor had neither the intellect nor the capital needed to gather correct information. If newspaper facts could not be trusted, neither could newspaper opinions. Protected by the public's gullible faith in the objectivity and and "impersonality of the editorial character," editors were free to praise what they liked and to damn what they did not like, to enthrone prejudice rather than truth.* Society, Cooper warned, had fallen under the influence of a privileged "press-ocracy" dominated by men who had little to lose even in matters of reputation, since their editorial masks gave them a measure of anonymity not enjoyed by other men of influence. From this anonymous, irresponsible source flowed untruth, until the whole nation "in a moral sense, breathes an atmosphere of falsehood." The faceless ones were in power.[11]

Cooper tried to put a face on these professional mismakers of opinion in his two novels, *Homeward Bound* and *Home as Found*, which he projected as a return to the world of *The Pioneers* "in order to show the difference which half a century has made in the appearance and usages of an American village." His hero is Edward Effingham, one version of the good gentleman of Cooper's dreams, who experiences the same disillusioning experiences with American society as his creator. Two villains stand for the sources of corruption in society. The lawyer-politician, Aristabulus Bragg, is a political technician who deals in majorities as a merchant deals in flour. Abstract principles of right and wrong have no place in his scheme of things; wrong is simply resistance

---

* In *Notions* Cooper had argued that the variety of opinions arising out of the profusion of newspapers in America acted to cancel each other out in the readers mind, so that newspaper became only sources of factual information. A decade later, he argued that the intense competition among newspapers for patronage and readers made "editors reckless and impatient to fill their columns." Cooper by the end of the 1830s had rejected the faith in competition so characteristic of his Liberal friends.[10]

to the popular will, particularly if that will be manufactured by himself. Bragg plainly is no gentleman, but, significantly, he is a model of honor in comparison with the newspaperman, Steadfast Dodge, one of the most odious characters in American fiction.

Dodge is a natural sycophant. Since in a democracy the people are sovereign, he naturally makes the popular will his god. Far from being an ideal man of integrity and independence, he is a creature of the mass mind, "accustomed to think, act, almost to eat and drink and sleep, in common." Dodge is a coward, but, when assured of the support of a majority, he becomes as brave as a lion in attacking those who choose to differ from the majority: "It is aristocracy, and has an air of thinking one man is better than another." Since he cannot act without the support of some kind of majority, if none is available, he works secretly to create it. Sensitive to popular views, shrewd in his ability to popularize an idea, this master manipulator lacks both intellect and integrity. When Effingham suggests that principles are important, the journalist hastily agrees, but he can only spout clichés, all of which reduce to the windy proposition that "one man is as good as another."

Dodge, a pompous, meddlesome, loose-thinking, and vulgar bully, symbolized for Cooper the new society, a society that had ceased to have any real leaders. Having been encouraged to repudiate the efforts of gentlemen to exercise their leadership talents, the average American, denied proper models, had become the slave of the dominant "we" and "they" of public opinion as expressed by the Braggs and Dodges of the nation. The "natural leaders of society" still survived, but they could not effectively challenge the new powers. Deprived of cultural capitals where they might concentrate their influence and talents, scattered throughout a largely rural population, they themselves were prey to the meddlers, who had gained control of the organs of opinion. "Public men and writers" lived in dread of the press, bowing to a debased version of the very opinion they should have led. As a result, even the countryside was being corrupted by those powers that had won control of the cities.[12]

Cooper's ideal gentleman was caught in a dilemma. To abandon the field to the technicians would be to abdicate in favor of forces that were destroying the republican community. But to fight back against the opinion-makers meant risking what remained of the public reputation needed by gentlemen to win the voluntary support of the people. Cooper decided to take the risk. Between 1837 and 1845 he carried on a one-man war against the press. In the battle of words that ensued, his access to the public was limited chiefly to his own novels and to the *Evening Post,* which opened its columns to him on request. A frequent visitor to Bryant's office, Cooper exempted the editor from his indictment of the Press:

> I place the name of Bryant as near the top of American literature, as any man has yet attained. In my view, he is not only one of the noblest poets, but one of the best prose writers of the age. A profession could never be totally degraded while it has such men in its ranks.... This is not the opinion of a political partisan either, for while I think generally with Mr. Bryant, on political subjects, we are widely separated on many essentials.[13]

Cooper underestimated the differences that separated him from Bryant, but they shared both a devotion to Jackson and a contempt for the Whig press. By publishing his open letters in the ultra-Democratic *Post,* Cooper made certain that he brought a swarm of Whig journalists down on his neck. Leggett's old enemy, James Watson Webb, in his *Courier and Enquirer,* vilified the novelist as "a base minded catiff" who had traduced his country in order to win the patronage of aristocratic Europe and who had boasted of his noble blood when he was actually, said Webb the son of "a highly respectable WHEEL-WRIGHT of New Jersey." Other Whig newspapers took up the refrain, while the *Knickerbocker Magazine* advised its readers to boycott *Home as Found* so as to "correct misplaced alliance with unprofitable or interdicted subjects. Books that are not read, are not sold and books that are not sold, are not written." And so it went. In less than two months in 1841, Thurlow Weed reprinted in his *Albany Evening Journal* references to Cooper, most of them unfavorable, from twenty-two different newspapers.[14]

In his war against Whig opinion-makers, Cooper received little support from Democratic editors other than Bryant, for most of them preferred to ignore a man who was so outspokenly critical of the press and of the public. His chief allies in the battle were the courts and the libel laws. By December 1841 he had initiated three indictments for criminal libel and twelve civil suits. Before he buried the legal hatchet, he had sued the Whig journalists Webb, William L. Stone (Bryant's old sparring partner), Park Benjamin, Horace Greeley, and, a total of five times, the influential Thurlow Weed who was a politician as well as a journalist.[15]

Cooper defended his resort to the courts as needed to protect individual integrity from the kind of public opinion expressed in, and manufactured by, the newspapers. Although he admitted that the press had the right to criticize his novels in any way it wished, he contended that no newspaper had the right to malign the character of an author. It was through such attacks on the characters of individuals, he argued, that the new mass opinion had weakened that mutual respect between the people and gentlemen so essential to good society: "Men cannot hear character coarsely assailed from day to day, and maintain a just appreciation of its importance." Contrary to the old saying. words, as well as sticks and stones, could hurt, and in a most fundamental way.[16]

Cooper was so successful in his suits that in 1843 he could boast that he had "beaten every man I have sued, who has not retracted his libels." But the taste of victory was far from sweet. It was true that he taught the American press some manners. "He put a hook into the nose of this huge monster, wallowing in his inky pool and bespattering the passersby," said Bryant; "he dragged him to land and made him tractable." Few persons, however, recognized that Cooper was striving not only to teach manners but also to save a cherished way of life from ultimate destruction. Bryant did condemn the Whig attacks as a threat to the purity and integrity of literature, but not even he fully appreciated Cooper's concern. "He is a restless creature," the editor wrote to a mutual friend in 1837, "and does not seem well satisfied with his position in this country, though his great reputation, his handsome fortune, his fine health, and very amiable family ought to make him so." If even his old friends found it difficult to see the world through his eyes, was it surprising that the majority of Americans should view Cooper's battles with indifference, perplexity, or hostility?[17]

Cooper entered the final chapter of his career with a feeling that he lived virtually alone in the midst of a mass opinion beyond his control. "The newspapers are the moral lungs of the nation, and what they tell the people they think, the people do think." If Cooper indeed were challenging the democratic Leviathan, than what chance did he have to win? None:

> He who suffers under the arbitrary power of a single despot, or by the selfish exactions of a privileged few, is certain to be sustained by the sympathies of the masses. But he who is crushed by the masses themselves must look beyond the limits of his earthly being for consolation and support.

Measured in terms of the challenge, his successes in using libel laws to beat antagonistic newspapers into silence seemed of little consequence. In the face of hostile public opinion, the libel laws were awkward and ineffectual defenses for any person, particularly since juries were likely to side with the public rather than with the individual, a point he made almost to the point of tedium in his last novel, *The Ways of the Hour*. As for his victory over the press, it had the effect of driving the newspapers to ignore him almost completely, without in any appreciable way reducing their hold on the public mind.[18]

There was defeat even in his victories. Not only did they result in Cooper's partial eclipse (at a time when Bryant was consolidating his fame), but they were won at the expense of strengthening hostility toward those two institutions on which he relied: the landed gentry and a judiciary independent of the popular will. Both were vulnerable to the charges that they were privileged deviations from the democratic norm; both were to be weakened in the 1840s. Bryant and his liberal friends were to contribute to this defeat. Indeed, for Cooper, there was little consolation on earth.

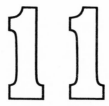

THE BARNBURNERS (1840-46)

On 29 May 1839 a martyr was made for the cause of Liberal democracy. William Leggett had stumbled through four years of despondency to life's ultimate defeat. In 1835, harassed by illness and faced with financial ruin, he had cried out of his enemies: "They are killing me." When he lost *The Plaindealer* in 1837, he retired to his New Rochelle home, the gift of his actor friend, Edwin Forrest. But he found no peace there. Worn out by his labors, he gave way before a series of "bilious" attacks, which depleted his strength and left his complexion the color of "saffron water." In the spring of 1839 his worried friends persuaded President Van Buren to appoint him chargé d'affairs in Guatemala in the hope that his health would "be renovated by a sea voyage and a residence of a few months in the benignant climate of Guatemala." It was too late. Four days after the announcement of his appointment, William Leggett died. A special steamboat was run to New Rochelle for his funeral.[1]

Leggett had a talent for defeat. His fiery dogmatism, by alienating friends as well as enemies, helped destroy his career in journalism, just as years before his pugnacious disposition had ruined his naval career. In 1838 he narrowly missed a Democratic nomination for Congress, chiefly because of the widespread feeling that his uncompromising spirit would alienate his fellow congressmen. Whatever his faults in life, however, in death he became a symbol of purity—the "true American Democrat," said Bryant:

His love of truth, too warm, too strong
   For Power or Fear to chain or chill,
His hate of tyranny and wrong,
   Burn in the breasts he kindled still.

Others agreed with Bryant. Leggett alive had frequently been a nuisance; dead he became the unapproachable, a point of hope in a disturbing world. Even Tammany Hall bowed to death by erecting a bust of the hero in the very room from which had come his excommunication from the party in 1835. As in the cause of other martyrs, his life acquired a mythical quality, embracing both the good and the evil of the world. In the myth, he was laid low not by his own defects but by the political prejudices of the times. Leggett had preferred principles to party, said Bryant's son-in-law, Parke Godwin, in 1842. "What was the result? Desertion and poverty for the time—to be followed but not till he was cold in his grave, with monumental honors and eulogies." The persecutors were politicians.[2]

There was need in the early 1840s for a point of hope, for a myth. Although the tumults of the 1830s were passing slowly away, the times were hardly secure, for they brought a renewal of the depression precipitated by the Panic of 1837. They also brought an acceleration of that social change that so disturbed Cooper; not even depression could long slow the increasingly rapid tempo of American life. Politics, newspapers, railroads, telegraphs, factories, immigrants, and nativists formed only a part of the vertiginous and variegated scene. In the 1830s New York City's population had increased by 54 percent to 312,000; the next decade would make it a metropolis of more than half a million people. The old, comfortable Gotham was giving way to a strange new city, a dangerous and exciting city.

Among the mature and the aged, change breeds nostalgia. By the 1840s such transplanted Yankees as Bryant sentimentalized on the innocence and stability of their native villages. In 1843–44 Bryant and Theodore Sedgwick joined with other ex-Berkshirites of the city to plan a homecoming, the Berkshire Jubilee, "for the purpose of renewing acquaintance and strengthening our attachment to our natal soil." The Berkshires stood for stability, noted the *Knickerbocker Magazine* in 1844, where tradition had escaped "the crushing foot of Innovation." And they stood for personal identity too: "You may know a Yankee everywhere, because he *has* a home, while the origin of the metropolites and cosmopolites one meets all over the world is as doubtful as the stormy petrels."

This sentimentalized but not inaccurate picture of the Berkshires provided a convenient symbol of the kind of society desired by Bryant and other liberal Democrats. For such men, tranquillity and harmony were part of the rural and natural order outside the cities. There in the countryside a purer, more stable form of life continued to flourish. And yet by the 1840s there were disturbing signs that even the countryside had not wholly escaped the chaotic change so characteristic of the cities. In 1843 the *Evening Post* described the plight of Bethlehem, Pennsylvania, a place Bryant had probably visited on one of his walking tours. Once, everything in this village had been "in harmony with the natural beauty of the place;" here was morality, hope, a sense of permanence—all that was needed to make the inhabitants happy and content. And so the villagers were—until some of them invested their money and hopes in local banks. "The great distemper of the time, overbanking and excessive confidence in banks, has made sad havoc with the prosperity of this prudent, laborious, and economic community."[3]

Undoubtedly, Bryant intended the story of Bethlehem as an allegory to warn rural folk as well as city dwellers of the dangers, moral and economic, of defying the "natural way"; for by the early 1840s Bryant, as a journalist, had widened his scope to include not only New York City but much of the state as well. The *Evening Post* was entering its heyday of state and national influence as the voice of liberal democracy. A new phase of an old battle had begun. By the early 1840s the new Free Banking Act had taken much of the edge off the bank controversy in New York, but hard times provided plentiful materials for the continuation of the dispute over economic policy, not only between Whigs and Democrats but among Democrats themselves. In fact, the disturbing conditions inflamed and enlarged the conflict between Locofocos and Bank Democrats to the point that it split the state party into two warring factions: The "Radicals" or, as they were called later, the "Barnburners" who generally upheld the Bryant-Leggett brand of liberalism, on the one side, and, on the other, the "Conservatives" or "Hunkers." These names have some significance. The Barnburners apparently received their name from their alleged willingness to risk political and economic turmoil in their pursuit of unrealistic ideals—i.e., to burn down the barn in order to get rid of the rats. Hunkers were accused by their enemies of "hunkering" after political office. The Barnburners, of course, were not indifferent to political spoils, but, generally they were more strongly committed to the laissez faire philosophy and less interested in maintaining party unity than were the Conservatives.

Early in 1843 the Barnburners tried to elect Bryant as state printer in place of Edwin Croswell, whose *Albany Argus*, long considered the official newspaper of the state organization, they identified with banks and with the Conservatives. This effort to make the *Evening Post*, with its radically liberal views, the voice of the party was defeated by a sizable majority in the legislature, but the war had only begun. Although Bryant had not promoted himself for state printer, this abortive effort had the effect of strengthening his involvement in the struggle for patronage and principle, which was to disturb state and national politics for over a decade. Little did he realize that 1843 was only the first scene of a political drama that was to reach its finale with the formation of the Republican party in the mid-1850s.

Soon after Bryant's defeat, an upstate newspaper commented that his "political opinions are considered quite too visionary and impracticable, by the sound and common sense Democracy of the country, to receive their countenance and support." Unsafe city Democrats versus sound country Democrats? Nonsense, replied Bryant; the "radical democrats" in fact were the safe men, because they maintained the "tranquil and regular order of things . . . It is your conservative who is rash and visionary; it is he who proposes and upholds the grand schemes which explode in general ruin." Radicals who were conservatives, conservatives who were destroyers—a paradox perhaps, but a valid insight into the nature of American society and politics. Certainly, Bryant in 1843 thought he had sound reasons for the judgment, for, as he saw it, the Conservatives were guilty not only of causing the bank "distemper" but of that most fundamental of sins, the misuse of government power.[4]

Between 1838 and 1842, a coalition of Whigs and Conservatives in the legislature had more than doubled the state debt in order to expand the New York canal system. Expansion was necessary, they argued, both to consolidate New York's hold on the western trade via the Erie Canal and to tap some of the more inaccessible regions of the state through branch canals. Optimistic, anxious to commit the state to their plans, the coalition planned to borrow for construction as long as the surplus tolls from the existing canals enabled them to pay the interest on the debt; the principal would, so they hoped, be paid off by the expected sharp increase in future tolls.

This plan was considered sound by men such as Verplanck, who had confidence in the dynamic nature of the American economy and in the "aggregate good sense of the community" in solving society's problems. In 1839, as a member of the Senate Finance Committee, Verplanck argued that public credit was "the inexhaustible treasury of every well-governed community . . . its surest agent in every effort it may be called to make to protect the liberties, or increase the happiness of the people." Credit was power that the government could use wisely and had used wisely in the canal program, for the new canals would encourage economic growth in the state, which in turn, by increasing tolls, would enable the government to pay its debts without increasing taxes.[5]

It was somewhat ironic that Verplanck, who was considered tightfisted in private life, should be an advocate of government spending; but it was an understandable irony, for he had faith in the benevolent uses of power. In contrast, Bryant's suspicions of power had deepened with time; public credit, as he saw it, was the "inexhaustible treasury" of public ills. He was disturbed by the inflationary tendencies inherent in the canal program, for they reminded him of "the speculations of 1836," which had caused the economic troubles of the times. Having suffered from his efforts to save the *Post,* he could see only the dangers of debt: "There is no healthiness of condition, either in public or private affairs, while there is a necessity to obtain money from others." The Whigs, in their faith in the boundless resources of the nation, had condemned such anxieties as "the melancholy dreams of sickly visionaries," said the *Post.* But were the visions of ruin so sickly when, in fact, the state bonds in 1842 were selling for as much as 30 percent below face value?[6]

The only gain, said the *Post,* was "a multitude of extravagant and worthless works," a point which it hammered at during the early 1840s. In fact, the Whigs and their Conservative allies by their heavy spending had committed the state to a form of transportation that in the next two decades was outmoded by the rapid advance of the railroad. Even as the Erie Canal achieved its operational peak, New Yorkers such as Bryant began to doubt that the canal system, which had proven such a boon to the city in previous decades, could give the metropolis sufficient access to its expanding hinterlands. The attack on the canal system seems to have come from two totally disparate interests: Merchants who complained that the canals were too small and too inflexible (they froze up for five months each year) to meet their need for cheap transportation and eastern farmers hurt by the rising tide of western farm products over the canals. In particular, city merchants, anxious to maintain their dominance of the western trade in the face of continued rivalry from Boston and Philadelphia, now began to see the canals as a potential obstacle to their ambitions. As both the *Post* and *Hunt's Merchant's Magazine* complained, the canal system interfered with New York's efforts to reach the West by railroad. Not only did the system drain off capital needed for railroad construction, it also restricted the operations of railroads already in existence, for by law the rail lines paralleling the Erie Canal (the best natural route to the West) had to pay canal tolls on the freight they carried during the season of navigation. The plain intent of the law was to protect the revenues of the canal; the greater the debt for canal improvements, presumably the deeper would be the state's interest in discouraging competition from the railroads.[7]

Bryant took his usual pleasure in pointing out how government meddling had again interfered with sound economic progress. Merchants and farmers, the great interests of the country, were being hurt to the benefit of "speculators" and politicians who waxed fat on the public debt. Bryant favored reorganization of the entire state government on a permanent basis. "The financial question," said the *Post* in 1845, "was the mere occasion, or what be called the eternal sign, around which the deep convictions of reformers gathered." In fact, the mid-1840s did see the culmination of that drive for reform that had first stirred in the 1820s and had been given force by the equal rights battles of the 1830s. As they unfolded their plans, it became evident that Bryant, Theodore Sedgwick, III, and like-minded Barnburners were early "mugwumps" in rebellion against the influence of the political technicians, whom they saw as usurping the powers and rights of individuals.

By 1846 the liberals had resolved to reform the state government in conformity with their ideals. They demanded both rigid constitutional restraints on the legislature's propensity to spend and the extension of the principle of general incorporation to manufacturing and transportation as well as banking, so that potential incorporators would be freed from legislative interference. They also proposed that both the governor and the legislature be stripped of their patronage powers, in part by giving lesser administrative officials greater security of tenure against "mere party proscription" (the seed from which civil service was to grow), in part by making important executive and judicial offices elective. They hoped that such changes would weaken the influence of the politicians, most of whose power seemed to rest on the use and the abuse of patronage. Nor did the reformers spare the judiciary, for they attempted to lessen the discretionary powers of judges not only by subjecting most of them to popular elections but also by simplifying and codifying the legal system so as to make the law as understandable and as automatic as possible.[8]

In 1846 the liberals apparently won their battle for a root-and-branch reform of the state government. The previous year, the Barnburners, heartened by the election of their hero Silas Wright as governor in 1844, pushed through the legislature a proposal for a constitutional convention; significantly, and ominously, the proposal was almost unanimously opposed by the Hunker Democrats and almost unanimously supported by the Whigs. In June 1846 the convention, dominated by liberal-minded Democrats, began 131 days of toil to create a new government suited to the people and to the times. When it finished, it had fashioned a new constitution embodying the liberal ideal of the negative state.

By an overwhelming majority, the delegates established a permanent debt limit of $1,000,000; any future peacetime loan that pushed total indebtedness above that limit was to be submitted to the people for their approval or rejection and, even when approved, was to be accompanied by a direct annual tax sufficient to pay off the loan in eighteen years. The same article also prohibited the use of the credit of the state to aid any individual, association, or corporation; earlier Verplanck had favored and Bryant had opposed aid for the Erie Railroad. While the constitution restricted government as a source of favors for the few, it also granted individuals greater freedom from state control by abolishing state inspection of merchandise and by repealing the special charter system for all but municipal corporations. At the same time, the convention struck a blow against an old Locofoco enemy by denying to owners of stock in note-issuing banks the same privilege of limited liability enjoyed by stockholders in other kinds of corporations.[9]

The delegates also tried to strike down another old enemy, the technicians. The constitution decreased the number of patronage positions by providing for the popular election of important administrative and judicial officials, including the controller, treasurer, and the justices of the supreme court. At the same time, the convention also paved the way for legal reform—Harry Sedgwick's old dream, which had been carried on both by his nephew, Theodore, III, and, more fervently, by another Berkshirite, David Dudley Field, who had been first a clerk and then a partner in the Sedgwick law office. By 1850 Field had achieved the first successes in revising the archaic laws and simplifying the tangled legal procedures of the state. As a result of Field's efforts, said Bryant, "not only has the cause of legal proceding been made more intelligible to those who are interested in them. . . . but the opportunities for pettifogging and chicane, before tribunals which are prompt in perceiving and inflexible in doing their duty, have become impossible." Here was a "great civil revolution," which promised to make law less pliable in the hands of the legal technicians, the lawyers and judges.[10]

In a broad sense, Bryant, Sedgwick, Field, and other liberals hoped that by substituting general for specific law they could reduce the human factor in government and also reduce the influence of government itself. In 1846 Field estimated that of the 8,343 laws passed by the state legislature since 1823 only 433 were general laws applicable to everyone. Was it not possible, then, that reform by doing away with most legislation would make the government a simple and efficient machine? General law would weaken the influence of insiders in government, whether they be favored charterholders or technicians. By restricting the state to the largely negative duty of enforcing general laws, liberals hoped to return most of the powers over life to local communities, private associations, and especially to individual people. Having no privileges to give, government would escape the corrupting influence of favor-seekers, and so become truly the agent of the people. Only then would government become the guardian, not the enemy, of free society.[11]

An honest, efficient political mechanism—that is what the Liberals tried to create in the constitution of 1846. Essentially, they hoped that New Yorkers, now freed from most government interference, would turn from politics to their own affairs; that by weakening government, they would deny men the privileges that had permitted some to threaten the interests of the many. A noble dream but, as events soon proved, an impossible one. By the 1840s the great drive for wealth was falling full force on New York, city and state alike. In 1842 Moses Yale Beach had begun to publish his *Wealth and Wealthy Citizens of New York,* an annual register restricted to persons worth $100,000 or more. By 1846 there were fourteen millionaires in the city. And there were thousands more who dreamed of entering the circle of gold, with the help of government favors, if possible. Such men found others willing to sell them the favors desired, for the constitution, far from weakening the reign of politicians, appears to have given greater opportunities to the less responsible members of that species. Even the *Post* sensed the danger in 1846, when it warned that the provision for the direct election of supreme court judges by district (rather than by general ticket as it suggested) would give politicians control of the elections and so produce "incompetent and unworthy judges." In a more general way, the efforts to bring government closer to the people by making more offices elective and by increasing the responsibilities of local government had the effect of increasing the influence of the political manipulators. Faith in local government suffered a severe setback when in 1852 the New York Common Council was discovered to have corruptly handed out valuable railroad franchises in the city. The resulting outcry against the "forty thieves" led the state legislature to vest the power to grant franchises in itself; less than a decade later, the legislature also abused the franchise power. The struggle for patronage and for favors and the corruption of government, had only begun. By the 1850s Fernando Wood had appeared on the political stage in New York, and in the wings, smiling, waited Boss Tweed.[12]

In December 1845 the *Post* observed that "in our new country, faster than in any other, society outgrows her garments, and new garments become necessary." It was true that such garments as the special charter system had grown tight on the growing economy, but the liberals threw out the good clothes with the bad, for, while they did not succeed in eliminating corruption from government, they did succeed in weakening government as a constructive power for the public good. In trying to expand the freedom of the individual, they left him naked before the new forms of power required to organize Americans in an increasingly massive democratic and capitalistic society. As far as responsible government was concerned, the Barnburners, indeed, had burned the barn, but the rats—corporations and political machines—survived.

Liberals found 1846 a banner year. Not only had they apparently established the negative state in New York, they had also seen the national government nearly destroy the protective tariff and, through the establishment of the Independent Treasury System, seemingly end government association with, and support of, state banks. The Independent treasury had initially been established in the last year of the Van Buren administration, but then it had been repealed by the Whigs.[13] With free trade, the "separation of Bank and State," and the reduction of government in New York, the year saw the establishment of free trade liberalism as the touchstone of American policy. But if the ideals and the rhetoric were enshrined in the American mind, practice and devotion were not; for in 1846, the very year of the liberal victory, the great champion of the Barnburners, Governor Wright, was defeated for re-election by a Whig. In the next years, reformers of all kinds increasingly turned their attentions to the slavery issue; when they were again able to concentrate on politics, they discovered that their ideals had been debased and their hopes disappointed. If they had listened to an old friend, they might have been forewarned, for from the deepening well of his isolation James Fenimore Cooper was able to discern, in his own apparently eccentric way, the course of the stars.

12

COOPER: DISSENT AND DEATH

By the mid-1840s the members of Bryant's generation, no longer young, had begun to settle into the places that life had found for them. Bryant was becoming more content with his lot. After nearly a decade of struggle, the editor not only had saved the *Evening Post* but also had made it one of the influential—and profitable—journals of the Liberal cause in America. Financially, he was beginning to acquire the means to escape from city life to Europe, to the Berkshires, or to his newly purchased estate at Roslyn on Long Island. William Gilmore Simms came close to the truth when he commented of his friend's "new charac-ter of farmer" that Bryant "deserves to be 'on his own ground,' and in the sacred homestead which he can call his own, must experience (for an American democrat) the very proudest of feelings." Bryant had greater security even in the urban world. Not only had be established himself as a respected spokesman for apparently triumphant Liberalism, he had also become one of the idiols of literary America, revered, if not always read, by the public. Socially, this shy man who confessed that his sympathy for fellow humans was decidedly "imperfect" had acquired a host of friends and followers.[1]

He was even able to pick up some of the strands of his friendship with Verplanck. After his withdrawal from politics in 1841, the New Yorker had turned gladly to a manifold life as a Shakespearean scholar, vice-president of the New York Historical Society, trustee of the Society Library, vestryman of Trinity Church, president of the Board of Immigration and director of the New York Life Insurance Company. Despite his political disappointments, life served him nearly as well as he served life. This inveterate clubman, as "round, plump, short, and jolly" as St. Nicholas himself, was the beloved founder and creative spark of the Century Club, established in 1847 to preserve the humor, the tolerance, and the dilettantism of old Knickerbocker New York. Although Bryant was a cofounder, he and other members of the club made it plain that Verplanck was the reigning spirit:

> Hexamiters I abandon, but very humbly pray
> That from our goodly nights, you will no longer stay....
> The pith of all is, you're away
> And we are all dull—we therefore pray
> You'll join us without delay.[2]

Both the doggerel and the club were reminiscent of the 1820s. With the tumultuous 1830s behind them, the two old friends now could join in an effort to revive the conviviality of the Bread and Cheese Club. But the new group lacked one essential feature of the old, the presence of James Fenimore Cooper. By the 1840s Cooper was settling into a physically and intellectually narrower circle than that of his New York friends. Although he was a frequent visitor to the city, he had identified himself with his native Otsego, which, having been by passed by the main transportation routes of the state, had become partially isolated from bustling America. Culturally, Cooper was losing contact with the literary scene. He had never shown much interest in other writers, and this indifference grew as a new literary generation appeared.

And America seemingly returned this indifference. Although his works sold well during the 1840s, intense competition in the publishing industry, which was troubled by masses of cheap reprints of European authors, drove down Cooper's profits from his books. His *The Wing-and-Wing*, for instance, sold twice as many copies as *The Last of the Mohicans* (1826) but returned only one-third as many dollars. Forced to grind out on the average two novels a year, dependent on European sales for much of his diminished income, Cooper felt as if he were losing ground in America, particularly since such social novels as *The Crater* won little public attention. In 1846 he wrote: "My time...is nearly done. At 57 the world is not apt to believe a man can write fiction, and

133

I have seen that this country is already tired of me." In his more optimistic moments he comforted himself with the thought that his works still found favor with "the better classes," but this gave little pleasure to a man who once had been the great American novelist.[3]

Cooper's growing sense of isolation from American society was a form of retribution, for from the beginning of his career he had openly avowed himself to be a member of a small elite from which he verbally exiled, as vulgar, most of the men and women who were pushing and rising to the top of the new society. Cooper was no snob; probably he had greater respect for the average person than did most of his contemporaries, but he made no secret of his contempt for the *nouveau riche* and the *nouveau grande*. In a limited sense, the new classes, having been excluded from his society, proceeded to exclude him from theirs. Unlike Bryant and Verplanck, both of whom made their way into a wide circle of business and literary men, Cooper fell back on a class that itself was becoming an isolated minority in American society, the class of his father and his wife, the landed gentry.

The greater the disturbing tendencies of American life, the greater was his identification with the stable values and outlook of the gentry. The element of conservatism that permeated the liberalism of his friends had by the 1840s become central to Cooper's philosophy. Traditions and conventions—these he increasingly considered as necessary to restrain human wickedness. Man, he asserted in *The Chainbearer,* was not the rational creature the liberals, in their more optimistic moments, thought him to be. "We are the creatures of conventions and the slave of opinion that come we know not whence," says his hero, Mordaunt Littlepage (*né* Temple and Effingham). "I had got the notions of my caste, obtained in the silent insinuating manner in which all our characters are formed." Better, then, that men be governed by the conventions of the landed gentleman than be slaves to that unstable master, public opinion. The conventions sustained "manners, taste, general intelligence, and civilization at large." In contrast, Cooper wondered whether public opinion left the American with any character at all, for the typical new man appeared to be "a jumble of the same senseless contradictions in his social habits, as he is fast getting to be in his political creeds and political practices; being, that is, *in transitu,* pressed by circumstances on the one side, and by the habit and imitation on the other; unwilling, almost unable to think and act for himself." Twenty years before Cooper had advanced the liberal notion that republican society was giving birth to men superior in character to Europeans.[4]

Cooper wrote with the feeling that both his caste and his principles were falling before forces beyond his control. Just as the popular pre-occupation with the new seemed to be swamping necessary traditions in a sea of senseless novelties, so did it seem that the American stress on the sovereignty of the people threatened the property rights essential to the existence of the landed gentry. In 1837 Cooper himself had experienced the "awful power" of the people in the Three Mile Point Affair: "The public—the all-powerful, omnipotent, over-ruling, law-making, law-breaking public." Five years later, he was shaken by the "anti-rent war," which rocked the society and politics of central New York state.

For generations, the great landowners of the Hudson Valley had lived like feudal lords on rents collected from their long-term tenants. The controversy started over efforts of some landlords to collect back rents that their predecessors had allowed to accumulate, but the funda-mental issue was the desire of the tenants for greater security of possession —that is, for ownership. That desire took the form of opposition— armed opposition in some cases—to attempted rent collections, thus raising a storm that, though it did not win widespread sympathy for the anti-renters, brought widespread disapproval of the landlords.

Alarmed by this popular disregard for property rights, by this "increas-ing demoralization of the people," Cooper came to the defense of the gentry in his trio of antirent novels: *The Redskins, The Chainbearer,* and *Satanstoe.* Criticizing the popular hostility to the landlords, he wrote in *The Chainbearer:* "It is this gradual undermining of just opinions that forms the imminent danger of our social system; a spurious philanthropy on the subject of punishments, false notions on that of personal rights, and the substitution of numbers for principles, bidding fair to produce much the most important revolution that has ever taken place on the American continent." The gentry, he argued in a public letter in 1844, were the natural and safest leaders of all communities. If they were destroyed, their place would be taken by "the attorney-usurers, who abound in, and disgrace the state."[5]

The gentry was needed to preserve tastes, manners, and correct prin-ciples, but who would preserve the gentry? The Whigs again won Cooper's enmity by denouncing the landlords in the name of popular rights. Out of power in the state, they were prepared to convert the controversy into political capital. The Democrats, in power, were obliged to oppose the lawlessness of the anti-renters. The Barnburner hero, Governor Wright, with the support of such liberals as Bryant, vowed to restore law and order with armed force if necessary. Again, Cooper had reason to consider the Democrats as the true defenders of the Republic. However, the Democrats did not actually defend the landlords. Wright may have denounced lawlessness, but he was also critical of the leasehold tenures against which the anti-renters were fighting. More shattering was the work done by the Democrats in prohibiting, through the new constitution, all feudal tenures and all leases on agricultural lands that ran longer than twelve years—the very kind of tampering with property rights that Cooper condemned in his anti-rent novels.[6] The manor system was doomed.

And so in a more fundamental way were most of Cooper's few remaining hopes, for the reforms of the liberal Democrats weakened the conventions and leadership with which Cooper was identified. Codification of the laws and popular election of judges, for instance, strengthened the popular will at the expense of the judiciary, to which Cooper looked for the protection of both individual character and property rights. In his novel *The Ways of the Hour* (1850) he warned that the changes, by weakening the authority of the judges, had converted juries (public opinion) from salutary checks on authority into irresponsible powers that threatened the rights and integrity of the individual. In a broader way, both Democrats and Whigs had upset the unseen system of checks and balances that had maintained harmonious relations betweem the gentlemen and the people. Reform had opened the way for domination of society by the prejudices of the masses.[7]

But society was not to be dominated by the masses themselves. Bryant hoped that great popular participation in government would lessen the concentration of power in the hands of the few. Cooper thought otherwise. In *The Crater* (1847) he advanced "the great and all-important political truth," which he wanted "written in letters of gold at every corner of the streets and highways in a republic":

> THAT THE MORE A PEOPLE ATTEMPT TO EXTEND THEIR POWER DIRECTLY OVER STATE AFFAIRS, THE LESS THEY, IN FACT, CONTROL THEM ... MERELY BESTOWING ON A FEW ARTFUL MANAGERS THE INFLUENCE THEY VAINLY IMAGINE TO HAVE SECURED TO THEMSELVES.

Mass democracy, then, served only to shift power from a responsible political elite to the new breed of technicians, the politicians and journalists, who made much of the popular will but who had little of the elite's devotion to principle and to the real interests of the people.[8]

In this new society, who would protect the individual against economic exploitation? Cooper had long scoffed at the free-trade ideas of the liberals as doctrinaire and naive. Bryant defended free trade as the basis for a social order in which every individual was free to pursue his own ambitions; the novelist feared it as encouraging the pursuit of the dollar, "perhaps the most corrupt and corrupting influence of life," at the expense of the old values and the integrity of the individual. Reform was opening the way for exploitive capitalism. In his *Autobiography of a Pocket Handkerchief* (1843) Cooper mocked the dream economy of the liberals. Eudasia Halfacre, a prattler of free-trade clichés, sees an expensive handkerchief in her possession as the end product of a benevolent process that "has given employment to some poor French girl for four or five months. . . . She has earned no doubt some fifty of the one hundred dollars I have paid." In fact, "the poor French girl" was poor indeed, for she received less than $ 10 for months of labor, the rest going to middlemen who took advantage of her helplessness. In their impossible quest for a completely free economy the liberals had weakened the "true elite" of gentlemen, who "ever shrink from affixing a value to the time and services of others," in favor of men whose rule of life was to buy cheap and sell dear, regardless of the human cost. In both politics and economics, as Cooper saw the situation, the effect of liberal reform was to leave the individual defenseless before the soulless power of corporations, newspapers, and political parties.[9]

Cooper had discerned, in their early stages, some of the major maladies of nineteenth-century America; unfortunately for his reputation, however, his report seemed more the work of a coroner than that of a doctor. Personally, he retained much of his old zest for life, but though the habit of life was strong, he had lost faith in the immediate future. Although American successes in the Mexican War excited his national pride and temporarily stimulated his hopes, he could not avoid the feeling that the people were rapidly dissipating the promise of the Republic. Even at home, he encountered signs of defeat. In 1848 he noted with disgust how the local public had spoiled Three Mile Point: "This place is a monument to the 'people's' honesty and appreciation of liberty. I know them and would as soon trust in convicts." Having lost faith in both the people and their leaders, he placed his trust in Christianity, that power which alone could "give the world that liberty and happiness which a grasping spirit of cupidity is so ready to impute to the desire to accumulate gold." Yet even his deepening piety gave him faith not in this world but only in the next.[10]

Cooper's pessimism appears strongly in the concluding chapters of *The Crater,* a novel with which he was particularly pleased. Most of the book is red-blooded adventure, but then comes a chapter headed "Vox Populi, Vox Dei," and misadventure begins. The story is that of Robinson Crusoe in reverse. Mark Woolston, the hero, brings civilization to an isolated island, capping his work with a stable government run by nine elected officials who hold office for life. Under the enlightened rule of this elite, society prospers, free from "the corrupting influence of politics." Alas, prosperity brings degeneration, for the people, forgetting both God and gentlemen, begin to believe that they are responsible for their happy state Then, to play on this pride and egoism, come the demagogues: "Factitious ministers" whose narrow zeal splits society into contending sects; lawyers who turn the law into an instrument of "speculation and revenge;" and, worst of all, journalists who whip up popular opposition to the rule of the elite Corruption has come to Eden—and destruction, too. Faced with mounting hostility, Woolston temporarily flees from the island; when he tries to return, he discovers that it has been obliterated by the eruption of a volcano.

This novel was not a literal summation of the Cooper version of American history, past, present, and future. As Thomas Philbrick has suggested, the novelist attempted in these scenes to combine his pet grievances with the conventional romantic theme of growth, decay, and destruction popularized by the painter Thomas Cole. But there is no doubt that Cooper would have liked a similar divine judgment to obliterate the growing armies of technicians who were corrupting American society. Certainly, by this time, he anticipated no such judgment from the American people. Popular feeling having triumphed, he lamented in *The Ways of the Hour,* "we see the oldest families among us quietly robbed of their estates . . . ; the honest man proscribed, the knave and the demagogue deified; mediocrity advanced to high place; and talent and capacity held in abeyance, if not trampled under foot." In this novel the heroine, Mary Monson, is found guilty of murder, chiefly because she is independent and aloof and, therefore, unpopular. She is saved at the very end, not by a repentent public nor even by a judge, but by fate, when one of her alleged victims appears in the courtroom just after she is sentenced to die.[11]

Cooper expected no last-minute reprieves either for himself or for the landed gentry. To the very end, he retained a measure of optimism, but his hopes lay in lands far distant from contemporary America: for himself, in that other world beyond death; for society, in the far distant future In 1842 he had expressed the hope that once American society had matured, had lost much of its unsettled and fragmented state, then intelligence, breeding, taste, and integrity would again rise to the top. He even had a good word for New York City:

> No one knows better than myself, how much there is that is excellent in principles, capacity, acquirement, and deportment, existing in New York; and no one knows better how much it is all an encampment, or a caravansary, quite as much as it resembles regulated community. The evils are, in a degree, inseparable from the extraordinary growth of the place. ... If New York were left to the real New Yorkers, in my poor judgement, it would be a town that, while it might want some of its present formidable "energies," every man who has a real desire to see his country respectable and happy, might be proud of.

New York, then, might become that capital of gentlemen, that concentration of the public virtues, which he saw as the hallmark of civilized societies. But this possibility lay in the distant future beyond his own lifetime. Unlike Bryant, Cooper at least dimly recognized that the growth of the cities as centers of commerce and money was producing profound, perhaps disastrous, changes in American society. Although he did not foresee that the society of his day was spawning such poisonous progeny as Boss Tweed and Jay Gould, he sensed that the rapid mobility of American life, which had broken down his ideal order, would not soon be stemmed. The "Great Descent" had only begun.[12]

Cooper is a classic example of alienation from society as a result, not of emotional maladjustment, but of a too-precise adaptation to one particular milieu. Within his own circle, on his own grounds, the novelist was a contented man, perhaps more contented than his liberal friends. But, by identifying himself so closely with the conventions, manners, and interests of one restricted group, he made it certain that he would suffer a sense of isolation and loss in a rapidly changing society of many

groups and interests. In this period other Americans, particularly southerners, experienced the tensions arising out of their identification with
landed interests in a nation that was becoming increasingly urban and
commercial. Most of them, however, whether planters or yeomen,
had identified with interests that had kept up with the general expansion
of the United States. In contrast, Cooper aligned himself with one of
the most restricted social groups in America, the landed gentry of the
Hudson Valley and eastern New York. It was characteristic that the
novelist should feel that the gentry was threatened not only by the
technicians but also by a socio-cultural group which was then enjoying
its heyday: As a self-conscious "Yorker," he had long been contemp-
tuous and suspicious of Yankees, an attitude that grew stronger as he
grew older, at a time when the Yorker element was virtually being sub-
merged in New York by the rising numbers and importance of transplanted New Englanders.[13]

Politicians, journalists, capitalists, Yankees—Cooper's inclusion of
these major constituents of society in his shooting gallery gave him the
critical freedom that made him, in some ways, the most perceptive critic of
his day. But his choice of so many important targets also helped make
him one of the most ignored critics, for it enabled Americans easily to
dismiss him as a crank with a monomaniac's devotion to an inconse-
quential class. Despite his brawls with the press and his blasts at the
public, most persons did not take his criticisms seriously.

In 1850, soon after finishing *The Ways of the Hour,* Cooper fell ill.
When he visited New York City in November , his friends were shocked
to discover how far his health had declined. Early in 1851 they began
plans for a public dinner to proclaim their esteem for him, but they were
too late. Illness kept Cooper at home until September 1851 when, after
months of discomfort, he died the day before his sixty-third birthday.
And so in February 1852 his friends and admirers who had hoped to
dine with him in honor of past times held a great meeting to honor
his memory. Bryant was prevailed upon to give the principal speech.
Although he had long shared common political affiliations with his
friend, the poet neglected Cooper the social critic in favor of Cooper
the heroic creator of red-blooded heroes. He mentioned Leatherstocking; he did not mention Temple, Effingham, or Littlepage. And thus
began the process that would soon, for the popular imagination, rework
the reputation of Cooper—this would-be defender of the social order—

into that of the author of tales of forest and sea—for boys.

This final indignity was foreshadowed by a special note of irony at the memorial meeting. The one man who perhaps came closest to being the embodiment of all Cooper's enemies was Daniel Webster, politician, Whig, representative of commercial interests, and Yankee. In 1850 Cooper had one of his characters say sadly: "Heaven knows what the country is coming to. There is Webster, to begin cramming a Yankee dialect down our throats for good English." The chairman selected by the meeting was Daniel Webster.[14]

13

DISSENT FROM THE LEFT: PARKE GODWIN

In September 1846 Bryant wrote to his wife from New York: "Since I took my seat I have been run down with beggar women—a young Italian female with a baby a month old—and Mr. Poe's mother-in-law, who says her son-in-law is crazy, his wife dying, and the whole family starving." Five months later Mrs. Poe died. Bryant had little compassion for suffering humanity. The inhabitants of his ideal world consisted of the strong and the moral, of persons able to take care of themselves. "He is always to me a pleasing person," wrote Emerson of Bryant, "but Miss Sedgwick complained of his coldness; she has known him always and never saw him warm." It is true that Bryant lent his name to the movement to abolish capital punishment, but he did this in defense of the principle that human life is sacred, rather than out of any sympathy for the man whose neck was in the noose. Unable emotionally to touch his fellow men, he expressed his benevolence through the defense of those principles that he thought essential for the happy, harmonious society.[1] In 1854, for example, the *Evening Post* praised President Franklin Pierce's veto of a bill to distribute ten million acres of public lands among the states for the purpose of improving the care of the insane. It admitted that the care was often "deplorably inadequate," but it called the bill a dangerous violation of the constitution: "the breach made by putting forth a measure with a good object opens the way for a host of corrupt measures."[2]

Bryant gave little thought to the growing numbers of urban poor spawned by the depression and by increasing immigration from Europe, but there were others who had at least recognized poverty as a challenge to American ideals. It was during the 1840s that Catherine Sedgwick discovered the urban poor by way of a route typical of the times, prison reform. In 1844, her nephew, Theodore Sedgwick, III, helped form the New York Prison Association with the aim of converting prisons into retraining centers to prepare convicts for a normal, moral life. There were women as well as men in the jails. In 1845 Catherine joined the newly organized Ladies Prison Association. Getting out beyond the homilies of her novels, she got to know the women, their children, and their "homes" in the city slums. Her good Unitarian soul rebelled at the human waste:

> With the means of universal education and sustenance, we see creatures with the powers and faculties out of which heroes and martyrs are made, covered with putrefying sores. My whole soul is sickened; and today, when I went into our church filled with people in their fine summer clothes...and thought of the streets and dens, through which I had just walked, I could have cried out, "Why are you here!"[3]

Catherine held closely to the conventional lines of help set down by a strongly moralistic and individualistic society. Each Sunday she conducted Bible classes at the Isaac T. Hopper Home for recently released female prisoners. She had already learned, however, that quoting scripture to the poor was not enough. If individuals could not save themselves from moral and physical degradation, she believed, then it was the obligation of the "more favored class of society" to bring salvation by supplying those individuals with the necessary education and employment. Catherine appealed to the rich, both to supply jobs for former prisoners (she employed several in her home) and to give money for a boarding school on Randall's Island, where pauper children could be exposed not only to proper education but to Nature, that influence that "exalts the angelic portion of our nature, and depresses the sensual and brutal."

But what if most of the favored class felt little responsibility for the less fortunate brethren? In her most popular novels in the 1830s Catherine unintentionally had encouraged the ready tendency among Americans to associate wealth with virtue and poverty with vice. In 1854 she noted bitterly that pharisaism rather than Christian charity marked society's attitude toward unwed mothers: While society permitted wealthy men and women, no matter how corrupt, to "ride in the world's chariots," a poor girl "ignorant of her own nature, with opportunity thrust upon her, and love blinding her, is the victim through life of a single offense. It is perpetual punishment." Some rich men did respond with something more valuable than pious words, but much of their money went to aid the most obviously unfortunate, the deaf, the blind, and the insane. There was little time and money left for the growing numbers of urban poor. In 1848 Catherine wrote in discouragement: "Some good is achieved—I see that—but the work is struggling and inefficient. If the sea were to roll over the adults and leave the children, we can devise a future, perhaps attain it for them." The sea did not roll in to obliterate the influence of adult poverty and crime on the young, nor did the rich respond with batteries of wealth in the war on degradation.[4]

After 1848 Catherine began to lose faith in her ability to cope with the city. She shrank from the moral and intellectual mediocrity of the new rich as well as from the proliferating slums. In the 1850s she spent much of her time at Lennox with her sole remaining brother, Charles; but in 1856 he died, leaving her alone in her sixties to face an increasingly impersonal world This reminder that she was of a passing generation weakened her faith in the effectiveness of her writings. In March 1857, while preparing *Married or Single?* (aggressively justifying her own choice of singleness), she asked whether it was not folly at her time of life to write a novel "only to supply mediocre readers with small moral hints" on daily life. And in April she wrote plaintively of her sense of loneliness, "when I think of all those whose hearts beat for me ... at the publication of my early books, all gone." After she completed a short *Memoir of Joseph Curtis* in 1858, she never wrote again; most of her last decade of life she spent at her ancestral home in Stockbridge, isolated from the restless and impersonal urban life she once had hoped to conquer.[5]

In *Married or Single?* Catherine had expressed concern over the growing gulf between the rich man and the average American, a problem posed not only by the concentration of wealth but by the growing indifference of the new rich to the needs of their less fortunate brethren. If voluntary benevolence did not fill the gap between rich and poor, what then? Like most Americans, Catherine had no answer. But there were a few men who in the 1840s believed they could reorganize society so as to make true benevolence possible. In 1844 a young man quoted with approval the prophecy of Catherine's longtime friend and Unitarian mentor, William Ellery Channing:

> Our present low civilization, the central idea of which is wealth, cannot last forever; that the mass of men are not doomed hopelessly and irresistibly to the degradation of mind and heart in which they are now sunk; that a new comprehension of the true dignity of a social being is to remodel social institutions and manners.[6]

With such a hope in mind, the young man had already launched his quest for utopia; he was Bryant's son-in-law, Parke Godwin.

Godwin was one of those "sensitive and dreamy" young men, intellectually and emotionally at odds with their society, who emerged from the middle class in both America and Europe during the years of the Industrial Revolution. Born in 1816 the son of a merchant and manufacturer at Paterson, New Jersey, he spent a youth "full of dreamy thought, full of feeling, and full of romance"—and also full of uncertainty, for early he began that youthful quest for something worthy to do. After his graduation from Princeton in 1834, Godwin, like Bryant, tried law as a career. Like Bryant, he soon discovered that this traditional path to fame and fortune was not for him. He returned to Princeton to study for the ministry; he abandoned that aim after six months, perhaps because formal religion did not satisfy his strongly religious disposition. The year 1836 found him in New York, "a briefless barrister in a great city," but what appeared to be a dead end soon became the prelude to a new and vital life.

By chance, he took a room in the same boarding house where Bryant was staying after his return from Europe. Godwin, like many other persons, was kept at arm's length by Bryant's reticence; he was surprised when the editor, after "several months of casual intercourse," suddenly offered Godwin, who had no experience in journalism, a place on the *Evening Post*. He accepted, and thus began a lifelong but stormy partnership, which was sealed in 1842 by Godwin's marriage to Bryant's daughter, Fanny. Surely, Bryant hoped Godwin would fill Leggett's place. He got his wish—in more ways than one. Godwin had Leggett's editorial ability and was a scholar to boot, but he also had the uncompromising spirit that had made Leggett so troublesome to his friends.[7]

During his first years with the *Post* Godwin shared Bryant's devotion to individual freedom and hostility to centralized power, but it soon became evident that he decidedly did not share Bryant's rather skeptical views of human nature. Widely read in the literature of France and Germany as well as that of the Anglo-American world, he responded strongly to the perfectionism inherent in the Unitarian and Romantic movements of his times. If man's nature could he perfected, then why was man neither good nor happy? In the early 1840s, as the depression dragged on, Godwin grew impatient. Poverty, degradation, and materialism all posed a challenge to any man in search of something worthy to do and Godwin thought that the institutions of society had not met the challenge. The Democratic party, on which Bryant had placed his hopes for reform, "has talked," said Godwin, "until it has not only exhausted its breath, but its life," while the Church, the agency of Christian brotherhood, had not even protested at the "huge social evils stinking in its very nostrils."[8]

In February 1843, having lost confidence in both the programs and the ideology of his elders, Godwin raised the flag of rebellion by publishing a new weekly, *The Pathfinder,* in which he soon challenged Bryant to point out in what way the Democratic party hoped "to improve the condition of the masses." *The Pathfinder* failed after three months of struggle, but not before Godwin had definitely identified himself with the utopian movements that had appeared in the North under the pressure of the depression and the growing disillusionment with politics. Early in the year, he discovered the writings of Charles Fourier, the French utopian, who he soon decided was one of the great geniuses of the age. Fourier, he thought, had both diagnosed the ills of society and prescribed their cure. Armed with his new-found faith, Godwin poured out a stream of books and articles that formed one of the first chapters in the nineteenth-century radical indictment of contemporary capitalism.[9]

He focused his attack on the complacent liberal faith in competition as a beneficient regulator of human affairs. Bryant and the Sedgwicks had argued that in a state of perfect legal equality competition would force each man to respect the welfare of his fellow men. For them, perfect legal equality meant perfect individualism, since no man would have the power to dominate another. But Godwin and other utopians saw competition in existing society as turning man against man in a war that encouraged selfishness, brutality, and the drive for dominance. While liberals thought in terms of the village community, Godwin constructed his social analysis in terms of the Industrial Revolution. More than Bryant, he recognized that the machine was revolutionizing social relationships. Under existing conditions, he warned in 1844, machinery threatened to become a substitute for human labor, which would give a few capitalists power and wealth at the expense of the many:

> Thus we have stated that blind competition tends to the formation of gigantic monopolies in every branch of labor; that it deprecates the wages of the working classes; that it excites an endless war between human arms, and machinery and capital—a war in which the weak succumb; that it renders the recurrence of failures, bankruptcies, and commercial crises a sort of endemic disease, and that it reduces the middling and lower classes to a precarious and miserable existence..., that while the few rich are becoming more and more rich, the unnumbered many are becoming poorer. Is anything further necessary to prove that our modern world of industry is a veritable HELL...? [10]

This description evidenced, perhaps, a greater knowledge of European criticisms of European capitalism than of American reality. Certainly, except for the reference to commercial crises, the picture pertained more to the England of the Industrial Revolution than to the still primarily agricultural United States, but Godwin believed he saw signs that America was moving down that same road to human ruin. In New York State, he declared, one of every seventeen persons depended on charity in the early 1840s, while in New York City some 40,000 people, one in eight, were destitute—and this in the city of John Jacob Astor and Moses Yale Beach.

In short, while the liberals dreamed of establishing the ideal republican society in the belief that they were working with social forms distinct from those of Europe, they were in fact pushing the nation in the same direction as Europe by their encouragement of competition in an increasingly industrialized society. Far from establishing the ideal community of prosperous and neighborly men, they were, thought Godwin, encouraging class war by stimulating the concentration of wealth and power. Blinded by their rural bias, they unthinkingly were surrendering control of the economy to a few commercial cities. The widening gap between capitalist and producer was rapidly becoming the problem of the century. It had to be solved if mankind "wishes to prevent the commotions with which nearly all civilized society is menaced—a question which in Europe, and perhaps ere long in this country, will leave the studies of philosophers...to take up arms in the streets." This was four years before the Revolution of 1848 and the Communist Manifesto.[11]

What could be done? The general answer was radically to reorganize society so as to suit it to the true nature of man. Evil and misery were not natural to life. God, the benevolent "great Engineer of the Universe," had created all that was needed for the good society. God had given man both the reason and the passions needed to live morally and happily in an ideal order of freedom. But man's natural goodness had been corrupted by existing society to the point where the passions, designed by the "Great Engineer" as part of his benevolent order, had been perverted into their opposites. Man had a natural passion for unity, for brotherhood, but competition had changed this "pivotal passion" into suspicion and hostility. Such social evils could "not be met by the ordinary methods of benevolence, because they are organic." To redeem man's natural goodness, man must alter the conditions of society.

Neither Godwin nor his Fourierist friends ever seriously considered revolution. Far from trying to gain control of government as an instrument to reshape society, they hoped to educate the masses to gradually rework their lives independently of government. In this hope Fourierists differed little from the liberals. Both rejected government because both mistrusted the politicians who managed it. The true agency of reform, they agreed, was a voluntary association of individuals who committed themselves to achieve a mutual aim. For the Fourierists, however, the association was to enable men not to achieve group aims within the existing social order but to secede from that order with its destructive industrial organization.[12]

In 1844 Godwin proposed that Americans organize themselves into "townships," or "philansteries," of some 400 families each, on the following Fourierist lines: First, the members of each proposed community were to pool as much of their capital as every man saw fit to contribute. Once the community was established, each individual was to be permitted to work as he pleased without direction. There would be no encouragement to laziness here, since the community would retain the profit motive; each person was to share in its profits, not on the basis of need but of productive contribution—namely, on the basis of capital invested, the difficulties and length of work performed, and "intelligence, activity, or vigor." Every person would then share in the common wealth in proportion to the capital, labor, and talent (the "three great productive faculties") he contributed.

This new organization of labor and capital would have four results: First, by making each township largely self-sufficient, it would decentralize the economy, thereby weakening the economic power of the cities. Second, it would teach men to work in harmony for the common good, because all would share in the general prosperity. Third, cooperation would enable the community to increase productivity by eliminating the waste caused by competition. Last, but the most appealing, cooperative society would permit the radical division of labor, which would produce contentment as well as efficiency, since each task could be related directly to a basic human talent. Tasks would become so simple and so diverse that each worker would be able to take part in some "thirty different kinds of labor, so as to employ alternatively all the physical and intellectual forces that he possesses." Association under Fourierist rules, then, would both increase human efficiency for the general good and create true individual freedom in which every person could develop his own personality. It would also engender the conditions for brotherhood, wherein each man would recognize that all other men were "parts of one great whole, living links in the great organism of Humanity. Thy neighbor is most truly our brother—nay, more than brother—he is our other self; his crimes, our diseases; his sufferings, our cause." Here in association was the way back to Eden, the way to incorporate the machine into the Republic, here in the village community.[13]

In one sense, Godwin was trying to establish (to use Leo Marx's terms) "the machine in the garden"—i.e., to reconcile the need for the machine with the desire to maintain the agrarian and "natural" Republic seemingly threatened by industrialism. Only in association, said Godwin in 1848, "can mechanical improvements be made available to the whole community; at present they come into competition with the laboring people, and throw them out of work."[14]

Godwin plunged into the associationist movement as if his emotional salvation depended on it. It is notable, however, that he did not commit himself physically or even psychologically to any of the numerous petty utopias that sprang up in the 1840s. When pressed to join the Brook Farm experiment, he admitted that his chief interest "has been the work of classification and method, and it now has so many attractions for me that I cannot relinquish it for other pursuits." In truth, Godwin was a theorist, not an activist. Even before he adopted Fourierism, he had been drawn into the nineteenth-century search for a" science of society," which would enable man to control his social environment just as science had already enabled him to control the physical realm for his use.

In 1844 he set out on what for him was the great intellectual adventure, the quest for the key to Fourier's "science": "the Law of the Series—the generating formula of the Divine Wisdom, in its distribution of universal order." For a time, in his enthusiasm, he believed that he was on the verge of discovering this law that governed the distribution of everything in the universe, including man's passions. What he hoped to find above all was a social science based "on mathematical certainty, such as exists in optics and astronomy." But the magic key eluded him. By the end of 1844 he had worked himself into a physical and mental breakdown, which, though it passed quickly, left him for a time intellectually in a "state of half-stupor."

Although he did not join any utopia, he did experience the same sense of alienation and frustration in urban life that drove scores of sensitive souls to the groves of Brook Farm or elsewhere. New York at times he found intolerable. "This city is worse than Babylon—mother of Harlots and Merchants," he wrote in 1844. "Its life seems utterly to have died out, and the few who labor sincerely in the Love of God and Man, we poor—and but for ourselves, quite friendless [sic]. Often as I walk the streets, I think of the words of poor Jean Paul, 'How lonely are men!. . . . But the breath of the Divine Spirit will soon have poured upon the skeletons of true men—and they will clothe themselves in the flesh and blood of humanity.'"[15]

Ironically, a major cause of Godwin's frustration was Bryant, who as a young man also had squirmed at his confinement in an intolerable place. In the eyes of his son-in-law, the editor plainly had been missed by the "Divine breath." He was too concrete a thinker and too committed to his own views to sympathize even with transcendentalism, much less with the imported utopianism of Fourier. Bryant closed the Post to Fourierist propaganda, an action that led Godwin to contrast Bryant with his great journalistic rival, Horace Greeley, who had become enamored with Fourierism: "Bryant is the most accomplished editor and by long odds the most accomplished writer—but his heart is not in it; he wants human everyday sympathies, and is a little malignant." In 1844 Godwin sold his interest in the Post, but continued as a writer and occasional editor until the fall of 1846 when he slipped some Fourierist doctrine into the newspaper while Bryant was away. When the editor returned, the two quarreled, and Godwin withdrew in a huff (although by 1850 Godwin had partially resumed his relationship with the *Post*).[16]

Before he made his break, Godwin had gotten a job in the New York custom house. Freed from Bryant's presence, he was able to concentrate his energies on the Fourierist movement—chiefly on saving it from its friends as well as its enemies. He had already acquired a strong distaste for Albert Brisbane, Fourier's first apostle to the Americans, primarily because of Brisbane's "rude steam-engine like hardness with which he treads upon all the more delicate and beautiful graces of the soul." Having joined the movement in his search for personal harmony with life, he also developed a veritable Yankeephobia against those New England members who were prone to go charging off against any and all of the world's evils; he was particularly disturbed by those who strayed off into abolitionism, for he feared that the attack against black slavery would disrupt the efforts to end the slavery of the working class.

Godwin was pleased, therefore, when in the spring of 1847 *The Harbinger,* the Fourierist journal he had helped establish in 1845, was moved from Brook Farm to New York. Brook Farm had been taken over by the Fourierists in 1845; for a time, they revived it, but in 1847, after a destructive fire, they gave up the experiment. The New York Fourierists were able temporarily to revive the journal; however, they could not save it from those implacable enemies of the movement in general— public indifference and a shortage of money. When Godwin became editor in November, he announced that he would make the "paper pay for itself," but despite his efforts to attract new readers by lessening its "abstract character," he had to suspend publication in February 1849. Godwin was optimistic to the end. "The cause of Social Reform. . . is the most momentous which now engages the public mind," he wrote in the last issue. "It sums up and completes all the progressive tendencies of the age." Although he promised that *The Harbinger* would soon reappear, Fourierism did not engage the public mind, and the journal vanished forever.[18]

The most tangible reason for this failure was Godwin's loss of his customhouse position in the wake of the Whig victory in the presidential elections of 1848, but more fundamental was his loss of faith in the Fourierist future. By 1849 he had learned what every radical in America was to discover: that the American people did not want any "organic" reform of their society. The Fourierists issued heroic pronunciamentos calling on the masses to break their chains; the response was not a roar but the polite applause of the few and the unnerving indifference of the many. On the title page of one of his books Godwin quoted John 18:23. "If I have spoken evil, show me wherein I have erred; if I have spoken good, why smitest thou me?" Godwin was not smitten but ignored, hardly encouragement for a crusader.

Perhaps it was his fellow Fourierist, Horace Greeley, who in 1868 best summed up the reasons for the failure of radicalism to break through the "stubborn indifference" of Americans: "Those who were in good circumstances, or hoped yet to be, wished no such change." Greeley went on to say that "the ignorant, stolid many" were too devoid of hope to rally to the radical cause; but Greeley and other Fourierists failed to see that few Americans had no hope—that the many, in fact, expected to be "in good circumstances." The simultaneous return of prosperity and the victory of free trade in 1845-46 made certain that the great majority of Americans would treat the utopians as absurd aspiring saviors of a society that had already been saved.

Godwin himself began to lose his enthusiasm for the movement several years before he lost *The Harbinger*. As early as 1846 he had termed the Fourierist plan for ideal communities "a pretty idea" but too mechanical to succeed: "Society is more than everything else a growth, a development, a life, like the human body, and you can no more change its structure by any outward mechanical efforts than you can change a boy into a man." In the early 1850s, he abandoned his borrowed Fourierist gloom over the fate of competitive society in favor of an almost mystical faith in the progressive, evolutionary tendencies of an essentially good world.[19]

This was not so radical a change as it appeared on the surface, for Godwin had simply used Fourierism as an instrument to express his dissatisfaction with the stuffiness, the deadness, and the harrassments of the times. His was fundamentally a rebellion against the politicians and others who seemingly had dissipated the promise of American life. Even as a Fourierist he had a strong affinity for the Young America movement with its stress on the benevolent and expansive character of American society. In the early 1840s, Godwin frequently wrote for the *Democratic*

Review, which by the mid-1840s had become the journal of the Young Americans. His chief grievance against the New England utopians was their hostility to the annexation of Texas and the Mexican War. In 1846 he refused an office in the American Union of Associationists because the Union had resolved to oppose the war. "The spirit of annexation which is here indirectly stigmatized," he wrote in refusal, "is the most vital thing that has shown itself in our politics for some years.... The question of extending *constitutional republican institutions* over this whole continent is one of the broadest, noblest and most important that was ever presented to any nation...I hold the government of the United States to be one century in advance of other governments and I would gladly see the principles extended over the whole earth."[20]

The political and social tensions of the early 1850s intensified Godwin's loyalty to the spirit of "Young America." Writing as an editor for *Putnam's Monthly,* freed from his commitment to Fourierism, he argued that the natural destiny of the United States was *peacefully* to expand north into Canada and south into Mexico, Central America, and the Caribbean, owing to its superior social system. By this time 1854 Godwin had identified himself with the antislavery movement, but he did not follow most antislavery men in condemning efforts to annex Cuba, probably because he considered expansion more important than the restriction of slavery. Americans, he wrote in 1854, were intrinsically no better than any other people, but their policies were more just, because of "our free and open institutions through which the convictions of men, and not the interests of monarchs" could influence decisions.

The exact connection between expansionism and democracy in Godwin's mind was rather nebulous, but he apparently believed that the popular pride and enthusiasm raised by expansion would help regenerate the nation by stimulating devotion to the principles and promise of democratic society.[21] As an intellectual, he had little use for the politicians and capitalists who, he felt, had mismanaged the affairs of society. To counter both, he identified the progressive tendencies in American life with "the general mind," which under the direction of science, philosophy, religion, and art was moving toward greater unity and freedom. Like Bryant and other literary men of the 1820s, Godwin tried to find a place for the intellectual in a practical-minded society by relating him directly to the people as copartner in the creation of a superior national character, but his views were more romantic and less moralistic than Bryant's. Great art meant a great nation, he said, where "the imagination was kindled by some great sympathy, and the whole soul . . . of the *nation* aroused into an intense and almost preternatural life." Godwin saw the basis for the national spirit not in a large centralized entity but in an aggregation of village communities. In 1855 he praised the prevalence in America of decentralization and local self-government as promoting both individual development and human brotherhood: "The people are the state, and grow into each other as a kind of living unity. Thrown upon their own resources, they acquire quickness, skill, energy, and self-poise."

Like Bryant, Godwin even expressed the hope that progress would, by reducing the machinery of government, virtually eliminate the politicians, "a pernicious class." Dreams! The politicians continued to exist, while society seemed to be as far from unity and harmony as it ever was. In 1856, writing now as a member of the newly formed Republican party, Godwin lamented: "The dream that this young land, fresh from the hands of its creator, unpolluted by the stain of time, should be the home of freedom and a race so manly that they would lift the earth by the whole breadth of an orbit nearer heaven . . . has passed away from us as nothing but a dream—we yield ourselves, instead to calculation, money-making, and moral indifference."[22]

Why had this promise failed? It was easy to blame the politicians and capitalists, but by 1856 Godwin thought he discerned behind them the essential force that had turned the nation away from greatness—slavery. He had been caught up in the movement of the times as it drew more and more of the ardor for reform into the antislavery cause. With that cause in mind, he called for the return of "great deeds" to touch the human heart and kindle it into purifying enthusiasm. Soon enough, Americans would have their opportunity to perform great deeds, to purify their society in the fires of war.

14

THE RISE OF THE SLAVE POWER

In February 1831 Harry Sedgwick, in that last year between insanity and death, rose before the Stockbridge Lyceum to pay tribute to an old family friend long dead. Elizabeth Freeman, or Mum Bett, as she was known to Harry and his brothers, had been the Sedgwick family servant for many years, but she had always been more family than servant. When Shays' rebels invaded the Sedgwick home in 1786, it was she who, in the absence of the Sedgwicks, discouraged them with the aid of a "large kitchen shovel" from wrecking the house. For the children, she had been more mentor than drudge. More to the point, Elizabeth Freeman was a Negro and an ex-slave.[1]

Harry's father had helped Elizabeth Freeman win freedom after the courts had ruled that the Massachussetts' Bill of Rights prohibited slavery in the state. Massachusetts so easily removed the blot of slavery because there were few slaves within its borders. But what of those southern states with their large populations of Negro slaves? Southerners had long argued that slavery, evil though it might be, was necessary, since the inferiority of the Negro made him inefficient as a free worker and socially dangerous as a freeman. In 1831 Sedgwick tried to refute this argument. Having known Elizabeth Freeman as well as he had known his own parents, he said, "I cannot believe in the moral or physical inferiority of the race to which she belongs."

But at this time, Negroes as a class *were* inferior to white men. "The truth is," said Harry, "that human nature is the same in all mankind. We are, for the most part, creatures of circumstance—and character is formed by condition." Even when Negores were freed from the degrading influence of slavery, they still faced the more pervasive discouragement of the caste system that existed in the North as well as the South. Taught by society to consider themselves as inferior, excluded from much of the civilizing influence of society because of their color, Negroes could not achieve their true potential, even if technically they received equality of legal rights. If only Americans would recognize that prejudice was responsible for inferiority, then the problems of slavery and race would be easily solved, for white men would see that it was to their advantage to treat the members of other races as equals. Negroes, given the status of free workers instead of slaves, would acquire the efficiency and reliability of free wage labor to the benefit of their employers and of the South in general. "The lands would be better cultivated. Population would increase, and land consequently rise in value."[2]

Harry's arguments agreed with the prevailing faith in enlightened self-interest, but would southerners sacrifice short-run interests to dubious long-run gains? Harry's nephew, Theodore, III, thought not. In 1833, writing to his parents during the early days of abolitionist agitation, Theodore warned that unless slavery were cut out of the nation "by bold and able hands" it would eventually disrupt the union. Like most of his contemporaries, however, Theodore was not "bold" enough actually to make the cut, for he felt that the South had reason to maintain its caste system. Whatever their potential, Negroes were inferior: "Is it rational to think in a generation to overcome the consequences of centuries? There the black population is; nearly 3 millions increasing at the South with frightful rapidity. How can you think to educate them up to an equality with us?" Slavery must be removed; yet slavery would remain so long as Negroes were inferior, and Negroes would be inferior as long as slavery remained. The only solution to this puzzle was to "get rid" of Negroes by colonizing them in Africa or the West Indies, but the problem of removing three million persons was so immense that few Americans dared to grapple with it.[3]

Cooper put his hopes in what he thought was a lower Negro birthrate which in time would make abolition practicable by reducing the proportion of Negroes to whites in the slaveholding areas. Harry Sedwick had denounced colonization as "trivial and indaquate." Legget expressed favor for the "rational and practicable" plan of the colonizationists to remove Negroes from the United States, a plan the abolitionists denounced as ineffectual at best and, at worst, a prop for slavery.[4]

Nearly every person preferred to leave the problems posed by Negro slavery to the slaveholding regions themselves. Northern anti slavery liberals were content to prevent the further spread of the institution in the hope that, if it were restricted, its inherent defects would ultimately lead southerners to abolish it. In sum, liberals were satisfied to consider the South's "peculiar institution" as a local evil, destined to die some time in the future at the hand of someone else.[5] But was slavery only a local matter? In the 1830s the abolitionists challenged this rather complacent liberal consensus by demanding that all Americans treat the institution as a national sin. Most liberals instinctively rejected abolitionist "fanaticism" as at best an annoying interruption of economic and political reform and at worst a threat to national unity.

The violent hostility shown in both North and South to the abolitionist crusade, however, put both abolitionism and slavery in a different light. On 7 July 1834 a riot broke out in New York City when a white mob tried to prevent a group of Negroes from using the Chatham Street Chapel for a belated Fourth of July celebration. As subsequent attacks proved, the ire of the mob was directed at abolitionists as well as at Negroes. Leggett in the *Post* lashed out at the persecutors for violating "the undoubted rights of the blacks." It was plain, however, that he was concerned more with abstract rights than with the plight of the persecuted. After warning that further persecutions would drive the blacks to listen to the "frantic ravings" of the abolitionists, he went out of his way to declare that the thought of "immediate emancipation and of promiscuous marriage between the two races is preposterous and revolting alike to common sense and decency." Eight months later, he assured southerners that northern Democrats were hostile to any program that would release slaves to become competitors of free white workers.

As the persecutions continued, however, Leggett shifted his emphasis from the evils of abolitionism to evils identified with slavery, particularly when in 1835 the Jackson administration, in deference to the South, closed the federal mails to abolitionist literature. In August 1835 Leggett warned that, while northern liberals would support any constitutional defense of the South, "we cannot trample on the charter of our national freedom to assist the slave-holder in his war with fanaticism." When Democratic leaders banished him from the party for this defense of free speech, Leggett concluded that slavery, if only indirectly, was a menace to the equal-rights philosophy. He gave full force to his new view in 1837, when in one of the last issues of *The Plaindealer* he warned that he would never support any effort to crush a slave rebellion:

> We confess with the keenest mortification and chagrin that the banner of our country is the emblem, not of justice and freedom, but of oppression; that it is the symbol of a compact which recognizes, in palpable and outrageous contradiction of the great principle of liberty, the right of one man to hold another as property; and that we are liable at any moment to be required, under our obligations of citizenship to array ourselves beneath it, and wage a war of extermination if necessary, against the slave, for no crime but asserting his right of equal humanity....

Would we comply with such a requisition? No![6]

Until he died, Leggett continued to deny that he favored, in any way, abolition by force; but could not southerners perceive between these lines the hint of coming catastrophe, the suggestion, perhaps, of an early-day John Brown?

Bryant, on his return from Europe in 1836, willingly inherited the *Post*'s defense of free speech for abolitionists. Although he had said little about slavery in the past, when Congress decided systematically to ignore petitions for the abolition of slavery in the District of Columbia, he denounced this "gag-rule" as part of a deliberate effort to break down "the liberty of speech and press." By 1838, in the face of continued assaults by northern mobs on abolitionists, he had come to associate slavery both with government restrictions on free speech and with dangerous social and political pressures within the North itself. This double-barreled threat aimed at the heart of free society was the "Slave Power" that he vigorously attacked in the future.[7]

In the late 1830s and early 1840s, however, neither Bryant nor young Theodore Sedgwick adopted the aggressively hostile stance taken by Leggett or the abolitionists. The Slave Power was little more than a half-formed abstraction that touched only lightly on their economic and political concerns. For them, slavery itself was still almost exclusively the problem of southern whites. They had no desire to sacrifice reform to any crusade against the peculiar institution, particularly since they had the opportunity in the early 1840s to see slavery, not as an abstract evil, but as a human—if not humane—way of life. Neither returned from his experience with a hatred of slavery or a passionate sympathy for slaves.

When in the summer of 1841 Sedgwick took a trip through Virginia, he readily heeded a Virginian's warning to avoid discussing "our Black People." Even in his personal diary, he made only one direct comment on slaves, and it is hardly critical of their condition: "No one can doubt that the Negroes in this state are a happy race. . . . They have few very great enjoyments but on the other hand they have few sufferings and they are spared the curse of discontent." An advocate of slavery could not have but it better.[8] Sedgwick, however, did enter into a discussion with a southerner on the adverse effects of slavery on "the industry and enterprise of the whites," a favorite concern of anti slavery men.

Bryant made similar observations when he first toured the Southeast in 1843. Much of his time was spent on the plantation of his friend, William Gilmore Simms, so that his opportunity to study slavery under all conditions was limited. Of his few references to the institution at this time, none were unfavorable, although he did note the existence of a contest between planters and slaves over the eternal question of to work or not to work: "The result is a compromise, in which each party yields something, and a good-natured though imperfect and slovenly obedience on one side is purchased by good treatment on the other." His experience did not leave him with a high regard for Negroes. In one of his letters written from Simms' plantation, he described "the humors of the Carolina negroes" as if to him they were comic figures, ludicrous in their efforts to imitate the white man. It was probably on this trip that Mrs. Bryant lifted the dresses of some Negro housemaids to see how they were dressed underneath. Her action revealed something more than the housemaids' petticoats.[9]

Liberals could tolerate slavery itself in the same way that a family might tolerate a disreputable uncle—to be accepted so long as he remained unseen and unheard. In the 1840s, when the persecution of abolitionists seemed to ease off, men such as Bryant were inclined to ignore slavery in favor of concerns closer to home. They were not, however, ready to tolerate the Slave Power, that aggressive force that had impinged on their affairs in the 1830s; they made this plain in 1843 when the nation took up an issue that revived the Slave Power idea in a new form. The issue was the annexation of Texas.

Bryant was not hostile to the westward movement. He had used the rhetoric of "manifest destiny" some twenty-five years before that term was coined by his friend John L. O'Sullivan. In 1820 he had spoken grandiloquently in his Fourth of July oration at Stockbridge of "futurity" and "destiny," of a time when the westward thrust of the American people would reach the Pacific. His concept of "futurity," however, did not include slavery. When in the midst of the free speech controversy of the mid-1830s a slaveholding Texas requested admission to the Union, Bryant warned that to comply would strengthen "a great evil, a great misfortune, and a monstrous anomaly" that had already caused enough mischief, "moral, social, and political." In September 1837, cautioned by his friend James K. Paulding that the slavery issue might split the Democratic party, he agreed to moderate his tone. "As to changing his course," wrote Paulding to President Van Buren (who apparently had instigated Paulding's request), "I did not attempt it for on this subject he is somewhat fanatical." Fortunately, perhaps, for Bryant's standing in the party, Van Buren himself vetoed the annexation scheme, but the issue would not stay dead for long.[10]

When in November 1843 Bryant heard rumors that southern Democrats, in cooperation with President Tyler, were planning to revive the annexation scheme, he was ready for battle. Northern Democrats, he wrote, had no intention of tampering with slavery in the southern states, "believing that causes are already in gradual operation which will inevitably bring on its extinction," but they would "resist to the uttermost" any effort to prolong its life. In December Theodore Sedgwick III entered the fray. Writing under his old pen name, "Veto," he warned that the Texas issue not only violated the moral sensibilities of liberal Democrats in the North but directly threatened their political interests by forcing on them a dilemma that they could hardly resolve. On the one hand, since part of their political appeal stemmed from their identification with individualism and freedom, they could not accept the expansion of slavery without losing much needed support in their own constituencies. On the other hand, if they were driven to take a hostile stand to slavery, they ran the risk of antagonizing the southern votes needed to acquire national power for their party and for their program of free trade. How, asked Sedgwick, was it possible to harmonize the interests of northern and southern Democrats? "How to serve God and Mammon?"[11]

The only hope was to keep slavery out of national politics by deflating the annexation movement within the Democratic party. In early 1844 the *Post* urged the renomination of ex-President Van Buren who, while he was no hero of the liberals, had both favored their economic program and opposed the annexation of a slaveholding Texas. Expansionism, however, was too strong to be stopped. The Democratic National Convention, after heated balloting, rejected Van Buren in favor of James K. Polk and annexation. When he learned of Polk's nomination, Bryant poured out his wrath in the *Post*: "The fiery and imperious South overrides and silences the north in matters of opinion.... The north is degraded." Later, he warned southern Democrats that if they tried to strengthen and perpetuate the slave system they would drive northern liberals out of the party. But, rage though he did, in the end he had to bow to the fact that Polk was a Jacksonian liberal, while his Whig opponent was none other than the archprotectionist, Henry Clay. Bryant and other liberals swallowed their pride and backed Polk.[12]

They did not, however, swallow Texas. In July Bryant, Sedgwick, David Dudley Field, and four others sent out a secret circular to some twenty party leaders in the state proposing that New York Democrats support Polk for the presidency but repudiate the Texas plank in the national platform. The leaders ignored the proposal. The chief effect of the circular was to weaken the political position of its authors, for a copy was published by pro-Texas Democrats as evidence of a liberal plot to prevent a Democratic victory in the November elections. Challenged, the signers published an open letter in the *Post* openly rejecting the Texas plank on the grounds that slavery was inimical to the principles of the true Democratic party, no matter what the "selfishness of mere partisans" might decree. If they were forced to choose between loyalty to party or loyalty to principle, they warned, they would stand by their principles, a resort to a form of "higher law" in politics that grated on the nerves of political regulars.[13]

The circular marked the beginning of another stage in the struggle between Barnburners and Hunkers for control of the state Democratic organization, since the Barnburners generally adopted a stand against Texas, while the Hunkers, anxious to strengthen their position with the national party, supported annexation. In effect, slavery had become a factor in the politics of New York, inflaming a dispute that ultimately would not only weaken the Democratic party but help bring on the Civil War. Intraparty tensions, however, were eased temporarily when in September the state Democratic convention nominated as its candidate for governor Silas Wright, the Barnburner hero and an opponent of annexation. With Wright at the head of the state ticket, the *Post* was able to proclaim the Democrats the party of freedom, while virtually ignoring the Texas issue. When Polk carried New York by a slim plurality, the liberals claimed that by playing down the annexation issue they had won for Polk the state and (since New York's vote was vital) the presidency Polk, they pointed out, had polled some 6,000 votes fewer than Wright. Was not this an indication that annexation was unpopular among New York Democrats? For a time, the liberals could believe it possible to protect their interests, their integrity, and their pride within the Democratic organization.

It is true that early in 1845 Congress, by joint resolution, committed the United States to annex Texas, an act which the *Post* denounced as threatening to transfer "the whole substantial power of the country...to the slave-holding states." But when in November Polk carried through with the commitment, the response of the newspaper was, "What has been done, has been done." Bryant, who was in Europe at the time, mildly criticized this softening of his anti-Texas position, but even he acquiesced to the fait accompli, if only because the twin victories of Polk and Wright promised liberal reform on both the national and state levels. While the Slave Power had won a victory, it had not seriously interfered with essential political, economic, and social aims; liberals were not yet compelled to make the choice between God and Mammon, between democracy and slavery. But if, seemingly because of slavery, the liberals were to lose influence both in state and national politics— what then? In April 1846 the United States declared war on Mexico. In November Governor Wright was defeated for re-election. The prologue had ended; the tragedy had begun.

15

THE FREE-SOIL REVOLT (1845-52)

By 1845 slavery had become a major national issue, but the antislavery cause as yet had found no political agency other than the weak and unpopular Liberty party of the abolitionists. Although the South's insistence on Texas had antagonized liberal Democrats such as Bryant and Sedgwick, they were reluctant to join an antislavery movement for fear of disrupting their party. The political and economic controversies of the previous fifteen years had accustomed them to see the Democratic party as the great agency of reform. Was it wise to jeopardize reform or their own personal standings? Participation in party affairs had given each man a role, status, and often money. Having a reputation as a Democratic journalist, even Bryant was reluctant to risk the loss of influence, prestige, and a share of government patronage when the Democrats were in power.

Liberals, like most other Americans, preferred to ignore slavery in the hope that the "peculiar institution" would ultimately die a natural death. To men anxious to avoid the terrible tumult and sacrifice of civil war, the American faith in the inevitability of Progress was a great comfort. But Bryant and other liberal Democrats rested their faith on two conditions: that they retain control of the party for liberalism and that slavery be a local and passive institution that in no way obstructed national progress. Neither of these conditions would be met in the decade after 1845.

The hope that slavery would die quietly had already been shaken both by the persecution of the abolitionists and by the annexation of Texas. It flickered in the turbulence generated by the Mexican War. The Slave Power had brought Texas in 1845, and Texas brought war in 1846. Bryant had earlier declared that an armed conflict over Texas would violate the democratic character of the nation. and yet in the end his nationalism triumphed over his liberalism. After some hesitation, he supported the war as one of defense provoked by a Mexican attack on American soil—the soil of Texas. Initially, he opposed an invasion of Mexico as inconsistent with the peaceful character of a republic, but he was soon caught up in the wartime enthusiasms aroused in the people by the heroics—reported in detail in the *Post*—of the American armies invading Mexico. His old friend Catherine Sedgwick had condemned the annexation of Texas and had condemned the declaration of war on Mexico; yet she confessed:

> My pulses beat quicker at the valor, indominable spirit, skill and hardi-hood of our people. If there were virtue in those Mexicans..., there might be sympathy for their wrongs. But as it is, it seems to me that it is the ordination of heaven that this stagnant, putrefying race should give place to the fresh young current that is settling upon them.[1]

Having acquiesced to a war of conquest, the liberals vowed to keep it from being a victory for slavery. When in 1846 Congressman David Wilmot of Pennsylvania proposed that Congress bar slavery from any lands acquired as result of the war, the *Post* supported him, as did a great part of the northern press. Critics argued that the "Wilmot Proviso" was unnecessary, since the new Southwest was not suited to slavery. Why, then, provoke useless sectional discord? There were slave states, replied the *Post,* such as Virginia that looked on the new territories as safety valves for their burdensome surplus of slaves, as a "place of refuge from the impoverishment into which the old age of slavery is certain to fall." It was true that much of the Southwest had neither climate nor soil suitable for slavery, but there were pockets of fertile land where slaveholders could establish themselves. Although they might be only a small minority of the population, a "few slaveholders have always an extensive influence in any community," so that they could maintain slavery, once established over the interests and will of the majority. Assuming this, Bryant and other liberals concluded, when southern congressmen united against the proviso, that the Slave Power had determined to advance its own interests at the expense of free men by turning untainted soil into slave land. In short, the liberals added the slaveholder to the privilege-seeker and the politician in their rogues' gallery of enemies of democracy.[2]

The identification of slavery with the traditional liberal foes was strengthened when in 1846 and 1847, in the midst of the controversy over the proviso, slavery emerged as a major factor in the politics of New York State. Between 1844 and 1846 the Barnburners had been able to gain the upper hand in their intraparty conflict with the Hunkers, but their victory was short lived. In 1846 Governor Wright was defeated for re-election by a Whig, a disaster that Bryant ascribed to the treachery of the Hunkers; for, while Wright had carried New York City by a substantial majority, he had lost some of the upstate districts where the Hunkers were strong. The resentment of the Barnburners deepened when in the summer of 1847 Wright suddenly died at the age of fifty-two. Their hero now became, like Leggett, a martyr to politics, a symbol around which partisan bitterness gathered. A month after his death, when the Democrats met in Syracuse to nominate candidates for state offices, Wright's presence was there. The Barnburners urged the convention to honor his memory by agreeing to liberal candidates and a liberal platform. The result was a political explosion. Reportedly, when one Hunker replied, "It is too late, he is dead," James B. Wadsworth leaped on a table to shout, "It is not too late to do justice to his assassins." The Barnburners had the indignation, but the Hunkers had the votes. They blocked the renomination of two of Wright's associates, Attorney-General John Van Buren (son of the ex-President) and Azariah C. Flagg, who as controller had checked the spending propensities of both Hunkers and Whigs. The Hunkers had won control of the party.[3]

The angry Barnburners concluded that the intrusion of the slavery issue into New York politics had given the Hunkers the leverage they needed to defeat the "true" interests of the people. In 1844-45 the Hunkers had tried to embarrass their opponents politically by making support for Texas an index of party loyalty—particularly when Polk's victory set off the quadrennial scramble for federal offices. When the Polk administration divided the spoils in 1845, the Barnburners, while they received some important offices, complained that Polk had denied them recognition commensurate with their importance in New York.

Possession of office meant possession of power, a political fact that convinced the Barnburners that the administration had used the patronage as punishment for their hostility to Texas, to weaken them in favor of their rivals. Thus they attributed Wright's political martyrdom in 1846 indirectly to Polk, Texas, and slavery.[4]

By 1847 liberals had formed the habit of blaming slavery for at least some of their political troubles. The Slave Power appeared to have become a meddlesome influence in both politics and policy. "Talk of an acquisition of territory," complained the *Post*, "and you are met with a demand that it shall be open to the introduction of slavery. Propose a scheme of finance, and you will find it opposed because it is feared that it may affect the interests of slavery." To eliminate these dangerous digressions, the Barnburners tried to close the slavery issue by committing the party to the Wilmot Proviso, the assumption being that the South would acquiesce to a fait accompli. In 1847 they launched a drive toward that end, warning that failure to respond to the rising antislavery sentiment of New Yorkers, as Bryant pronounced it, "would be suicidal." When the Hunkers openly supported the Polk administration in its hostility to the proviso, they strengthened the suspicions of their enemies that they were willing to sacrifice the state party in order to remain in the good graces of the slaveholders. A collision between the two factions was inevitable. At the Syracuse convention in 1847 Bryant's friend David Dudley Field tried to submit his "cornerstone" resolution committing New York Democrats to oppose the extension of slavery into any territory acquired from Mexico. He was ruled out of order. When the violent debate set off by this ruling had ended, the Hunker majority consolidated their position by adopting resolutions praising the policies of the Polk administration. Having failed to maintain either their power or their principles, the Barnburners bolted from the convention, they met a month later at Herkimer, where they adopted Field's resolutions. The Free-Soil revolt had begun.[5]

The Barnburners, when they left the Syracuse convention, probably did not intend to start a political revolution. Despite their earlier threats and despite the blandishments of some politicians who favored a third party, the majority of liberals initially had little thought of breaking with the old organization. To leave the party was costly, as Bryant pointed out to his brother John, who out in Illinois was seriously considering the idea of a free-soil party. "All parties formed for a single measure are necessarily short-lived," warned Bryant. "I never mean to belong to any of them unless I see some very strong and compelling reason for it. The journalist who goes into one of those narrow associations parts with the greatest part of his influence." For him and for other Americans, slavery was an issue not to excite but to suppress, so that they could return to more conventional concerns. The Barnburners hoped that by letting the Hunkers go down to defeat in the state elections of 1847 they could regain control of the party machinery. They failed. The Hunkers did in 1847 lose to the Whigs, but the chief political result was to discredit the Barnburners in the eyes of Democratic regulars throughout the country. Too late, the liberals recognized that they had actually weakened their position in the state and national organizations.[6]

Earlier in 1847 Theodore Sedgwick, III, had urged the young men of Union College to "disregard the menaces of political majorities, the influence of government patronage, and all the blandishments of office, and fail not, on all proper occasions, to denounce *Slavery* as the opprobrium of the age, the curse and cancer of your country." These were brave words, but Sedgwick began to have second thoughts about disregarding majorities and government patronage. In early December, after consulting with Bryant and Field, he published an anonymous letter in the *Post* urging northern Democrats to refrain from efforts to make the Wilmot Proviso an issue at the Democratic National Convention in 1848, because the issue would split the party and threaten what he had long feared, the disruption of the Union. Probably Sedgwick hoped to ease the way for the renomination of his old acquaintance, Martin Van Buren. Certainly, he was anxious to avoid a head-on confrontation that might force the Barnburners to break with the national party. As the 1850s would soon show, he was far more hostile to the idea of an antislavery party than was Bryant. Reluctantly, the editor acceded to Sedgwick's proposal in the hope that the liberals could protect both their position and their principles within the party.[7]

Events in the next five months crushed that hope. Early in 1848 the Barnburners and the Hunkers, meeting in separate conventions, selected separate delegations to the Democratic National Convention scheduled to meet at Baltimore in May. Their actions dropped the factional disputes of New York State into national politics, since the convention would have to determine which of the two delegations represented the state party. The status of liberals as Democrats was to be decided in a forum where the influence of slavery was strong. Clutch at straws though they might, the Barnburners were headed straight for rebellion, as they fully recognized when in May the two rival New York delegations appeared at the Baltimore convention. Faced with a factious situation, the convention offered to admit both delegations—if they would agree to share equally New York's convention votes and if they pledged to support the presidential nominee to be selected at Baltimore. The Hunkers agreed to the conditions and were admitted. The Barnburners rejected both—the first because they thought it an attempt on the part of the South to nullify New York's influence on party matters, the second because the nominee was likely to be Lewis Cass, an anti-proviso man. Southerners, complained the *Post,* were trying to force the liberals to play "a game in which the stake is. . .human freedom and the rule of the game 'heads! slavery wins—tails! liberty loses!'" On the eve of the convention, Bryant had warned that efforts to destroy the political influence of "the friends of Silas Wright" would end hopes of a Democratic victory in New York. The Barnburners gave effect to the editor's warning after their delegation returned home. In June, they issued a call for a convention at Utica to nominate their own candidate against Cass, the Baltimore nominee.[8]

Bryant now favored the idea of a third party. To acquiesce to Cass's nomination, he warned, would mean virtually disbanding the Barnburner organization during the campaign, which was political suicide. Power was a factor and so was pride. New York liberals, he raged, had suffered the "indignity" of being ignored as if they were unimportant; now "they will have their candidate; they will organize as New York Democrats know how to organize, and they will make their voices heard." To make those voices even louder, after the Utica convention in June had nominated Martin Van Buren for the presidency, Bryant urged the Barnburners to give their movement a broader character: "The other states of the north and west swarm with our natural allies." Already he had been apprised of strong free-soil feelings in Illinois. What had begun as an intraparty feud in New York was beginning to snowball into a northern sectional party as it picked up all those northerners—Whigs, Democrats, and abolitionists—who had chafed at the power of politicians and of slavery. Late in June came the call for a national convention of Wilmot proviso men to meet in Buffalo. In early July, "some of the strongest, most consistent, and influential

Democrats" of Berkshire county met to hear speeches by the native sons, Field and Sedgwick, and other Barnburner emissaries from New York. The Berkshire meeting implemented resolutions favoring free-soil and Van Buren by selecting a delegation to the Buffalo convention, headed by Bryant's old friend, Charles Sedgwick.[9]

In early August, thousands of free-soilers poured into Buffalo to launch their twin rebellions against the party system and the Slave Power. The convention proceeded to nominate Van Buren and, as his running mate, the Whig Charles Francis Adams on a platform that subordinated the traditional economic issues that had divided Democrat and Whig anti-slavery men to the campaign against the politicians of their old parties. Similarly, liberals and abolitionists, while they continued to differ in their approaches to slavery itself, proved at Buffalo that they could unite against the apparent efforts of the Slave Power to make slavery a national institution. The key resolution demanded that the federal government commit itself "not to *extend, nationalize,* or *encourage,* but to limit, local-ize, and discourage Slavery" by all constitutional means.[10]

Having committed himself to a third party, Bryant swung the *Post* vigorously into the campaign for "Free Soil, Free Speech, Free Labor, and Free Men." On election day the *Post* went all out to stir up enthu-siasm for the cause: "Never in the history of our existence as a people, has there been a greater issue at stake. It is no less than the salvation of our empire from the curse of slavery. . . . shall the United States no longer be known as the home of the free and the asylum of the oppressed, but as the home of the slave and the oppressor of the poor?" Enthusiasm, however, was no substitute for votes. In New York State Van Buren lagged some 12,500 votes behind Cass and far behind the victorious Zachary Taylor, while in the city he did much worse, polling less than 10 percent of the total vote. The *Post,* however, initially was optimistic, hopeful that 1848 had given birth to a powerful new party, which in the future would frustrate the designs of the Slave Power.[11]

The hopes were premature. It was true that, by helping to defeat Cass, the Free-Soilers had taught both Hunkers and southern Democrats a lesson in the importance of liberal support, but, while the *Post* was boasting of the great new antislavery organization, Barnburners such as Bryant's friend Samuel J. Tilden had concluded that the massive Whig victory in New York had left them with hardly any organization at all. Bryant might rest content with a great principle as the cornerstone of political organization; others believed that the foundations of political power lay in the possession of political offices. If this were so, the future was indeed grim for of the 128 seats in the legislature both Democratic factions won only 20, and of the state's 32 seats in Congress the Democrats won only 2. The fact that the Barnburners won 13 legislative seats to the Hunkers' 7 was meager consolation. Neither faction thought that the dispute over slavery was significant enough to risk the destruction of the Democratic party. In 1849 they united behind one slate of Democratic candidates for state offices, and in 1850 the reunion was sealed when they supported Horatio Seymour in his losing bid for the governorship. Party traditions, party loyalties, and party spoils triumphed over anti-slavery feelings. The Hunkers and the Barnburners vanished from New York politics.[12]

The more zealous anti-slavery Democrats such as Bryant viewed the restoration of party unity with mixed feelings. Having reluctantly joined a third party, he was now reluctant to abandon it or its guiding principle, the Wilmot proviso. In March 1849 he referred to his own experience as an advocate of free trade to prove how devotion to a great principle could ultimately triumph over the hostility of the politicians: "The doctrine of universal freedom in the new territories is one that fully commends itself to the moral sense of the people, and is in such perfect agreement with their best principles that it must be fully adopted." The next fifteen years would prove that Bryant was right, but the immediate future seemed only to fulfill his earlier prophecy that a third party formed on a single measure is "necessarily short-lived," for in the summer of 1850 Congress sharply reduced public interest in the slavery question by enacting a compromise acceptable to moderates of both North and South.[13]

Although the *Post* denounced Congress both for enacting a more stringent Fugitive slave law and for failing definitely to prohibit slavery in the territories acquired from Mexico, it reluctantly acquiesced to the Compromise of 1850 as a way of easing a controversy that had unsettled conventional politics. Bryant and other liberal Democrats were prepared to swallow defeat over the Wilmot Proviso, bitter as it was, for they were still deeply concerned with the old issues and the old policies. Even at the height of the free-soil fervor in 1848, they had looked with suspicion on their Whig allies. Their suspicions turned to outrage when the regular Whigs, having won power both at Washington and at Albany in 1848, again yielded to the temptation to spend the public's money. In 1850 the *Post* denounced a new canal program enacted by the New York legislature as a threat to the sacred "guarantees against public extravagance," which the liberals thought they had safely enshrined in the constitution of 1846. Just before the state elections the newspaper urged all Democrats to unite against the Whig spending policies: "The cardinal principles of public policy upon which the democratic and conservative parties have divided in this country for the last quarter of a century are not secondary to any issue of a more immediate origin." Having decided that the Free-Soil party would not protect correct principles, Bryant in 1852 backed the Democratic presidential candidate, Franklin Pierce, even though Pierce had pledged to uphold the Compromise of 1850. Bryant argued that he could better resist the aggressions of the Slave Power as a spokesman for an established party than for a splinter organization, but plainly he had decided at least temporarily to subordinate antislavery to reforms that benefited white society.[14]

Could antislavery be held separate from reform? Prior to 1844 Bryant, like most Americans, thought so. During the Free-Soil revolt, however, he and other liberals had grown accustomed to treating slavery as a menace to their vision of a society of free, prosperous individuals. Politically, as they saw the situation, the Slave Power had at least indirectly kept the party of democracy from maintaining its state and national power. Socially, slavery itself posed a threat to both the prosperity and status of the average white man, the backbone of democracy. "There are two classes of persons in the United States who take great interest in the future destiny of the blacks," complained the *Post*, "namely the slave owners and the abolitionists. A more important question than this...is, what is to be the destiny of the white man?" If the Slave Power could force slavery into the territories, the West—the land of opportunity— would be effectively closed to white yeoman and workers, for nowhere did slave labor and free labor co-exist except at the expense of degrading and impoverishing the free worker. In July 1848 the *Post* used an advertisement from a southern newspaper offering slaves for sale to illustrate the argument: "The heading which is prefixed to our article is often seen in the advertisements of Southern newspapers—'Mechanics for Sale!' How do you like the phrase, broad-shouldered workingmen of New York?" In 1849, when he visited the South, Bryant even praised the proliferation of textile mills there as promising to enhance the dignity of at least some white men "in a region where manual labor has been the badge of servitude and dependence." But the corrupting influence of slavery was pervasive. The next year the *Post* reported that at least one southern mill was experimenting with slave labor. All in all, the peculiar institution threatened further to degrade the masses of white men to the benefit of a few slaveholders. Such was the institution that the Slave Power intended to strengthen throughout much of the nation. Was it so far-fetched, then, to warn workers that the southern apology for slavery as a social good "would justify any kind of social inequality, even the forcible subjection of whites by whites?"[15]

Prior to the appearance of the Slave Power idea, most liberal northerners had been content to accept the existence of slavery, for they did not consider the welfare of Negro slaves important enough to risk a violent sectional conflict that might destroy the Union. Now, by concentrating on the Slave Power as a menace to white interests, liberals such as Bryant minimized both the racial and sectional implications of the slavery controversy. They could treat the controversy in conventional liberal terms as one between privilege and people, involving the interests of aristocratic slaveholders on the one side and the free white majority on the other. Hostility to the expansion of slavery, far from being wild, disruptive abolitionism, was simply a defense of the democratic social order. Was there any validity to the threat that the South might secede in the face of a strong antislavery stand? If slavery indeed threatened the interests of the majority of white southerners, would they permit the breakup of the Union in defense of slavery? Bryant and other liberals throught that despite their bluff and bluster, southern leaders would acquiesce to a show of antislavery strength.[16]

This is not to say that liberals had determined to take the offensive against slavery. They continued to act on the assumption that they had no constitutional right to interfere with slavery in the slave states; their strongly individualistic and localistic bias would have it no other way. It did mean, however, that they were prepared to take a firm stand against the apparent aggression of the Slave Power, particularly in the western territories. The Compromise of 1850, by deferring a final decision on the territorial question, had eased the tensions of the previous years. For a time, the liberals were able to return to traditional politics in the belief that the Slave Power was relatively quiescent. But if that menace did not remain quiet? In 1850, in reference to Calhoun's demand for a constitutional amendment to strengthen the power of the slave states within the government, the *Post* had warned slaveholders that they had better not disturb the existing situation, for the first new amendment to the Constitution "will not provide for the equalization of the burdens of slavery...but will prohibit forever the representation of slave property in Congress." In 1853 the newspaper reported the rumor of a southern conspiracy to prevent the creation of Nebraska territory. The political upheaval that had been brewing since the mid-1840s and had been averted in 1848, was now about to begin.[17]

16

THE REPUBLICAN TRIUMPH (1854-60)

In 1851 Parke Godwin glanced back over the previous half century and found it had been a great creative season of the human race. The last fifty years, he wrote in the *Evening Post,* formed "a destructive, and yet prolific period—in which many things have gone out and so many things come in, so many horrible errors and prejudices been killed, and so many new and beautiful truths born—that mankind, we believe, to the end of their days, will rejoice in this period."[1] Accustomed to view the grand sweep of human events through rosy spectacles, Godwin conceivably could have lapsed into complacent acceptance of the inevitability of progress, as indeed he sometimes did; more often, however, this student of society found his stimulus in the disparity between the promises of history and the ugly realities of the present.

Godwin had long believed that slavery was one of the ugliest of realities. In the 1840s he showed at least some interest in the plight of Negro slaves. While Bryant condemned the institution chiefly as a violation of the principle of individual rights, Godwin criticized it also as brutalizing and exploitive. "Inferior men they may be, imperfect men they certainly are," he wrote of Negroes in 1843, "yet neither their inferiority nor their imperfections can . . . excuse our treating them with injustice and outrage." Two years later, he expressed interest in the problems of some 400 ex-slaves in Virginia who, freed by John Randolph on the condition that they be removed to the free states, were having difficulties finding a place for themselves outside the South. He toyed with the idea of incorporating them in a Fourierist community: "Could these men be trained into freemen and productive loving Christians by the machinery of organization and mild juditive [*sic*], firm guidance, what becomes of your slavery question and slavery too?" The experiment was never tried and, to Godwin's disgust, slavery remained an issue.[2]

Although benevolently disposed toward the Negro, Godwin despised those who crusaded against slavery without offering a feasible way of freeing the slaves. Believing that the abolitionists only detracted from more desirable and practical efforts to reform white society, he denounced them in 1845 as "niggerloving and white-man hating fanatics." Slavery was a "foul and heartless Molloch" but then so was competitive capitalism. Of the two, capitalism was far worse, for it degraded the mass of white men. For a time, he was even willing to stomach the pro-slavery arguments of John C. Calhoun in the belief that Calhoun's insight into the exploitive character of society was "a thousand times to be preferred to the democratic simplism" of the liberals and the "simplistic moralism" of the abolitionists.[3]

So long as Godwin remained a critic of capitalism, he considered anti-slavery to be at best only a side show of reform; but, when he abandoned Fourierism, he soon joined the liberals in their attack on the Slave Power as an enemy of reform. He had been drawn into Fourierism partially because of his dissatisfaction with the nature and direction of the existing political leadership. When in 1853 he became political editor of *Putnam's Monthly,* he launched what in effect was a second critical career with an assault on "the flatulent old hacks, the queasy and prurient old bawds, who have so long had control of the old parties." The existence of these political prostitutes perplexed many of *Putnam's* middle-class readers. Like them, Godwin by the 1850s had concluded that the American social and economic system was fundamentally sound; it was not surprising, therefore, that both he and they should attribute the troubles of the times not to any faults in the system but to something extraneous to, and incompatable with, the democratic order. Slavery was logically the villain.[4]

Bryant and other liberals had begun to make this connection during the controversies over Texas and the Mexican Cession Territories. But Godwin's ardent expansionism had led him to discount the free-soil arguments; then, he had seen the antislavery movement as a barrier to progress. In 1854, however, the issue of slavery in the West was raised in a distinctly new form that did not involve the acquisition of new territory. In the spring Congress upset the precarious peace established in 1850 by passing Stephen A. Douglas's Kansas-Nebraska Bill, repealing the Missouri Compromise, which for thirty-four years had prohibited slavery in that part of the old Louisiana Purchase Territory north of the parallel 36°30'. Godwin responded to the repeal with a blistering attack on the Slave Power that equalled in intensity his earlier indictments of competitive capitalism.

In an article, "Our Parties and Politics," published in the September issue of *Putnam's,* he charged that slavery had corrupted the "free Democratic Republic" created by the founding fathers. Instead of withering away as Americans had hoped, the institution "has become interwoven with vast and intricate interests, and it is now sustained positively by political and philosophical argument." The slave "aristocracy" had not only maintained itself but had used its control over the Democratic party to subvert freedom in the North. It had long menaced freedom of opinion; now in the 1850s through the Fugitive Slave Act it had turned the free states into "a hunting ground for slaves"; worst of all, it had acted in the Kansas–Nebraska Act to open the West, America's land of opportunity, to "a form of society...whose highest achievement is a purchase of the wealth and freedom of one race by the eternal subjection of another....A single act of legislation, like Satan, when he entered Paradise, has reversed the destinies of the World."[5]

Godwin reserved his sharpest thrusts for those northern Democrats who, as he saw them, had acted with the Slave Power. Under Jackson, the Democrat alliance of northern liberals and southern planters had advanced the cause of freedom, but the growing ambitions of the Slave Power now made that alliance impractical and dangerous. In an effort to maintain a political alliance outmoded by the diminishing importance of the issues that had produced it, "machine democrats" had not only cast their party at the feet of slavery but had corrupted both politics and government in order to maintain their grips on the shaking throne: "Government, in short, is converted into a vast conspiracy of placemen, managed by the adroiter villains of the set who control legislation, defeat reform, and infuse gradually their own muck-warm spirit into the body of the community." Unfortunatly, even the people, deprived of the stimulus of great leaders, were sinking into a state of supineness and decay.

Slavery, then, was the most vital issue of the age, a challenge that had to be met if the nation was to achieve its promise. To redeem themselves and the nation, argued Godwin, northerners must unite against the Slave Power and, particularly, its supporters in the North who were responsible for nationalizing the corrupting influences of slavery. The destruction of the "little men," of the "toads" who had crawled into "the seats of eagles," would remove slavery as a force from national politics and revive the promise of the Republic. Once, the Democratic party had been the agency of revival; now, northerners, regardless of old political affiliations, must unite in a new antislavery coalition dedicated to:

THE REPEAL OF THE FUGITIVE SLAVE LAW—THE RESTORATION OF THE MISSOURI COMPROMISE—NO MORE SLAVE STATES—NO MORE SLAVE TERRITORIES—THE HOMESTEAD FOR FREE MEN ON PUBLIC LANDS.

In essence, this was soon to become the platform of the new Republican party, which by the autumn of 1854 had begun to appear in many areas of the North.[6]

The politically footloose Godwin could easily urge Americans to forgo their old political ties in favor of a new party, but what of men such as Bryant, whose careers were still rooted in conventional politics? By the 1850s the editor had settled down at his Roslyn estate where he spent long hours working in his garden with his wife, at his request, by his side. "I must do as my wife says," he wrote with his characteristically sly humor, "and how could that be if I had not her at hand to direct me." The *Post* had become a profitable venture, freeing him from the dirt, bad air, and noise of the city to retire not only to long weekends at Roslyn but in the decade after 1848 frequently to distant places: the South, the West, the Caribbean, Western Europe, and the Near East. From his Near Eastern trip in 1853 he brought back the beginnings of the long white beard that was to be his trademark in later years. Here at long last was the means to achieve his long-frustrated dream of withdrawing permanently to the countryside, but he stayed with the *Post,* for, dislike them though he might, journalism and politics had given him a role, a sense of purpose, which ironically his waning poetic talents no longer could supply. And so he remained to fight the political battles of the 1850s, a scarred and often weary warrior, reluctant to fight but prepared by his long experience to lead his readers into the fray when the occasion called.[7]

On matters of slavery, he hoped the call would never come. In 1852 he had returned to the Democratic fold in his pursuit of the traditional goals of public honesty and free trade. He and his associate, John Bigelow (assistant editor of the *Post*, 1848–61), had thrown the influence of the *Post* behind the election of Franklin Pierce, with the wishful thought that fate would prevent a duplication of Polk's administration: "Such presidents as he are only accidents, and two such accidents are not likely to be visited upon a single miserable generation." In a real sense, they had to believe that Pierce was a true Democrat, because, if he were not, they had no choice but to break with the old organization and risk a political debacle like that of 1848. For more than a year after Pierce's victory, they held to the hope that the new administration would follow correct principles. It is true that by the summer of 1853 the *Post* had become sufficiently critical of administration policy to be "invited" by the Washington *Union* to leave the Democratic organization; but its editors replied that they would stay, "because it is *our* party." The Kansas–Nebraska issue in 1854, however, finally convinced them that indeed there could be "two such accidents" as Polk in one generation.[8]

After Congress took up Douglas' bill in January, the *Post* helped launch a public crusade against its Northern supporters, most of whom were Democrats. The people of the North seemed to rise in wrath against "the Nebraska perfidy"—and yet the bill passed. Why had so many Democrats betrayed the people? In March, Bryant accused President Pierce of using his patronage power (shades of Polk) to whip reluctant politicians into line. The Slave Power, through political corruption, again had used the Democratic party to capture the seat of power.[9] But still Bryant was reluctant to consider the idea of a new party. Shaken by the tremors of political revolution, he clung to the hope that both slavery and the slave issue could be contained and the old political channels repaired, if only the northern rank and file could be persuaded to oust the politicians in control of the Democratic organization. When a correspondent proposed that northern Whigs and Democrats join in 1856 to back Thomas Hart Benton and William H. Seward for the presidency and vice-presidency, the *Post* noted that Benton was a free-trade Democrat and Seward was a Whig identified with government interference in matters of trade. Let the two parties continue to exist, it advised. "Both parties abound in great men, and the way to get a good President is for both to nominate good candidates."[10]

The traditional parties, however, did not nominate good men, nor did they act to unite northern opinion against the apparent aggressions of slavery. In the state and congressional elections of 1854, Bryant found that he had to choose among four major state tickets, all of them bad. The Democrats again had split over patronage matters, with the "Hard-Shell" and "Soft-Shell" factions each running their own separate slates. The *Post* rejected the "Softs" because they were aligned with the Pierce administration, and the "Hards" because though, they were hostile to Pierce, they were also hostile to the antislavery movement. Of the two other tickets, that of the Whigs was acceptably anti-Nebraska but also wrong in its economic principles, while the nativism of the American party was simply repellant. Liberal Democrats literally had no place to go. Bryant, Bigelow, and friends sat out the election like sideline spectators who believe they can play the game better than any of the players.[11]

Bryant soon had to agree with his brother Cyrus, who out in Illinois had already concluded that there was as much chance of converting Satan to the true faith as there was of persuading Democratic leaders to change their ways. By 1855 Bryant had decided that so long as those leaders managed political affairs the slavery issue would remain alive to excite discord and violence—and not the violence of political debates alone, for in that year blood had begun to flow in Kansas, apparently as a result of conflict between pro-slavery and antislavery settlers. Finally, he accepted the political revolution that in 1844 he had helped to start by opposing the annexation of Texas. When in 1855 the new Republican party ran its first ticket in the state elections, he supported it, even though his old friend and partner in the Free-Soil party, Samuel J. Tilden, was the "Soft" candidate for state attorney-general. Slavery, said the *Post* in justification of its stand, had become the great issue of the day; the old issues were dead—and so was the old party system. The people of the free states needed a new political agency to block the efforts to tranform slavery from a local institution, harmful only to the southern states, into a national institution protected by the federal government. Here in the aggressive efforts of the Slave Power was the chief source of corruption in government; here, too, was a menace to the good name and nature of the Republic. For Bryant now, the old party differences over the basic political and economic issues were to be suspended until the influence of slavery had been contained within its old limits. Little did he and other Republicans realize that they had set in motion forces which, far from restoring the old order, were to radically change the nature of American society.[12]

Blind to the great events which lay ahead, the editor joined the new party with much suspicion and little enthusiasm. When in early 1856, he was invited to attend a Republican convention at Pittsburgh he refused, because, as he explained to his brother John, he had little taste for politics and little faith in political parties: "The moment a party becomes strong the rogues are attracted to it, and immediately try to manage it." He was wary of the enforced marriage between Democrats and Whigs, although his uneasiness diminished when in the spring of 1856 the Republicans nominated the presidential candidate and approved of much of the platform which the *Post* had promoted. The candidate was John C. Fremont, the son-in-law of Thomas Hart Benton (Jackson's old political ally), and the platform ignored the protective tariff and other Whig policies, so that it was possible for Bryant and other cautious Democrats to consider the new party as the true descendant of Jacksonian Democracy.[14]

Godwin entered the fray in 1856 with more enthusiasm. Having already set down the fundamental principles of the early party, he now supplied Republicans with further ammunition by republishing a collection of his magazine articles from the previous three years. The book, *Political Essays,* served to strengthen the Republican image as the party of reform which would regenerate American society by eradicating both the Slave Power and political corruption. It offered Americans the hope that if they threw themselves decisively into the effort to contain slavery that just around the corner they would discover the true democratic republic.

This promise, however, had two edges. If it expressed the more idealistic side of the early Republican party, it also served to convince many persons in the North as well as the South that the Republicans threatened the existing order. By treating antislavery as a way to national regeneration, Republicans such as Godwin gave to their party the appearance of moral fervor similar to that of the abolitionists. In his essay, "Kansas Must Be Free," Godwin described the controversy over slavery as "one of conflicting civilizations," involving the fate of a "master-wrong," which would decide the future of the nation: "Slavery and freedom cannot both be national. . . . If slavery is not a local thing, peculiar to some of the states, then freedom is local and peculiar." From the Republican point of view, it was plain that Godwin spoke of containing, not abolishing, slavery. He had not lost his earlier hostility to "the 'fevered' abolition sentiments of New England." Given the tensions of the times, however, it was hardly surprising that his views, like Lincoln's later "House-Divided" speech, should strengthen southern fears of the Republican party and so pose the dread prospect of national disunity, secession, and civil war.[15]

One of those men who took this prospect seriously was Bryant's old friend and ally, Theodore Sedgwick, III. Theodore had been the editor's chief lieutenant in the battles against both Bank Democrats and Hunkers, but after 1848 the two men had gone their separate ways. Unlike Bryant, Sedgwick remained firmly committed to the Democratic party throughout the 1850s. Preoccupied with a lucrative legal practice and the preparation of a textbook on constitutional and statutory law, he played no role in politics until 1857 when briefly he edited the newly established *Harper's Weekly,* a magazine aligned in its editorial policies with wealthy conservatives in New York and Boston, chiefly merchants involved in the booming southern trade. Like most of these conservatives, Sedgwick was what Bryant contemptuously called a "Union Saver" prepared to make concessions to the South in order to preserve national unity.

Although he shared Bryant's concern with political corruption, he treated the question of reform as distinct from the slavery issue. On that issue, he warned again and again, northerners must compromise or risk driving the South into disunion. The real danger to national progress was not the Slave Power but the "wild frenzies" of the antislavery men, who had reacted violently to an institution that at worst was only a marginal threat to northern interests. He urged the North to acquiesce to the controversial Dred Scott decision (which the *Post* condemned as making slavery "a Federal institution, the common patrimony and shame of all the states,") because that decision would have "no practical effects injurious to our tranquility, or to our institutions." (Sedgwick argued that the ruling that Negroes were not federal citizens simply conformed with prevailing prejudices throughout the nation.) It was senseless, then, to agitate against slavery, especially since the peculiar institution was already being eliminated by the "immutable laws" of supply and demand. The free states, he argued, had nothing to lose by making concessions to the South and much to gain, for "when the sun of compromise in this country shall set, it will rise on a scene of civil conflict, and, in a probability, of bloody strife."[16]

Sedgwick's death in December 1859 saved him from the sight of the strife he feared, but death unfortunately did not save him from involvement in that kind of political situation that served to make Republicans. In late 1857 President Buchanan appointed him as federal district attorney for the Fourteenth District of New York to replace one John McKeon, who had been removed after he aided political reformers in defeating the controversial Fernando Wood as mayor of New York City. The appointment provoked a brief flurry of criticism, chiefly because it was identified with Buchanan's use of the patronage power to punish political dissent. "If Theodore Sedgwick accepts an appointment under the circumstances," warned the Berkshire *American,* "there will be a commotion in the old burying ground in Stockbridge, if the Sedgwick ghosts are not ashamed to come to earth again." He accepted the appointment.

Sedgwick's old friends had reason to disapprove even of the manner in which the Senate approved his nomination. Initially, the appointment was opposed not only by Republicans but by some southern Senators who remembered that he had opposed the annexation of Texas. In the end, however, he narrowly won Senate approval, twenty-nine to twenty-five—with the help of Senator Slidell of Louisiana and with the aid of a testimonial from an old Hunker that he had not broken with the Democratic party during the Free-Soil revolt. Less than two years later, he was dead at the age of forty-eight. *Harper's Weekly* praised its ex-editor as "emphatically a gentleman, in the old sense of the term," but ironically this magazine, which took pride in its illustrations, did not publish his portrait, for it found that "neither family nor friends possessed any likeness of the deceased." There was no poem from Bryant lamenting Sedgwick's death as there had been for Leggett some twenty years before.[17]

Sedgwick's position was for him realistic, but his realism seemed little more than moral obtuseness to men such as Bryant and Godwin who had learned to hate the Slave Power as an oligarchic threat to the liberal ideal. During the political campaign of 1856, the *Post* had compared the slavery controversy to the dispute over the "Money Power" during the 1830s: "The strife is not more sectional now than before. Then it was the effort of capital chiefly held at the North struggling against democratic principle"; now, it was a similar effort by those whose capital consisted of slaves. If essentially the controversy was not sectional, then, why should there be any real prospect of disunity? Republicans were simply trying to destroy the political influence of the Slave Power in national politics: "It is that slavery which we are to throw off, by a great concentrated effort, not the slavery of their black work-people, who must wait till Providence, in its own good time, shall interfere for them." Could not Americans generally recognize that the Republican party was an agency of defense, not a threat to the vital interests of the slaveholding states?[18]

Neither Bryant nor Godwin were ignorant of hostility shown the Republican party by southern leaders. Bryant's friend, William Gilmore Simms, by the 1850s had become a secessionist who defended slavery as eternally necessary for the Negro. But both Republicans were so preoccupied with the Slave Power idea that they failed to appreciate the depth and extent of southern feelings. When in 1859, for instance, John Brown launched his abortive effort to revolutionize the slaves of Virginia, the *Post* denounced the action but praised the man as showing "a nobleness and magnanimity of conduct such as we venerate in Plutarch's heroes." It even justified Brown's raid as a tit-for-tat response to such violent acts of the Slave Power as "Bully" Brooks' caning of Charles Summer in the Senate in 1856: "Brown is only a disciple of its own school." This kind of editorializing led the Washington *Constitution,* the official journal of the Buchanan administration, to damn the *Post:*

> With that journal the inky stream of deep and ruthless hatred flows on without ebb, and there is no calamity to which the South might be subjected over which it would not rejoice with savage exultation.... It is not fanaticism; it is not delusion; it is that 'study of revenge, immortal hate' ascribed to Satan in his fall from Heaven.

Bryant denied the charge, but in December the *Post* used the occasion of Brown's execution again to commend the man's heroism, fortitude, and hatred of oppression: "It is to such qualities as these, and not to the holy horror of mere disorder, that we owe our existence as a nation." Who would guess that in southern eyes Brown had threatened not "mere disorder" but that most horrible of all civil disorders, servile insurrection and race war? In the *Post* Brown was given a symbolic role more pleasing to the Republican eye, that of challenger of, and martyr to, the Slave Power.[19]

Because they conceived of their party as an agency of defense and reform, Republicans such as Bryant in 1859 and 1860 underestimated the seriousness of the sectional crisis excited by the prospect of a Republican victory in the national elections. Although he expressed some concern for national unity, Bryant gave more attention to the nature and appeal of the party, particularly to the problem posed by the persistent Whiggism of such Republican chiefs as William H. Seward and his partner, Thurlow Weed. Many ex-Democrats feared that the Whigs might gain control of the party with their obnoxious ideas, particularly when in 1859 Republicans supported efforts to re-establish the protective tariff. Bryant was disturbed. "Democratic Republicans regard their principles as essential to liberty," he warned, "and therefore more vital than the question of slavery itself." His meaning was clear: a successful Whig effort to use the party to propagate Whiggism would revive the old party antagonism and so jeopardize the chances of victory in 1860.

Since 1860 was a presidential election year, the intraparty rivalry centered on the nomination for the presidency. The leading contender for the nomination early in the year was Seward, who posed for Bryant and other ex-Democrats in New York the chilling prospect of Whig domination of both the national and state Republican parties. The best way to block a Seward victory was to find a powerful challenger. Bryant found his man in a state with which he had strong financial and emotional ties, Illinois. Abraham Lincoln, it is true, was himself an ex-Whig, devoted to the memory of Henry Clay, the apostle of protectionism; but at least he was not Seward. So it was natural that Bryant should agree to introduce Lincoln when in February 1860 the onetime rail-splitter came to New York to win eastern support in his bid for the presidential nomination.[20]

At the mass meeting at Cooper Union, Bryant himself was introduced by his friend, fellow Berkshirite, and fellow ex-Democrat, David Dudley Field. The poet–editor experienced a triumph. When Field instructed the audience, "Those of you who are in favor of Mr. Bryant will say aye," there was a thunderous "aye." "Those of you who are not in favor will say no." There was silence. "There is no No." Amid "laughter and applause," Bryant came forward, this shy man, now for a brief time "Mr. Republican," to introduce the greatest Republican of them all. Thinking perhaps of his brothers in Illinois, he presented Lincoln as a child of the "Great West," which "is a potent auxiliary in the battle we are fighting for Freedom against Slavery; in behalf of civilization against barbarism." For a moment, the bearded poet and the gangling prairie lawyer, the ex-Democrat and the ex-Whig, stood together on the platform, summing up between them the better nature of the Republican party.

Lincoln pleased his New York audience by ignoring the conventional economic and political issues in order to hammer away at the Slave Power as the aggressor and to emphasize the point that the Republicans, far from being dangerous radicals, were simply defending the American tradition. This was the kind of language Bryant wanted to hear. Privately, he called the Cooper Union Address the best political speech he had ever heard. Lincoln, having won the editor's goodwill, took care to keep it. On his return to Springfield, knowing that his words would reach Bryant's ears, Lincoln said: "It is worth a visit from Springfield... to New York to make the acquaintance of such a man as William Cullen Bryant." Lincoln gained a powerful ally.[21] When Lincoln won the nomination, the *Post* not only lauded him as "a personification of the distinctive genius of our country and its institutions," but lent the name of its august editor to head the Lincoln electoral ticket. Lincoln's victory in November 1860 was interpreted by Bryant as a successful conclusion to the revolt against the Slave Power that he had helped initiate in 1844; the American people, "by deciding boldly and firmly" for the Republican policy of containment, had effectively closed the slavery issue. With supreme confidence in this conclusion, he even warned that the election had destroyed the original bond of Republican unity; now party members had to find a substitute for their common hostility to the Slave Power in a common devotion to "the public welfare."[22]

The meaning of this warning became apparent when shortly after the election a struggle for power broke out between the Sewardites and ex-Democrats. Remembering how patronage apparently had been abused by the Polk and Pierce administrations, both Bryant and Godwin tried to use their influence to keep Seward out of Lincoln's cabinet. When the President-elect ignored their advice and appointed Seward as his secretary of state, Bryant proposed that Lincoln appoint the ex-Democrat, Salmon P. Chase, to the Treasury as a "counterpoint" to Seward's influence. This was done, but, when the patronage victories were totalled up, the former Democrats had won no better than a draw, a failure that had its effect even in the offices of the *Post*. Godwin had hoped to be appointed to the American consulate in Paris; instead, the post eventually went to Bryant's associate, John Bigelow, who had Seward's support. Godwin's failure completed his reconciliation with Bryant, since he took Bigelow's place as an editor and part-owner of the *Post*; but this was small consolation for the success of the Sewardites in winning a sizable share of Republican power. The whole question of patronage and power, however, soon was overshadowed by a new danger far more threatening than Whiggism.[23]

Secession, civil war—these threats the *Post* had discounted during the campaign as resting on the bluff and bluster of a small minority of southerners who had neither the will nor the power to put their words into effect. Settle the slavery issue by voting Lincoln into office, Bryant argued, and the majority of southerners would accept the results of the election. Republican control of the national government, the editor had predicted comfortingly, would even encourage southern unionists and antislavery men to challenge the Slave Power within its own dominions. He ridiculed the fears of such "Union Savers" as his old friends, Verplanck and Tilden, who like Theodore Sedgwick had convinced themselves that only a Republican defeat would preserve the Union. Although out of respect for friendship and fair play Bryant permitted Tilden to publish his warnings in the *Post,* the editor also took the trouble to refute his friend's arguments.

When Tilden learned that Lincoln had won the election, he appeared, "pale, haggard, and preoccupied," at the offices of the *Post*. There he was teased by some of his Republican acquaintances for his gloomy predictions. Finally, he could take it no longer. "I would not have the responsibility of William Cullen Bryant and John Bigelow," he told his tormentors, "for all the wealth in the sub-treasury. If you have your way, civil war will divide this country, and you will see blood running like water in the streets of this city."

Impossible! It could not happen!! The next day the *Post* reported that secessionists in South Carolina had set the machinery in motion that would carry that state out of the Union in December. By early February 1861 all seven states of the Lower South had seceded. The contest that the *Post* predicted had come to an end in fact had only begun. What would the future bring? In December 1861, a year after the secession of South Carolina, Godwin thought he saw the answer: "God's hand is in the whole thing more clearly than I ever before saw it in human affairs.

Slavery is doomed." The Republican revolt against the politicians was about to become a revolution.[24]

THE DEATH OF SLAVERY

Time passes and men die. In April 1860 Bryant rose before the New-York Historical Society to eulogize Washington Irving, who had died the previous year. Now the surviving member of the triumvirate that had made America's "literary springtime" in the 1820s, the poet paused to note the changes that had taken place in American life since those earlier and simpler days:

> The new inventions bring new calamities, and men perish in crowds by the recoil of their own devices. War has learned more frightful modes of havoc, and armed himself with deadlier weapons; armies are borne to the battle field and dashed against each other and destroyed with infinite bloodshed. We grow giddy with this perpetual whirl of strange events, these rapid and ceaseless mutations; the earth seems to reel under our feet.[1]

Just how giddy and how destructive the world was, Bryant had yet to learn. Even in the face of the secession of South Carolina in late 1860, he clung to the hope that disunion would not, could not, occur. Let "Union Savers" such as Tilden scurry in search of a last-minute compromise; Bryant advised a policy of "wise and masterly inactivity" and saw no need for constitutional amendments to protect the South. He thought that the traditional constitution, if redeemed from the perversions of politicians and slaveholders, already provided sufficient protection for all, including slavery as a local institution within the states. If only the federal government would enforce the laws as if nothing had changed, then those who had chosen to secede "out of mere jealous irritation and prejudice" would have time to reconsider, the majority of southerners (who had nothing to gain from the mad plans of a few slaveholders) would rally in favor of the Union, and in six months secessionism "would subside like the fretful impatience of a child."[2]

Bryant, himself a man of rigid self-control, could not appreciate the passionate power of pride, anger, and fear. Having forgotten his own militant zeal as a member of a self-conscious minority more than forty-five years before, he did not understand that southerners felt that they were defending home and homeland. Thus, when the guns boomed at Fort Sumter on 12 April 1861, he denounced the Confederate attack as an act of deliberate and unprovoked treason. In his poem "Not Yet," published in the summer, he urged all Americans to unite against the rebellion:

> Oh country, marvel of the earth!
>   O realm to sudden greatness grown!
> The age that gloried in thy birth,
>   Shall it behold thee overthrown?
> Shall traitors lay the greatness low?
>   No, land of Hope and Blessing, No!

The land of opportunity laid low by traitors—this was the heart of the dogma that was to govern the attitudes of Bryant and other Republicans. They believed that the Republican party was the party of American reform, that essential to that reform was the destruction of the Slave Power and the containment of slavery. Lincoln's election in 1860 was, then, a victory for national purity. As democrats and Americans, slaveholders should have acquiesced to the decision for reform, since that decision did not threaten their vital interests. By choosing secession, they proved the Republican charge that, far from simply trying to protect slavery, they had conspired to nationalize it. Having failed in this effort, now they were committing the unforgivable sin of seeking to destroy both democracy and the nation itself.[3]

The logic of this "Conspiracy Theory" soon led Bryant down the road to abolitionism. In the 1850s he had dissociated himself from the abolitionists, being careful to stress that he and his fellow Republicans were fighting to protect the freedom of white men, not to advance that of Negroes. Now that the Slave Power had committed the final sin of bloody rebellion, however, the editor readily concluded that the basic evil, slavery itself, must be destroyed. In January 1861 he warned southerners that if they persisted in their efforts to establish the Confederacy, their acts would "prove the suicide of slavery." A year later, as the Union armies began to accumulate large numbers of escaped or captured slaves, he urged the government to support the "practical emancipation" brought about by Union conquests of slave territory. To the fears of the "Union Savers" that a war against slavery would intensify southern resistance Bryant had a ready answer based on the prewar analysis of the slavery controversy: the majority of southerners had been dragged into war against their will by the Slave Power; destroy the foundations of that power, and the majority would be able to affect its will to work for peace. Moreover, emancipation was a necessary step toward the primary Republican goal, the regeneration of American society. On 4 March 1862, editorializing on Lincoln's first year in office, the *Post* called for a crusade to end slavery:

> It is yet to be shown whether we are in reality worthy of the great duty that has been laid upon us ...; whether this war is the sublimest event of the nineteenth century, or is to be allowed to dwindle into a sham and a farce; whether it is to regenerate our society thoroughly or merely to restore us to that state of venal policies and low morality out of which we have been caught for a time by its lofty enthusiasms; whether we are wise enough to terminate forever the hideous system which has been the cause of all our past corruption and degradation.[4]

In June Bryant, less than three years from his seventieth birthday, accepted the presidency of the New York Emancipation Society. When in September Lincoln made his preliminary commitment to emancipation, both Bryant and Godwin came strongly to his support.[5] (It was Godwin who, at the Republican-Union party's state convention at Syracuse, reported the platform and praised the Emancipation Proclamation. When the party lost the state elections to the Democrats, who opposed emancipation, the *Post* attributed the defeat to popular resentment of the indecisive war policies of the Lincoln administration, not to hostility to emancipation.) The *Post* praised the Preliminary Emancipation Proclamation as returning the nation to its true nature:

> It is only now that we begin to feel our own greatness truly, as a part of the human family, called upon to wake up from a long dream of

happiness and prosperity on a false basis, and to renew our social life in the proportions required by the vast improvements of the modern times.

And in January, when the proclamation (freeing all slaves in rebel territory) went into effect, the newspaper made acceptance of emancipation virtually a test of loyalty: "Either we must give up our Union or give up slavery."[6]

There were many northerners, however, who felt that the choice was not between the Union and slavery but between the Union and emancipation—men wearied of the apparently endless war, men who were hostile to Republicans, abolitionists, and Negroes, men sympathetic to the South, all anxious to end the bloodshed in the hope of restoring through compromise the old Union as it was. In 1863 the strength and activity of Peace Democrats and the almost treasonable "Copperheads" in New York City seemed to grow day by day. Having been defeated in the state elections in November 1862, Republicans and War Democrats were in no mood to tolerate "Copperheadism," as the *Post* made plain when in February it denounced a meeting of Peace Democrats headed by Samuel J. Tilden as a "Reactionist Conspiracy" that aided the rebellion. Nor was Tilden the only one of Bryant's old friends to feel the lash of war-born zeal, for the next year Verplanck suffered for the third and last time loss of office for his stubborn adherence to his version of the right.[7]

Verplanck had intended to withdraw permanently from active politics when he refused to run for re-election in 1841. At the very time that Bryant was being drawn into national politics by the slavery issue, the New Yorker had retired into the close and fading Knickerbocker world he knew so well. He had founded the Century Club as a way of preserving that world, but even in "the Century," he could not escape the passions and prejudices of a society at war. A man of tolerance, accustomed to the easy-going ways of the face-to-face politics of early New York, he had little sympathy for mass movements in general and none for abolitionism, believing that the abolitionists could do little actually to benefit the slave, while they most definitely did damage the spirit of compromise and accommodation needed to preserve the Union. With the rise of the Republican party, he became a Democrat and "Union Saver." "Old Verplanck," wrote George Templeton Strong in 1856, "has pronounced for Buchanan! Talks like a filibuster, a South Carolinian, Brooks, or Captain Rynders. Marvelous, but gratifying. I never knew old G. C. Verplanck to be on the winning side anywhere."[8]

During the war, Verplanck condemned the Lincoln administration for its arbitrary arrests of suspected traitors and also for its resort to paper money as legal tender. So did Bryant, but the editor subordinated his dissatisfaction to the overriding objectives of the war. Verplanck wanted peace. By 1863 he had aligned himself with two journals that the *Post* denounced as Copperhead and proslavery, the New York *World* and the *Knickerbocker Magazine*. What was worse, he could not keep his hostility to the war out of his role as president of the Century Club, where he was the leader of a substantial peace faction. As such, he proved intolerable to many of the younger members, and in February 1864 this man who had been the guiding spirit of the club was voted out of office by a great majority in favor of the New Englander, George Bancroft.[9]

Bryant opposed the move, but even he later conceded that his friend was blind to the great issues of the war. The attitude of the majority was probably best expressed by George W. Curtis in *Harper's Monthly*. The removal was regrettable, wrote Curtis, since Verplanck was "a true Knickerbocker," but with the Union in peril, "indifference is impossible. . . . Such indifference is the most positive partisanship. It is passive co-operation with the assault. It is strength withdrawn from the resistance; and when every man counts it must be, and will be, and ought to be treated accordingly." G. T. Strong agreed with the general judgment, though he hardly considered Verplanck to be passive: "How unpleasant it is to vote for a snob like Bancroft, and against my old friend Verplanck! But Verplanck's Copperhead talk is intolerable. . . . He does not see how times have changed and how fast they are changing. He looks on the great national movement that is growing stronger every day and already controls the conduct of the war just as he looked on the ravings of. . . the Abolition Society twenty-five years before." Such was the fate of a man who had adjusted too well to a world that was passing away.[10]

Verplanck's fellow peace men in the club bitterly resented this triumph of what one of them called the "puritanical faction," and retaliated by unsuccessfully trying to blackball the next Republican who applied for membership; ironically the near victim of their rage was that old enemy of puritanic zeal, Parke Godwin. Verplanck took his defeat with his usual good grace and outward equanimity, but how must he have felt when in November the "puritanical faction" gathered at the club to celebrate Bryant's seventieth birthday? Bryant was applauded both as a poet and a patriarch of the great movement that had swept his friend aside. One of the many poems sent to honor his birthday concluded:

> Before thee Error howled and fled,
>   And in thy path, though bold and strong,
> Oppression quailed. From thy hand sped
>   The glittering shafts that crippled wrong...
>
> O may thy happy eyes behold
>
> Fair Freedom's triumph, and hold the sway
>   Of Peace, which after strife and pain,
> Shall usher the illustrious day
>   Of a great People born again.

Verplanck sent only a letter coldly declining an invitation to attend the celebration, because "peculiar circumstances put it out of my power to be present."[11]

"A Great People born again"—it was this hope that the death of slavery would regenerate America that preserved Bryant and Godwin from much of the anxiety and disgust so evident in Verplanck's criticisms. But what was to protect that hope from the frustrations of a prolonged war? By the spring and summer of 1864, as the Confederacy fought on, the two editors feared that the mounting war-weariness of northerners might force a peace without victory. From the Berkshires in that year came a letter from Catherine Sedgwick, who had initially supported the war, calling for men "of great brains and clean hands" to restore the peace. Having lost a nephew at the battle of Antietam, she had no desire to continue the bloodshed. "Why not act," she asked Bryant, "like sensible Christians in common affairs? Let bygones be bygones?— declare boundaries—agree upon some mode of settlement?"[12]

Such attitudes were doubly disturbing in 1864, the year of a presidential election. How to keep the Republicans in, and the Peace Democrats out, of national power? This question particularly bothered New York Republicans, since New York City was a stronghold of peace sentiment, which had tipped the last state elections in favor of the Democrats. Early in 1864 both Bryant and Godwin concluded that the Democrats drew much of their strength from public dissatisfaction with the indecisive policies of the Lincoln administration. On 21 March the *Post* urged Republicans and War Democrats to postpone their Union National Convention scheduled for 7 June: "Should our affairs continue to prosper, then Lincoln will continue in the favor he now enjoys. . . . But if we shall encounter only reverses and calamities, would Mr. Lincoln then be the proper standard bearer of the loyal party?"[13] If necessary, the Great Emancipator was to be sacrificed to the cause of emancipation and reunion. But Lincoln's critics had neither the power nor the candidate to replace him. When the Union convention met at Baltimore as scheduled and renominated the president, Bryant acquiesced, although not with much grace. Godwin hardly acquisced at all. In August he joined with his old Fourierist ally Horace Greeley and with David Dudley Field to circulate privately a proposal for another Union convention to consider replacing Lincoln with a stronger candidate, possibly General Grant. The movement, however, faded away with the news of Sherman's victories in Georgia. Forced to choose between a strengthened Lincoln and General McClelland, who had been nominated by the Democrats on a peace program, the dissidents backed the Emancipator.[14]

Lincoln's success in carrying all but three states in the November elections indicated that neither Bryant nor Godwin had accurately gauged public opinion in the country at large, but their fears for New York were largely validated by the fact that the president won the state by less than 7,000 votes, having lost New York City by more than a two-to-one margin. Whatever the state of politics in 1864, Lincoln's re-election marked the end of uncertainty and doubt. By the end of the year, the promise of victory, held off for so long, was rapidly becoming reality as the hammer blows of Sherman and Grant reduced the Confederacy to rubble. Bryant was elated. On 1 January 1865, he urged the Union army to hasten the advent of that new era he had long awaited:

> Be strong; be hopeful! Your crowning triumph cannot be far distant. When it arrives, our nation will have wiped out a dark stain and will stand in the sight of the world a noble commonwealth of freemen bound together by ties which will last as long as the common sympathies of our race.[15]

Both Bryant and his son-in-law hoped that the new era would be very much like the old liberal ideal. The death of slavery, they dreamed, would reopen the way to the old Republic of moral and happy individuals, free from the corrupting influence of power. In March, with victory in sight, the *Post* urged Lincoln to concentrate not only on completing the wartime goals of reunion and emancipation but also on solving the problem posed by the "enormous and almost unlimited centralization of functions and forces" produced by the war. Already, Bryant and Godwin were beginning to look forward to a return to conventional economic and political interests, now that the "dark stain" was in the process of being eradicated.[16]

Emancipation, however, brought the new and perplexing problem of integrating the freed Negro into a society predominantly white. Although neither Bryant nor Godwin had totally ignored Negroes in the past, much of their interest in Negroes had been forced on them by the slavery controversy. Were southerners right when they argued that the natural inferiority of blacks made their enslavement natural and necessary? Bryant and other anti-slavery men thought not; to them, much of the Negro's inferiority, far from being natural, was in fact the product of slavery itself. But few were prepared to follow this line of reasoning to Harry Sedgwick's conclusion that Negroes were fundamentally equal to whites. In 1853, for instance, the *Post* attempted to answer southern arguments by serializing the "complete study of the comparative anatomy and psychology of the Negro" made by Hermann Burmeister, a German zoologist. Burmeister concluded that Negroes were not so inferior as to justify their enslavement, but he also asserted that "the black man is hardly capable of elevating himself to the heights of civilization." Two months later the *Post* concurred with both statements when it said in reference to the degrading influence of slavery that "the disproportion between whites and blacks intellectually is great by nature; we never could see the propriety of increasing it by legislation."[17]

During the Civil War, when black troops fought and died to suppress the treason of white slaveholders, the *Post* adopted a more favorable view of Negroes, particularly when it seemed necessary to defend the practicability of emancipation. Slavery, Bryant argued, had encouraged slaves to be indolent and irresponsible. Destroy the slave system, treat Negroes as free men, and they will respond as free men, for they were "human beings operated upon by the same motives that control others." Early in 1866, he even went so far as to argue that the "natural effect of a state of freedom" would be to place the wealth and power of the South in Negro hands, because the freedmen were "laborious, orderly, temperate," while "southern whites are indolent, proud, disorderly, with constitutions tainted by an hereditary thirst for whiskey."

Throughout this period, Bryant's attitudes, like those of many other

Americans, were influenced less by what Negroes actually were than by what he believed, under the circumstances, Negroes should be. With the death of slavery, he hoped that the nation would soon return to the conventional economic and political issues, particularly to those wartime policies that threatened the liberal system established before the dispute over slavery reoriented politics. Could white Americans rid themselves of the centralization, the tariff, the taxes, and the paper money produced by the war, if, because of the Negro's inability to stand as a free man, they had to concentrate on the race problem? The freedmen, therefore, *had* to have the ability to stand on their own feet with little support from the federal government.[18]

Both Bryant and Godwin did believe that the crusade against slavery included the commitment to establish the principle of equality for all races. Bryant had long favored granting Negroes in New York equal voting rights with white men as a way of strengthening the equal rights principle. In 1860 the *Post* pointed out that this would have little practical effect, since the proportion of Negroes in New York was small. Despite such assurances New Yorkers rejected proposals to abolish voting discrimination by some 140,000 votes in 1846 and again in 1860. On the other hand, in 1865 and later the editors opposed federal efforts to impose complete Negro suffrage on the South, fearing that such efforts threatened, as Godwin put it, "the danger of dangers," the further centralization of power. They preferred to entrust southerners with the race problem. Bryant proposed that the nation commit itself to equal rights by ratifying the Fourteenth Amendment, leaving the states and the courts to protect those rights.[19] Bryant argued that the provision in the Amendment reducing a state's representation in Congress and the Electoral College in proportion to that part of its population denied the right to vote would encourage the southern states to enfranchise Negroes. This provision, if it had ever been enforced, would have had little effect on northern states, where the population of Negroes was small. Once the amendment was ratified, once the principle was enshrined in the Constitution along with the abolition of slavery, "then the Negro question will be settled, and the nation would turn to other matters." The alternative was the use of force, which threatened not only to increase the power of the federal government but also to stir up a new version of the old slave controversy, which for so long had disordered politics.[20]

Fortunately, perhaps, for his peace of mind, Bryant had little editorial responsibility when in 1867 Congress, under the domination of the Radical Republicans, rejected his conservative solution and intensified efforts to reorganize southern political society by force. Soon after his wife died in September 1866, he left on a ten-month tour of Europe. When he returned the following September he effectively removed himself from political matters for much of the next four years in order to concentrate on his last great literary endeavor, the translation of the *Iliad* and the *Odyssey*. His few references to Reconstruction during these years, however, indicate that he had had his fill of the Negro question. In June 1868 he urged his old Democratic-Republican ally, Salmon P. Chase, who had returned to the Democratic party, to prevail upon that party to accept the "policy" of Negro suffrage as both just and necessary for "domestic peace." Soon afterwards, when he learned that the Republicans had nominated General Grant for the presidency, he expressed the hope that Grant's election would convince southerners that they would have to accept the principle of equal treatment for Negroes. Bryant was an old man who sought domestic peace and dreamed that the lurid and disturbing book of slavery would be closed forever.[21]

The nightmare of the Grant administration strengthened Bryant's desire to end the controversy. Far from bringing peace and a return to reform, Grant's election ushered in eight years of tumult, corruption, and bad policy both in the national government and in the South. Bryant—already hostile to the Radical experiment in imposing Negro suffrage on the South—showed little sympathy for the Radical regimes that appeared as a result of that experiment. When in 1875 federal power (in the form of General Sheridan) intervened to protect the Radical regime in Louisiana, the editor was enraged. He helped to organize a meeting in New York to protest the intervention, warning in the *Post* that "the country cannot always endure the questionable experiments which have been making for ten years. There must be an end to this theory, or there will be an end to the Republic in its original purity." Just as earlier he had joined the Republican crusade in the conviction that the Slave Power was the enemy of reform, now he abandoned the crusade in the belief that Reconstruction seriously interferred with needed efforts to maintain the Republic.[22]

Prior to 1865 Bryant's sympathies for Negroes as victims of the Slave Power had grown stronger; now they diminished as Negroes became identified with Radicals and spoilsmen. Once the editor had viewed southern white leaders as victimizers; now he saw them as victims of harsh and corrupting forces. Bryant's personal experiences strengthened his distaste for Reconstruction. In 1868 he had renewed his friendship with William Gilmore Simms, and in the same year, on Simms' recommendation, he hired the one-time editor of the *Southern Literary Messenger*, John R. Thompson, as literary editor of the *Post*. Memories of the favor shown his poetry by the South before the war were revived, and other memories as well. When in the spring of 1873 he traveled through the Southeast on his way to Florida, he fell in love with the region, just as he had done in the 1840s. On this trip he noted that Negroes seemed less healthy and more poorly clad than during the days of slavery, and he did not perceive any compensatory improvement in character and intelligence. To the end he officially held to the hope that education and experience would ultimately redeem the Negro from the effects of slavery, but he put his hope in the distant future beyond the sphere of his own life. If little could be done in the present, then why trouble the politics and consciences of whites? In 1875 he wrote off-handedly in reference to the prospect of closer relations with the Chinese ("our pig-tailed brethren"): "I prefer the Caucasian race. The Negroes are a source of trouble, and there is no knowing what may happen as a consequence of the mutual jealousy of the races." In sum, he had concluded that it was senseless to stir up sectional and racial antagonisms in a vain effort to achieve an artificial equality between the races.[23]

The *Post* criticized the Civil Rights Bill of 1875 as at best ineffectual and at worst an inflammatory interference with the natural relations between the races. It applauded those who opposed a provision for integrated schools: "Intelligent observers ... agree that the establishment of mixed schools in the South would defeat all plans for public education of blacks. If free schools were required by law to be thrown open without distinction of color, there would probably be no free schools in some states." It placed its hopes in "separate schools" with "equal facilities," essentially that "separate but equal" doctrine that in the future was to permit the South to segregate the Negro in a decidedly unequal position.[24]

Such attitudes can be attributed to the hardening of an old man's mind, yet there was also a reflection of both past and future feelings in the United States. White Americans were long accustomed to conceive of their nation as a white man's society with white man's problems.

It was natural that Bryant and even the more humane Godwin should treat the problem of racial adjustment as tangential to the main issues of the day. Neither the editor nor his son-in-law repudiated the anti-slavery commitment to establish the principle of legal equality, but by 1875 both were satisfied with the embodiment of that principle in the Fourteenth and Fifteenth amendments. The implementation of the principle was left to the states, to individuals, and to nature.

Bryant and Godwin interpreted Reconstruction in the traditional terms of liberal democracy: federal intervention, directed by politicians, had produced the corruption and disorder; the solution to racial and sectional problems was to end such interference, so as to permit the natural order to work out the proper relations between the races. It had been necessary to destroy slavery, because, like the system of economic privilege, it had obstructed the natural order, but, now that this had been done, further efforts to force the advances toward freedom would prove self-defeating. It was true that Negroes, once deprived of federal protection would fall under the influence and control of upper-class whites, but this was simply a natural relationship. "Men of superior culture and position," said Godwin in 1877, "always exercise a sort of unconscious despotism over their inferiors, and it is hardly to be regretted." Such subordination would not mean any greater inequality than already existed among white men. Basic Negro rights—the freedoms needed for self-development—would be preserved by competition, competition for Negro labor and competition between parties for Negro votes. "We do not see how society at the South," said the *Post* in reference to the final withdrawal of federal troops from the South in 1877, "can escape the natural laws which control society elsewhere."[25]

Bryant admitted that white prejudice was a danger, but he argued that with the abolition of slavery—the chief source of prejudice as he saw it—intelligent southern whites would eventually recognize that fair treatment of Negroes would benefit both themselves and their region. Characteristically, Godwin adopted the more general line that the end of slavery had radically altered the entire social system of the South, forcing men to alter their opinions and their ways in order eventually to conform with the new reality. Neither man ventured to predict how long this natural process would take before the Negro received the rights reserved for him in the Fourteenth and Fifteenth amendments. Neither gave much thought to the Negro's tomorrow.[26]

On such a note did the antislavery movement end. Bryant had once conceived of the Civil War in terms of apocalypse—as a divinely decreed event that ripped asunder the ordinary fabric of history in order to regenerate the spirit of man. The war was a turning point in American life, to be fought "until the grand dragon shall be bound and cast into a pit." A stirring thought—but apocalypses have their ends, their definite conclusions, and if extended beyond their time lose their inherent drama. For Bryant and Godwin, the drama ended with the death of the great dragon, slavery. The aftermath, Reconstruction, had little emotional appeal; the apocalypse had dwindled into a dirty tempest in the mundane realm of politics. The crusade was over. The death of slavery, said the *Post* on Thanksgiving day in 1875, had created a "new order of things.... We are more truly a united and homogeneous people than we have been at any time during the last half century.... There is now no longer a disturbing difference in creed and practice between the citizens of the North and those of the South." The time had come for reconciliation among Americans long divided. The race problem? That was not important. The real problems to be faced and conquered were the traditional economic and political problems of white America.[27]

THE END OF REFORM (1870-80)

In 1875, when the *Evening Post* moved into its imposing new building at Fulton Street and Broadway, it took the occasion to celebrate the fiftieth anniversary of Bryant's first contributions to its pages, noting with pride that since that day "it has enjoyed many triumphs of its guiding principles. In the new era which begins to-day, it forecasts the enjoyment of many more." It then presented a long list of triumphs for the cause of political purity and free trade. Like the editor whom it celebrated, the *Post* proudly adhered to past principles, questioning neither the principles nor the views of human nature and the social order on which they were based. In ideas and style it had become, in the words of a member of its staff in the 1870s, "an old fashioned newspaper of uncondescending, uncomprising dignity . . . conducted by gentlemen for gentlemen." It is true that in 1875 it made an effort, by reducing its price from five cents to three, to reach "the greater multitude who are compelled to labor with little leisure, " but its voice remained that of men whom the past had treated well, who saw in their successes indications of the progressive tendencies of the existing social order.[1]

Bryant himself had reason to be satisfied that the principles he had long advocated were the basis for progress, for the past had brought him both fame and fortune. Poetry, most of it written decades before, had made him an American institution. Journalism had given him influence and wealth. By the late 1860s, he was finally able to seize the leisure for literary endeavors that for half a century he had pursued. His creative powers had dwindled but at least wealth enabled him during his few remaining years to withdraw emotionally from the social world to the world of self, which had been so strong in his younger years.

This sage and basically modest old man recognized what was occurring. On his seventieth birthday in 1864 he had remarked: "Much has been said of the wisdom of Old Age. Old Age is wise I grant for itself but not wise for the community. It is wise in declining new enterprises, for it has not the power nor the time to execute them. . . . But this is not the wisdom for mankind at large by whom new enterprises must be undertaken." The crusade against slavery was Bryant's last new enterprise. To be sure, the old enterprises remained, particularly the problems of corruption and fraud, which had spread like cancer in the war and postwar eras. Hostility to the Weeds, the Tweeds, and the whole tribe of amoral political technicians had become a reflex, sustained by decades of suspicion of government. Years of conflict had given Bryant a role he neither would nor could abandon, that of a crusader against bad measures and bad men. But the crusader had by the 1860s felt that sharp decline in zeal, which men often call the mellowing of age.

"Old Age is wise I grant for itself"—how true, for the strain of self-interest so strong in Bryant's youth had grown as the man grew old. Behind the poet and liberal worked the ambitious Yankee, who having fought his way to wealth now was anxious to preserve that wealth for his posterity. In 1870 one Rufus Peet, in a letter criticizing Bryant for not more strongly advocating free trade, touched a sensitive nerve when he noted that when Peet learned the poet was worth $500,000, " 'the poetry' of your *character* vanished." Although he normally refused to retort to such personal criticism, Bryant replied sharply with a defense of both his freetrade views and his wealth.[2]

As Godwin had already discovered, the editor could be equally defensive about his investment in the *Post*. By the 1860s the newspaper had become a million-dollar enterprise and one of the most profitable journals of its day. Having little taste for financial matters, Bryant left the business affairs of the *Post* in the hands of his partner and business manager, Isaac Henderson. Shrewd and energetic, Henderson had brought prosperity to the newspaper ever since 1850 when he had first taken on the mundane responsibility for advertising, circulation, and dividends.

But his character conformed all-too-well with the age that produced a Jay Gould and a Daniel Drew. It was Henderson who in the 1870s reportedly pulled off one of the slickest coups in the history of New York real estate; he quietly bought up an unnoticed strip of land, all of two inches wide, on Broadway and sold it for $125,000. Earlier, he had been implicated in decidedly shady dealings. During the Civil War President Lincoln had fired him as navy agent at New York on charges that he had taken rake-offs on government contracts. Tried for this alleged crime, he was acquitted—to Bryant's evident satisfaction; but Godwin was convinced that Henderson had, in fact, taken illegal "commissions" totaling perhaps as much as $100,000.

Godwin felt that the *Post* could not attack with authority the corruption of others so long as this shady character was associated with the newspaper. In 1865 he proposed to Bryant that Henderson, who owned a one-third interest in the newspaper, be eased out of its affairs. Bryant refused. Faced with a choice between his often troublesome son-in-law and a business manager who produced good dividends, he chose the manager. Three years later Godwin again sold his share in the newspaper and left, being "ideal enough," he later complained to Bryant, "to be deluded to the extent of one-hundred thousand dollars at least." Henderson somehow had acquired one-half of Godwin's share—enough to match Bryant's voting power in the enterprise.[3]

In the 1870s Godwin and Bryant did join to fight the political corruption so prevalent during these years, but again the shadow of Henderson, "the wicked partner," fell between them. In 1870 Godwin expressed his disgust with the decay of American politics in an article for *Putnam's,* part of his attack being directed against the notorious Tweed Ring. The *Post* had already joined in the rising criticism of Boss Tweed, but it was by no means an ardent challenger of his power. Why? After having published a strong attack on the Ring, Charles Nordhoff, who was serving as editor during Bryant's prolonged absence, abruptly resigned under pressure from Henderson; it was rumored that Henderson was anxious to preserve some $5,000 a month in advertising that Tweed allegedly was buying in the *Post*. Although the newspaper did not totally suspend its criticisms of the Ring, it is notable that the next year its new editor, Arthur G. Sedgwick (the son of Theodore, III), also resigned when Henderson suppressed an article censuring a member of the parks department. Bryant did not intervene in either case.[4]

Again in 1872 it was Godwin, not Bryant and the *Post,* who showed the greater zeal for political reform on the national level. Disgusted with the scandals of the Grant administration, both men joined the Liberal Republican movement to prevent Grant's renomination; but to their disappointment the movement was a fiasco, in part because of the persistence of prewar political differences. In the spring a dispute broke out in New York over the election of delegates to the new party's first national convention at Cincinnati between those who wanted to reverse the trend toward higher protective tariffs and those who wanted to nominate for the presidency the ex-Whig and persistent protectionist, Horace Greeley. The freetraders lost, and Greeley was nominated; later he also received the nomination of the Democratic party.

Embittered by Greeley's nomination, Bryant and Godwin met with other Republican free-traders at New York's Steinway Hall to consider selecting another candidate. Someone suggested publicly that Bryant, who chaired the meeting, be given the nomination, an idea the editor treated as almost as bad a joke as the Greeley candidacy. He informed the public of his feelings in a published "card":

> Certain journals of this city have lately spoken of me as one ambitious of being nominated for the Presidency of the United States. The idea is absurd enough, not only on account of my advanced years, but of my unfitness in various respects for the labors of so eminent a post....It is impossible that I should receive any formal nomination, and equally impossible, if it were offered, that I should commit the folly of accepting it.

Bryant was then seventy-seven years old. The free-trade Republicans made no nomination.[5]

The failure of the Steinway Hall conference to find some route of reform between the Scylla of Greeley and the Charybdis of Grant led to another parting of the ways for Bryant and Godwin. In the name of Republican party unity, Bryant reluctantly permitted his newspaper (Henderson was anxious to keep it Republican) to support Grant's re-election. On the other hand, Godwin joined with a few other dissidents to form the Liberal Republican Reformer's party which nominated William S. Groesbeck of Ohio for the presidency on a platform drafted by Godwin that called for civil service reform, the abolition of national nominating conventions in favor of "spontaneous nominations," and the direct election of president and vice-president. This was essentially the same platform suggested by Godwin earlier at a reform meeting in the Fifth Avenue Hotel. At this time, he had also proposed the creation of "the American Democratic-Republican party" to run Charles Francis Adams for the presidency.[6]

Bryant could hardly be blamed for refusing in 1872 to follow his son-in-law down the road to nowhere. A realist, he accepted Grant as the lesser of two evils, a position that many of his political friends could understand. Many of these friends, however, were less satisfied when in the next presidential election he again remained with the Republican party. In the spring of 1876, Bryant and Godwin met with some 200 prominent reformers at the Fifth Avenue Hotel, this time to devise some way of keeping the Republican nomination out of the grasp of a spoilsman such as James G. Blaine or Roscoe Conkling. The conferees had somewhat better luck than they had had in 1872, for the Republicans nominated Rutherford B. Hayes of Ohio.

But Godwin refused to support Hayes on the grounds that the new candidate was a front for the same old corrupt leadership that had disgraced the party under Grant. When the Democrats nominated Samuel J. Tilden, Godwin went to his support in the belief that only through a Democratic victory could the nation escape the questionable leadership and the threadbare issues inherited from the Civil War. Like other reformers, he dreamed of restoring the relatively clear-cut and vigorous two-party system that had existed before the slavery issue had disrupted the Jacksonian political patterns. In 1870 he had argued that American politics had degenerated because neither party now held "to any creed of general principles" that would govern its policies. Now in 1876 he took the position that the Democratic party under its new leadership, like the old prewar party, stood against "the enormous centralization which has grown up since the war" and stood for the "thorough regeneration of essential political practices and doctrines."[7] Godwin was not the only ex-Democrat associated with the *Post* to return to the fold, for John Bigelow, Charles Nordhoff, and David Dudley Field also supported Tilden.[8]

Bryant also favored a realignment of the parties on the basis of conventional economic and political issues, but again he refused to follow his son-in-law. Although he and Tilden had been separated by the dispute over slavery, both men by the early 1870s were anxious to end the old quarrel over a vanishing issue. Soon after his inauguration as governor of New York in 1875, Tilden sealed the renewal of their friendship by inviting Bryant to spend a week at the governor's mansion. Bryant accepted and went to Albany, there to receive both Tilden's hospitality and a royal reception from the state legislature. Political ideals as well as friendship influenced Bryant in Tilden's favor, since the two men had fought together for liberal principles as Barnburners in the 1840s. Yet, when Tilden was nominated, Bryant not only refused the request of his friend, John Bigelow, that he run as a Tilden elector but even kept the *Post* in the Republican party.

Bryant said that he saw little difference between the two parties, for, while Tilden was the better candidate, the Democratic party itself was tainted both by its record during the Civil War and by its present disposition toward the heresy of "Greenbackism," the support of paper money. If the Democrats won, Bryant argued, Tilden would be so busy handling patronage problems that he would have little opportunity to reform the government. On the other hand, Hayes, because he represented the party in power, could concentrate on removing the bad apples from the government barrel. The editor was at least partially right, for Hayes did usher in the beginnings of reform, an achievement that led Godwin back to the Republican organization in 1880.[9]

In 1876, however, John Bigelow furnished a less attractive explanation of Bryant's conduct: that the editor had been influenced by the evil genius, Henderson. "Instead of editing the *Post*," Bigelow complained of his friend, "the *Post* is editing him. He is singularly ignorant of what has been going on at Washington and Albany during the past year." Had Bryant, out of ignorance and a desire to protect his investment, yielded to Henderson? When Tilden was nominated, the *Post* had praised his candidacy. On that day, Henderson, who was anxious to keep the favor of the Republican business classes in New York, had a long discussion with Bryant over editorial policy; the next important reference the *Post* made to politics was in the form of a bitter attack on the Democratic platform. Whether it was decisive or not, the influence of the "wicked partner" was there.[10]

The lack of zeal shown by the old crusader in the war on corruption was doubly disturbing to some of his friends, since both he and they continued to conceive of reform almost exclusively in political terms. Having learned to consider government as the primary source of society's troubles, Bryant assumed that the best way to promote the public welfare was to elect honest men who would adhere to correct principles, particularly the principles of free trade. He attacked the spoilsmen not only because they stole the public's money but also because they were identified with government interference with society and the economy. Such bad policy was responsible for the major social evils. Economic instability, speculation, business frauds—each was the natural product of the greenbacks inherited from the war and of general government meddling with the monetary system. In response to high prices, economic collapse, and poverty Bryant, a president of the Free Trade League of New York as well as an editor, supplied one well-worn explanation: The artificial restraints imposed on trade by the protective tariff, that monster which "revolts against the order of nature." To the problems of the day, the old solutions applied: Let there be free trade and an end to government interference in favor of special interest groups; let natural principles prevail.[11]

There was much in Bryant's outlook that deserved preservation. At its heart wast hat guiding principle whose triumphs the *Post* had applauded in 1875, a principle that formed the essence of liberal democracy: "self-government, or the freedom of the individual in all its relations consistent with the social order." This principle Bryant helped hand on to succeeding generations. In a more limited sense, he also contributed to the making of the new reform movements, which had just begun to appear in response to the problems of the urban-industrial age. His attacks on the tariffs helped to carry over from the 1830s the concern for equal rights and the hostility to monopoly that formed the basis for almost every reform movement up through the twentieth century. The blasts he vented against tariff protectionism as a violation of equal rights and as a prop for special interest groups, for instance, influenced in a small way the thought and rhetoric of the Granger movement of the 1870s.[12]

The old liberal and the future reformers, however, were miles apart in their understandings of "monopoly." The Grangers believed themselves threatened by concentrations of private power beyond their control and turned instinctively to public power to protect themselves. On the other hand, Bryant continued to define monopoly as government-granted privilege, as a political problem produced by the interference of public power with the principles of free trade. In 1877 western farmers applauded when the Supreme Court made its landmark decision in *Munn* v.

Illinois in favor of state regulation of the railroads. The *Post* denounced the decision as encouraging the bad practices of the past. The chief danger, it warned, lay in the fact that "while the power of the state and party in power is absolute, that of the corporation is immediately restrained by questions of patronage and competition" (two years later the Standard Oil "Trust" won control of some 90 percent of the petroleum refining industry). If the decision should establish a precedent, then "we may look for misdirected public zeal guided by the arts of demagogues, and visiting the corporation with unscientific and ill-devised penalties." Power, to Bryant, meant governmental power; governmental power—and this idea went back to his Federalist youth—meant demagogues and the consequent abuse of power at the expense of the individual.[13]

So long as Bryant edited the *Post,* it remained "an old fashioned" newspaper, fighting the battles that gentlemen were accustomed to fight, ill-prepared for the new problems of poverty, labor, corporations, and immigration that had appeared with the growth of urban-industrial America. After the poet died in 1878, the *Post* temporarily acquired a new tone when Godwin took the helm. More closely attuned to city life, more aware of the complexities of society, he was better equipped than Bryant to comprehend the changing power relationships of the new age. In 1879 he took the position that businesses, particularly corporations, that had received special favors from the public should be subject to some public supervision. The next year he spoke out in favor of state regulation of railroad rates on the grounds that railroads were monopolies and warned businessmen "who are promoting large enterprises and engaging in all sorts of combinations to take thought of possible measures which may be demanded by public opinion at no distant day."

In a limited sense, here were the beginnings of a twentieth-century reformer. It is true that, despite his recognition of the growth of private power, Godwin emphasized the old liberal panaceas, hard money and free trade, in the belief that American society remained fundamentally sound and fundamentally good.[14] But in this respect he was not much different from some of the later Progressive reformers, men who sensed the dangers of the concentration of business power yet clung to traditional solutions for the problems posed by that power—men who walked backwards into the twentieth century, creating in their efforts to revive the lost world of Bryant the beginnings of a new liberalism suitable for modern times. Perhaps if Godwin had remained in control of the *Post*, he might have carried the newspaper into the new currents of reform that had started to appear in the last quarter of the nineteenth century, but this was not to be, in part because for one last time the "wicked partner" intervened.

In 1868 Henderson had had his influence trimmed when Bryant discovered that he had run up debts on the *Post* in order to finance his private business transactions. But he remained a powerful and disturbing presence in the newspaper even after Godwin became editor in 1879. After more than two years of conflict with Henderson, Godwin, who was neither very patient nor very persistent, had grown weary of his job. It was then that he discovered that Henderson was secretly negotiating the sale of his (Henderson's) shares in the newspaper to a prominent capitalist, who Godwin suspected to be the infamous Jay Gould. Anxious to avoid any association with "a notorious speculator and gambler," Godwin determined to beat Henderson to the punch by selling the Bryant family shares to a respectable group of businessmen, headed by the prominent railroad man Henry Villard, who happened to be in the market for a newspaper. Henderson was pressured into selling his shares to the group, and so, after more than fifty years of association with the newspaper, the Bryant family disappeared from its affairs. The family received $450,000 as a result of the sale; the newspaper received a more conservative cast from its longtime editor, E. L. Godkin, which left it mired in the nineteenth century. Indeed, under Godkin, it fully achieved its destiny as "an old fashioned newspaper...conducted by gentlemen for gentlemen." The old era had died. The new era was yet to be born.[15]

19

THE ROAD HOME

Old New York was dying. One wet day in March 1870, the long hand reached for Gulian C. Verplanck. After having contracted a cold, the New Yorker spent one of his usual half-nights of conversation, and shortly fell seriously ill. His regular physician was unavailable, and a young doctor whom he had never seen before came to attend him. Verplanck uncomfortably asked the young man where he had received his training. "Paris" was the answer. Apparently displeased, the old nationalist turned his face to the wall and died. He was in his eighty-fourth year.[1]

Thus New York lost a native son who had seen the eighteenth-century town grow into a modern metropolis and who loved it still with the same serene confidence of his younger days. As a scholar, clubman, and vestryman of Trinity Church, he had known some of New York's oldest and finest families; as President of the Board of Emigration from 1847 until his death, he had helped comfort some of its very newest families, refugees from the oppressions of Europe. He loved the city's virtues and tolerated its weaknesses, accepting even its political corruption as a fact of urban life. In his last public speech three years before his death, he praised Tammany Hall as a "lofty watch tower" that protected principles and people against "usurping and unscrupulous power" (Radical Reconstruction?). His listeners would not have learned from this speech that the Hall was dominated by the Tweed Ring. Scarcely attuned to the great nation that was developing outside, Verplanck found his refuge and his world in Manhattan and the lower reaches of the Hudson.[2]

Long before, Verplanck had made New York a welcoming place for a shy young Yankee from the Berkshire Hills. Now it was Bryant who was chosen by the New York Historical Society to give the city's final adieu to this old friend. Bryant said that the vacancy left by Verplanck's death disproved the rule that there is always someone to replace any man: "When I look for one to supply the place of our friend who has departed, I confess I look in vain." Meant to be a tribute to Verplanck's solid, old-fashioned virtues and manifold talents, the remark also betrayed Bryant's sense of the passing not of time alone but of an age.

Bryant had lived long enough to bury most of his friends and contemporaries. Leggett, Cole, Cooper, Irving, Verplanck—all were gone. The last of the generation of Sedgwicks who had helped shape his life vanished when in 1867 Catherine Sedgwick died in her ancestral home at Stockbridge, after nearly a decade of genteel poverty. As early as 1860, with the death of Irving, Bryant had begun to feel that the world had passed him by. "Among other symptoms of age," he wrote to a friend, "I find the disposition growing up within me to regard the world as belonging to a new race of men, who have somehow or other got into it, and taken possession of it, and among whom I am a superfluity. What have I to do with their quarrels and controversies?"[3]

Bryant faced the prospect of his death with the dignity of a man who had long accepted its inevitability; but he did not welcome death, for life continued to treat him well. His health, maintained by a regimen of his own devising, remained good almost until the last; at the age of eighty, he could still vault over a four-foot gate. He also had wealth, which enabled him to escape from the disagreeable aspects of life. Soon after the Civil War he bought the old Bryant homestead at Cummington. Here in the house where he had spent most of his childhood, he found a comfortable retreat among the memories of his family and the familiar features of the Berkshire Hills. Emerson had once complained humorously that the poet had "suborned" all of Nature "to speak for him, so that there is no feature of day or night in the country which does not, to a contemplative mind, recall the name of Bryant." Here, in the Berkshires, in *his* landscape, he was truly at home.[4]

Bryant aged gracefully and remained what early life had destined him to be, a dignified, shy, gentle, and rather passive man. In 1875 he was described, while presiding over a Century Club meeting, as "Sphynx-like, measuring out short sentences now and then as if they were precious."[5] He remained essentially self-contained, but looked increasingly to religion for comfort. As a young Unitarian, he had considered the divinity as little more than a benevolent force. Now, as his friends and members of his family died, he turned to a personal God, a saving God, and to another world of supreme existence. In 1872 he expressed hope for the "vast enlargement" of the human intellect once the spirit had been freed from the restrictions and imperfections of the body. Almost indignantly, he repelled the threats to his faith, chiefly from the new Darwinian science. The new science, in its conceit, might challenge the spirituality of man and the existence of a personal God; Bryant clung to the science of his youth, which taught that all things were part of the divine harmony:

> The Great Founder, he who gave these laws,
> Holds firm the reins and sits amid his skies.

He spoke of the "law of love" as the way to personal happiness and to the elimination of "a large proportion of the evils which affect mankind." In May 1878, after listening to his minister read the psalms in which David denounces his enemies, the old man protested that hatred of one's enemies was in direct violation of Christian duty.[6]

The next week, on 29 May, the eighty-three-year-old Bryant spoke at the unveiling of a bust of Mazzini, the Italian patriot. Suffering from a severe cold, he kept his speech short , and concluded with an apostrophe to the bust itself: "Remain till the day shall dawn—far distant though it be—when the rights and duties of human brotherhood shall be acknowledged by all the races of mankind." Feeling weak after his speech, he accepted the invitation of General James G. Wilson to rest at the Wilson home. The two men reached the house, but, as Wilson went forward to open the door, Bryant, apparently dizzied, fell violently backwards and hit his head on a stone step. He suffered a brain concussion, and two weeks later he died.[7]

Characteristically, Bryant had instructed his younger daughter, Julia, to hold a quiet and private funeral for him. Characteristically, the world ignored his request. John Bigelow persuaded Julia that society would not approve of "burying so large a personality as if he were a favorite horse or dog," and so the funeral was lavish and public. Among those who attended the services at the Church of All Souls in New York were Peter Cooper, Henry D. Sedgwick, Jr., David Dudley Field, Samuel Tilden, Walt Whitman, and Thurlow Weed. A special train brought the body back to Roslyn, where it was buried overlooking Long Island Sound.[8]

Given the nature of the forty-year relationship between the poet and his son-in-law, it was almost appropriate that Godwin was in Europe when Bryant died and missed the funeral. Godwin himself was gradually retiring from the active world. In the early 1880s, after he had sold his interest in the *Evening Post,* he spent most of his time preparing both a two-volume life of Bryant and a four-volume edition of Bryant's poetry and prose. In 1884, though he had sworn to put his money into something "less precarious" than a newspaper, he made one last stab at journalism with his son, Harold, as editor and owner of the New York *Commercial Advertiser.* For a time, the newspaper took a lively, humane, and generally enlightened view of the problems of the day, but Godwin's fears were justified. The paper lost money, in part because he did not have the heart to fire the incompetents on his staff. In desperation, he finally resigned as editor-in-chief in favor of George Cary Eggleston, who soon turned the deficit into a hearty dividend.[9]

The mid-1880s closed out Godwin's career. Wealth and age led him to retire into the genteel society of upper-class New York, to share with Carl Schurz, John Hay, young Theodore Roosevelt, and others in the conviviality of the Author's Club, to glory during the gay and gray Nineties in the color and warmth of the opera world. A long-time student of Shakespeare, in 1900 Godwin published one last work, a study of the sonnets: the *Nation's* critic dismissed it as a "well-intentioned book" based on a series of guesses and on paraphrases of Shakespeare himself. This was the swan song of that often brilliant and sensitive man who once, long ago, had hoped to promote the regeneration of society. Less than four years later, on 7 January 1904, Godwin died at the age of eighty-seven.[10]

The radical had died long before the man, but Godwin's career was, above all, a monument to men of good will. Perhaps he best summed up his life's attitude in 1881 in a speech on the death of President Garfield:

> We profess politically to be built upon the doctrine of human equality... but does it actuate our conduct? Do we show by it that we heartily

believe that the meanest and humblest of our fellow men is an equal in all the essentials of humanity? ... Let the cesspools of our cities, which harbor unimaginable vice, answer; let our newspapers which some days seem to be nothing but records of crimes answer; let corruption in high places answer. Do you think if we took all men by the hand, in the genuine paternal spirit. . . that the whole moral atmosphere would not be clarified and regenerated?[11]

Such benevolence gave warmth and color to the often cold world of nineteenth-century liberal democracy. It is such benevolence that often gives strength and direction to the uncertain democracy of the twentieth century.

20

REFLECTIONS OF AN AGE (1820-80)

In the years between 1815 and 1830 it was possible for many young Americans to believe that their United States had reached its final phase of greatness. The troublesome days of the French Revolution and the Napoleonic Wars had passed, and, with them, hopefully, had gone the old fears and conflicts they had excited. America now could concentrate on attaining its natural destiny as a unique new nation, free and democratic, a world apart from the strife-torn, privilege-ridden society of Europe. Even more than most generations of young men, a Verplanck, a Bryant, or a Cooper could believe that he personally stood on the threshold of a new age of harmony, where all men would unite, where each would be free to achieve his dreams.

That age never came. Instead, the dream of an era of good feelings was shattered by political conflict and social discord. The New York City that in the 1820s had seemed a land of promise became in the next decade a world of broken hopes and frustrated ambitions. The reason for this failure was easily defined by that moralistic society: some Americans had not lived by the rules of liberal democracy. But what exactly were the rules? Who had broken them? How had they been broken? The growing complexity and diversity of American society guaranteed that there would be no one answer to these questions.

This fact became evident in the early 1830s when Bryant and Verplanck, after cooperating to support the election of Andrew Jackson and to oppose the protective tariff, split over the issue of the National Bank. Verplanck, who was very much a member of the established New York business community, sided with the Bank. For him, the political and financial disorder that accompanied the Bank conflict resulted from Jackson's mismanagement of governmental power; the solution was to re-establish enlightened administration of national affairs by experienced men. Thus Verplanck became a founder of the Whig party and a leading proponent of the positive state.

Bryant would not follow his friend out of the Jacksonian camp. A New Englander who had absorbed his social and economic views from his fellow Yankees, the Sedgwicks, he had little faith in the business community. In 1828 he had become the editor and part-owner of the *Evening Post* with the hope that a profitable newspaper would enable him to concentrate on his poetry; the economic troubles of the 1830s left him, as both a poet and newspaper owner, imprisoned in the increasingly obnoxious world of New York journalism. From the beginning, he sided with Jackson's war against privilege-seeking businessmen in the belief that they were the chief cause of the nation's problems. The cycle of boom and bust which disturbed the economy in them id-1830s inten-tensified his conviction that the Jacksonian party was an indispensable champion of liberal principles against self-seeking politicians and capitalists. In his eyes, the natural way to the liberal ideal was through the establishment of negative government, which would guarantee equal protection for all but otherwise not interfere in human affairs.

Bryant's commitment to the negative state was intensified by the influence of his assistant editor, William Leggett, whose hatred of authority made almost fanatical his belief that "the world is governed too much." Leggett's devotion to the ideal of a society of masterless men was too extreme for temperamental moderates like Bryant, but it made him the hero of the Locofoco movement, which grew out of the unstable economic conditions following the "Bank War." Long after his premature death in 1839 the memory of his zeal nourished the character of the *Evening Post* as the purest voice of liberalism in America. When continued economic and political tensions split the Democratic party in New York, the *Post* became the chief organ of the liberal "Radical" or "Barn-burner" faction and a major influence in state and national politics for the next twenty years.

The tumultuous 1830s set James Fenimore Cooper off on his own track. Although he shared Verplanck's faith in the possibilities of enlightened administration, his ideal policy-maker and leader was not the businessman but the landed gentleman. It was natural, then, for him to support the Jacksonian party as the best defense against the rising influence of commercialism. Far more than Bryant, however, the novelist was sensitive to the underlying defects of the society which was emerging with the Jacksonian movement. The growing influence of journalists and professional politicians as well as of businessmen he saw as a threat to the values and, indeed, the existence of gentlemen such as he conceived himself to be. Driven increasingly on the defensive, ever more critical and pessimistic in his social views, Cooper became isolated from the mainstream of liberal democracy, his warnings ignored as being no more than the mutterings of a reactionary advocate of an outmoded social order.

In the 1840s Cooper's fundamental dissatisfaction was mirrored (from the left) in the writings of Bryant's son-in-law, Parke Godwin. More sensitive than Bryant to the emotional side of human existence, far more confident of the natural goodness of mankind, young Godwin rejected the laissez-faire program of the Democratic party as an illusory defense against the inhumanity of modern capitalism. Convinced that established American institutions had betrayed the promise of liberal democracy, he advocated the reorganization of American society on the collectivist principles of the French utopian Charles Fourier. He soon learned, however, that Americans would not be converted to a European social philosophy. Although he never abandoned his romantic optimism, in the 1850s he joined his father-in-law in a crusade against the influence of slavery, which, even more than capitalism, then seemed to pose a direct threat to liberal democracy.

All members of the group had long considered slavery to be a gross anomaly in a free society; significantly, however, none except Harry Sedgwick showed much sympathy for the slave. Like most liberal critics of slavery, in contrast to the abolitionists, they were willing to accept its existence in the South, provided it did not threaten the national predominance of liberal democracy. Some were hostile to the abolitionist war against slavery. Cooper was naturally sympathetic to southern planters, especially since abolitionism was strongest in New England, a section that as a self-conscious "Yorker" he had come to despise in the years before his death in 1850. Verplanck, another Yorker, eventually rejoined the Democratic party in the belief that it was the best protector of national unity against abolitionist fanaticism.

Though the slavery issue drew Verplanck back into the old Jacksonian party, it drove Bryant out. During the 1830s he had begun to identify slavery with the much larger issue of preserving and expanding democracy. As journalists, both he and Leggett were particularly concerned with freedom of opinion. When mobs attacked abolitionists for their opinions and when southern sympathizers attempted to excommunicate Leggett from the Democratic party for his defense of free speech, both men began to conceive of slavery as a power that threatened the liberal ideal. Until the outbreak of the controversy over the annexation of Texas in 1844, this Slave Power was of relatively minor concern. After that date, however, Bryant progressively came to see slavery as a meddlesome and dangerous force that was seriously disrupting liberal politics in the North. Every defeat for the liberal wing tof the Democratic party, every defeat for liberal democracy, seemed to stem, directly or indirectly, from the Slave Power.

The apparently growing influence of slavery demanded a revision in the old Jacksonian political formula. The privilege-seeking businessman against whom the Locofocos had protested was replaced, as the chief enemy, by the privilege-seeking slaveholder. Thus, for Bryant, the earlier battle within the ranks of capitalism was transformed into a conflict between liberal society, of which capitalism was a part, and a southern quasi-aristocracy. One essential element in the old formula remained, however, in that the new struggle again centered on the power of self-serving politicians, the assumption being that only their betrayal of the people gave strength to the slave menace. Fundamentally, the liberal objective was not to destroy slavery but to reform government and politics by ousting rascals from power. Once this was done, then liberal democratic principles would prevail, and the threat posed by the Slave Power (and privilege-seekers generally) would vanish.

This logic led both Bryant and Godwin to unite with anti-slavery Whigs in the foimation of the Republican party in the period between 1854 and 1856. For them, the new party was a defensive organization intended to protect liberal democracy, not a radical, reorganizing force. They dismissed, therefore, the warnings of such old friends as Verplanck and Theodore Sedgwick, III, that the election of a Republican president would be treated by the South as a threat to its vital interests. Secession?—elect good men, purify government, and the majority of southerners would rally against the disunionists. When, in fact, the lower South reacted to Lincoln's election by seceding from the Union in 1860–61, Republicans such as Bryant and Godwin were forced to recognize that they had underestimated the influence of the Slave Power in southern society. The outbreak of the Civil War led both men to conclude that only by the elimination of slavery itself could America be preserved as a liberal democracy. And so the war became for them a great redemptive rite which, by exorcising the source of past political troubles, would purify the Republic.

In contrast, Verplanck condemned the war as an explosive destroyer of the established order. No better, in his eyes, was the ravaged peace brought in the years after 1865 by the reconstruction program of the Radical Republicans. Increasingly withdrawn in his political views, intensely localistic in his loyalties, he showed little awareness of the significance of the great upheaval that had begun in the 1840s. His personal world, once so wide and promising, had shriveled by the time of his death in 1870 to the narrow back yard of Knickerbocker New York.

Time may simply have passed Verplanck by, but its effect on his friends was more complex. Neither Bryant nor Godwin was intellectually prepared for the problem that at the war's end in 1865 supplanted the problem of the Slave Power. The question was no longer that of resisting the Slave Power but that of finding a place in liberal society for the ex-slaves. Both men had shown little sympathy for the slaves; although neither was an overt racist, they took for granted that the welfare of Negroes was of secondary importance in white America. They did in 1865 show some sympathetic interest in the freedmen, but their overriding concern was the traditional liberal one of reversing the strong centralizing tendencies encouraged in government and society by the war. They opposed, therefore, the Radical Reconstruction program for its emphasis on federal protection of southern Negroes. By the early 1870s they committed themselves to the liberal judgment that Reconstruction was simply another example of government meddling with the natural order. Their suggested solution was to end federal interference with the natural process of racial adjustment in the South; they preferred to ignore the probability that the southern caste system, inherited from the days of slavery, would severely restrict opportunities for Negroes.

Neither Bryant nor Godwin, however, could escape the continued effects of the dispute over slavery. When faced with the corruptions of the Grant administration, the two aging liberals again split. Bryant, out of loyalty and self-interest, kept the *Evening Post* within the Republican party, while Godwin joined the Democrats in the hope of reviving the old Jacksonian crusade against privilege and corruption. Unfortunately for such hopes, the slavery issue had permanently changed the configuration of American politics, dividing and weakening the ranks of liberal reform; this fact was driven home by Bryant's refusal in 1876 to publicly support his old friend and fellow liberal, Samuel J. Tilden, for the presidency.

The presidential election of 1876 marked the last major efforts for both Bryant and Godwin. The poet–editor died in 1878, and his son-in-law soon afterward retired from the *Evening Post,* selling some fifty years of family control over the newspaper. What had the two men accomplished? On the one hand, they had helped keep vital and alive the liberal democratic dream of a society of free men, without privilege, with equal opportunities for all. On the other, they had acquiesced to the exclusion of American Negroes from that dream. Moreover, they left behind an *Evening Post* that clung to the notion that the way to the good society lay through the elimination of governmental interference with the natural order. By elevating a principle devised for earlier and simpler times into a universal rule of politics, they served to hamper the efforts of more modern liberals to develop a role for government as a counterweight to the growing private power and privilege which was to be so troubling to the next century.

And so, like all men, the members of the group lived and died as creatures of their times.

NOTES

The following abbreviations will be used after the first citation:

B-G: Bryant–Godwin Papers, New York Public Library.

E.P.: New York *Evening Post.*

G, *B.:* Parke Godwin, *A Biography of William Cullen Bryant,* 2 vols. (New York, 1883).

G-R.: Goddard–Roslyn Papers (Microfilm), New York Public Library.

N.Y.H.S.: New-York Historical Society.

N.Y.P.L.: New York Public Library.

L. & J.: James Fenimore Cooper, *Letters and Journals,* ed. James Franklin Beard, 4 vols. (Cambridge, Mass., 1970, 1960).

CHAPTER 1

1. Parke Godwin, *A Biography of William Cullen Bryant* (New York, 1883), I: 3–8, 53–58, 62–66; Donald M. Murray, "Dr. Peter Bryant: Preceptor in Poetry to William Cullen Bryant," *New England Quarterly* 33 (1960): 513-20; Tremaine McDowell, "The Ancestry of William Cullen Bryant," *Americana* 22 (1928): 410–19; Elmer H. Miller, *Sketches and Directory of the Town of Cummington* (West Cummington, Mass., 1881), pp. 17–18, 30.
2. William Cullen Bryant, *The Embargo (1808),* ed. Thomas O. Mabbott (Gainesville, Fla., 1955); G, *B,.* I:22, 26–28; Tremaine McDowell, "The Juvenile Verse of William Cullen Bryant," *Studies in Philology* 26 (1929): 98–102.
3. G, *B.,* I:30–37, 85–93, 103–05; Tremaine McDowell, "Cullen Bryant Prepares for College," *South Atlantic Quarterly* 30 (1931): 125 ff.; Tremaine McDowell, "Cullen Bryant at Williams College," *New England Quarterly* 1 (1928): 444 ff.
4. G, *B.,* I:119–28, 132; William Cullen Bryant II, "The Genesis of Thanatopsis," *New England Quarterly* 21 (1948): 163–66, 175.
5. G, *B.,* I:129–30, 134–36.
6. *Ibid.,* I:138–39, 144; William Cullen Bryant, II, "Thanatopsis" and "The Waterfowl in Retrospect," *New England Quarterly* 30 (1957): 188; George Downs to Bryant, 6 July 1815 and William Baylies to Bryant, 24 Jan. 1816, B-G.

221

7. Richard D. Birdsall, *Berkshire County: A Cultural History* (New Haven, Conn., 1959), p. 52 ff.; Harry H. Peckham, *Gotham Yankee: A Biography of William Cullen Bryant* (New York, 1950), pp. 49–52; Charles J. Taylor, *History of Great Barrington* (Great Barrington, Mass., 1882), pp. 424, 442.

8. Tremaine McDowell, "Bryant and *The North American Review*," *American Literature* 1(1929–30): 14–15; William Baylies to Bryant, 8 Nov. 1817 B–G; George H. Ives to Bryant, 24 June 1816, B–G; Bryant to Edward T. Channing, 6 Sept. 1818, Autograph Collection, Houghton Library, Harvard.

9. Peckham, *Gotham Yankee*, p. 50; William Cullen Bryant, *An Oration Delivered at Stockbridge. July 4th, 1820* (Stockbridge, Mass., 1820).

10. E.R. Brown, ed., *Life and Poems of John Howard Bryant* (n.p., 1894), p. 9; Ernest R. Eaton, "William Cullen Bryant, The First of American Poets," *Quarterly of Phi Alpha Gamma* (1934), p. 4.

11. Explanations of Bryant's interest in nature vary; see G, B., 1:91, 104: Norman Foerster, "Nature in Bryant's Poetry," *South Atlantic Quarterly* 17 (1918): 17; Norman Foerster, *Nature in American Literature* (New York, 1923), p. 11. Tremaine McDowell, *William Cullen Bryant: Representative Selections* (New York, 1935), p. xxxiv ff.

12. Birdsall, *Berkshire County*, pp. 52, 265–78; Richard D. Birdsall, "Bryant and Catherine Sedgwick—Their Debt to Berkshire," *New England Quarterly* 28(1955): 355–56; McDowell, *Bryant: Representative Selections*, pp. xxxvi-xxxvii; Bryant, "The Rivulet."

13. G, B., 1:13, 26–27, 33; Gordon B. Wellman, "Samuel Hopkins, Rational Calvinist and Mystic," *Review of Religion* 3 (1938–39); 267, 275; Frank K. Foster, *A Genetic History of the New England Theology* (Chicago, 1907), pp. 139, 155–6.

14. McDowell, *Bryant: Representative Selections.*, pp. xxiv, xxvii; McDowell, "Bryant at Williams", pp. 456, 465–66; Foster, *Genetic History*, pp. 283, 287. Arthur W. Brown, *Always Young for Liberty* (Syracuse, N.Y., 1956), pp. 47, 53, 62–63, 74. H.D. Sewall to Bryant, 12 May 1821 and Andrews Norton to Bryant, 15 July 1823, B–G.

15. G, B., 1:100 ff. McDowell, *Bryant and North American Review*, pp. 15–26; *North American Review* 5 (1817): 338–40. A facsimile of the complete "Thanatopsis" (1821), annotated by Bryant, is in Misc. Papers, Bryant Folder, N.Y.P.L. Edward T. Channing to Bryant, 3 Sept. 1818, 8 March 1819, B–G; Willard Phillips to Bryant, 2 Dec. 1817, B–G.

16. G, B., 1:163–64; Gladys Brooks, *Three Wise Virgins* (New York, 1957), pp. 160–61, 169 ff.; Mary E. Dewey, *Life and Letters of Catherine Maria Sedgwick* (New York, 1871); Biographical sketches of Theodore I, Theodore II (designated as Theodore, Jr., in this book), Theodore III, and Catherine M. Sedgwick are in the *Dictionary of American Biography*.

17. Dewey, *Sedgwick*, pp. 93, 157, 160; John W. Francis, *Old New York* (New York, 1958), p. 155.

18. McDowell, *Bryant and North American Review*, p. 26. Bryant to Edward

T. Channing, 25 March 1819, Autograph Collection, Houghton Library, Harvard; Channing to Bryant, 8 March 1819 and 15 May 1821, B–G.

19. William E. Leonard, "Bryant and the Minor Poets," *The Cambridge History of American Literature* (New York, 1947), 1: 264–71. For some contemporary reactions to *Poems* see *North American Review* 13 (1821): 381–82; William Charvat, *The Origins of American Thought, 1810–1835* (Philadelphia, 1936), p. 22; G, B., 1:279. Facsimile of "Thanatopsis," Misc. Papers, Bryant Folder, N.Y.P.L.

20. *North American Review* 13(1821): 381–82; G, B., 1:179–80; Dewey, *Sedgwick,* p. 148. Verplanck to Richard Henry Dama, 8 Sept. 1821, Verplanck Papers, New-York Historical Society.

21. Birdsall, *Berkshire,* pp. 278–79, and *Bryant and Catherine Sedgwick,* p. 361; John B. McMaster, *A History of the United States from the Revolution to the Civil War* (New York, 1918–1919), 5:303; Baylies to Bryant, 8 Nov. 1817 B–G; Willard Phillips to Bryant, 21 Oct. 1823 B–G; Charles Sedgwick Henry Dwight Sedgwick to Bryant, 23 Jan. 1825, B–G.

22. John Bigelow, *William Cullen Bryant* (Boston and New York, 1890), pp. 36–39, 61. Bryant to Channing, 2 June 1821, Autograph Collection, Houghton Library, Harvard; Willard Phillips to Bryant, 3 Oct. 1821 B–G; Charles Sedgwick to Bryant, 5 Nov. 1824 B–G; E.R. Hallenbeck to Bryant, 9 June 1826, B–G.

23. Birdsall, *Bryant and Catherine Sedgwick,* pp. 361, 371; Charles Sedgwick to Bryant, 3 Sept. 1824, B–G; Henry Dwight Sedgwick to Bryant, 13 Oct. 1824, Jared Sparks to Bryant, 16 Oct. 1825, B–G; Bryant to Sparks, 1 Nov., 29 November 1824, Sparks Papers, Houghton Library, Harvard; *North American Review* 20(1825): 257. 24. G, B., 1:180–206; Bigelow, *Bryant,* pp. 55–56. Henry Dwight Sedgwick to Bryant, 16 January, 1825, 23 January 1825, B–G.

CHAPTER 2

1. Robert E. Spiller, *Fenimore Cooper: Critic of His Times* (New York, 1931), p. 78; Robert G. Albion, *The Rise of New York Port* (New York, 1939), pp. 10, 13–14, 390.

2. Charles King, *Progress of the City of New-York* (New York, 1852), pp. 74–75; Bayrd Still, *Mirror for Gotham* (New York, 1956), pp. 81, 90, 99, 114; McMaster, *History of United States,* 5:122–123; New York *Commercial Advertiser,* 28 April 1825, 6 May 1825.

3. Dixon Ryan Fox, *Yankees and Yorkers* (New York, 1940), pp. 196–97; David M. Ellis, "The Yankee Invasion of New York, 1783–1850," *New York History* 32 (1951): 9–17; David M. Ellis, *Landlords and Farmers in the Hudson-Mohawk Region, 1790–1850* (Ithaca, N.Y., 1946), pp. 20–22; James Fenimore Cooper, *Notions of the Americans* (New York, 1963), 1:135–36.

4. Rev. Samuel Osgood, *New York in the Nineteenth Century* (New York, 1867), pp. 56–57; Bryant, *Oration…1820,* p. 6.

5. *Commercial Advertiser,* 3 May, 1825; E.P. Richardson, *Painting in America* (New York, 1956), pp. 211–12; Van Wyek Brooks, *The World of Washington Irving* (Philadelphia, 1944), pp. 236, 242–4; James G. Wilson, *Life and Letters of Fitz-Greene Halleck* (New York, 1869), p. 282; Philip Hone, *Diary of Philip Hone,* ed. Allan Nevins (New York, 1927), I:372.

6. Brooks, *World of Irving,* p. 235. *The New York Review and Atheneum Magazine* 2 (1825–1826); 367–68.

7. Wilson, *Halleck,* p. 327; James G. Wilson, *Bryant and His Friends* (Mew York, 1886), pp. 45–49; G, *B.,* 1:217, 220; Dewey, *Sedgwick,* p. 341; Robert C. Sands, *Writings of Robert C. Sands in Prose and Verse* (New York, 1834), 1:3–30.

8. Robert W. July, *The Essential New Yorker: Gulian Crommelin Verplanck* (Durham, N.C., 1951), pp. 4–13; William Cullen Bryant, *Prose Writings,* ed. Parke Godwin (New York, 1884), 1:395–400.

9. Gulian C. Verplanck, *An Essay on the Doctrine of Contracts* (New York, 1826), p. iv.

10. Gulian C. Verplanck, *Discourses and Addresses on Subjects of American History, Arts, and Literature* (New York, 1833), p. 190; July, *Verplanck,* p. 14ff; Dixon Ryan Fox, *The Decline of Aristocracy in the Politics of New York* (New York, 1919), p. 205n.

11. Fox, *Decline of Aristocracy,* pp. 209–15; G, *B.,* 1:179–180, 208, 210.

12. McDowell, *Bryant,* p. 415; Nelson F. Adkins, "James Fenimore Cooper and the Bread and Cheese Club," *Modern Language Notes* 47(1932): 74; *Memorial of James Fenimore Cooper* (New York, 1852), p. 102.

13. Spiller, *Cooper,* pp. 59–75; Henry W. Boynton, *James Fenimore Cooper* (New York, 1931), p. 72.

14. Adkins, *Bread and Cheese,* pp. 72–73; A.H. Marckwardt, "The Chronology and Personnel of the Bread and Cheese Club," *American Literature* 6 (1934–1935); 394; Henry Brevoort, *Letters of Henry Brevoort to Washington Irving,* ed. by G. S. Hellman (New York, 1918), p. 161; James Fenimore Cooper, *Correspondence of James Fenimore Cooper,* ed. J.F. Cooper (New Haven, Conn., 1922), 1:107; *The New York Review and Atheneum Magazine* 1(1825): 44, 2 (1825–1826): 288, 306–08; Bryant to Verplanck, 29 Dec. 1828, Berg Collection, N.Y.P.L.; Verplanck to Bryant, 9 January 1829, B–G.

15. McDowell, *Bryant,* p. lxii n.; James Fenimore Cooper, *The Letters and Journals of James Fenimore Cooper,* ed. James Franklin Beard (Cambridge, Mass., 1960, 1964), I;172; *United States Review* 2 (1827); 264.

16. Verplanck, *Discourses and Addresses,* pp. 224–27; Gulian C. Verplanck, *An Address Delivered at the…American Academy of Fine Arts* (New York, 1825), p. 35.

17. Robert E. Streeter, "Association Psychology and Literary Nationalism in the *North American Review,* 1815–1825," *American Literature* 17 (1945–

1946): 244–45; William P. Hudson, "Archibald Alison and William Cullen Bryant," *American Literature* 12 (1940–1941): 59–68; Bryant, "Lectures on Poetry," *Prose Writings,* pp. 11–19 ff.

18. Arvid Shulenberger, *Cooper's Theory of Fiction* (Lawrence, Kans., 1955), p. 35; *L. & J.,* 1 :94, 173, 177; James Fenimore Cooper, *The Spy: A Tale of Neutral Ground* (New York, 1960), pp. lx–xl, 462–63.

19. *The New York Review and Atheneum Magazine* 2(1825–1826): 288; *L. & J.,* 1:243, 258, 263n, 287.

20. *United States Review* 2 (1827): 264; Charles I. Glicksberg, "Bryant and *The United States Review,*" *New England Quarterly* 7(1934): 689–701. James G. Carter to Bryant, 11 April, 3 May, 17 May 1826; Charles Folsom to Bryant, 30 Oct. 1826, B–G.; Bryant to R.H. Dana, 17 April 1830, G–R.

21. July, *Verplanck,* p. 109 ff. Bryant to Jared Sparks, 8 Nov., 16 November 1827, Sparks Papers, Houghton Library, Harvard; Bryant to Verplanck, 28 Dec. 1827, Berg Collection, N.Y.P.L.

22. Allan Nevins, *The Evening Post* (New York, 1922), pp. 122–34; G, *B.,* 1:229, 235.

23. Albert F. McLean, Jr., *William Cullen Bryant* (New York, 1964), 62.

24. William P. Trent, *William Gilmore Simms* (Boston and New York, 1892), pp. 69–70; John Pierrepont to Bryant, 8 Sept. 1827 B–G; Eliza Robbins to Mrs. Frances Bryant, 24 July 1829, B–G.

CHAPTER 3

1. G, *B.,* 1:229, 339, 2:36; Nevins, *Post,* pp. 138, 247–48.

2. Charles I. Glicksberg, "New Contributions in Prose by William Cullen Bryant," *America* 30(1936): 582; Bryant, "The Embargo," "The Ages," and *Oration...1820,* pp. 4, 11; *United States Review* 1 (1826): 346.

3. Mary L. Booth, *History of the City of New York* (New York, 1866), pp. 724–25; *Niles' Weekly Register* 29 (1825–1826): 52; G, *B.,* 1:222.

4. Bryant's review of *Redwood, North American Review* 20 (1825): 253; [Theodore Sedgwick] *Hints to My Countrymen* (New York, 1826), pp. 14–15, 35, 122–23, 130, 185.

5. *Ibid.,* p. 14.

6. G, *B.,* 1; 58; for Sarah Snell Bryant, see her manuscript diary in Houghton Library, Harvard; *United States Review* 2 (1827): 253, 312.

7. *United States Review* 1 (1827); 252–53; *North American Review* 9 (1819): 208; Sedgwick, *Hints,* pp. 18, 62, 156, 161.

8. Dewey, *Sedgwick,* pp. 51, 53; Catherine M. Sedgwick, *Redwood: A Tale* (New York, 1824), 1: 122, 124, 169.

9. Sedgwick, *Hints,* pp. 35, 62, 72, 76, 146.

10. Joseph Dorfman, *The Economic Mind in American Civilization, 1606–1865* (New York, 1946), 2:709; Gulian C. Verplanck, *The Influence of Moral Causes Upon Opinion, Science, and Literature* (New York, 1834), pp. 9–11, 26, 37; Verplanck, *Discourses, and Addresses,* p. 236; Verplanck, *Doctrine*

of Contracts, p. 75.

11. Verplanck, *Doctrine* . . . , pp. 11, 55, 101; July, *Verplanck,* pp. 209–10; *North American Review* 22 (1826): 259–65.

12. Verplanck, *Doctrine of Contracts,* pp. 11, 102, 120–26; *North American Review* 22 (1826): 264–65.

13. Verplanck, *Discourses and Addresses,* pp. 78–79, 205.

14. Birdsall, *Berkshire,* pp. 219–21, 244, 246. Charles Sedgwick to Bryant, 5 Nov. 1824, B–G.

15. Dewey, *Sedgwick,* pp. 434–35, 442. Henry Dwight Sedgwick to Verplanck, 20 Dec. 1825, Verplanck, Papers, N.Y.H.S. *E.P.,* 16 Oct., 18 Oct., 30 Oct., 3 Nov., 13 Dec., 1826.

16. [Henry Dwight Sedgwick], *English Practice: A Statement Showing Some of the Evils and Absurdities of the Practice of the English Common Law* (New York, 1822).

17. Birdsall, *Berkshire,* pp. 253–55; Henry Dwight Sedgwick, *English Practice,* pp. 33, 35; *North American Review* 19 (1824): 417, 419–20, 424, 430.

18. Henry Dwight Sedgwick *The Practicability of the Abolition of Slavery* (New York, 1831), p. 30; Perry Miller, ed., *The Legal Mind in America* (Garden City, N.Y., 1962), pp. 142–43.

19. Dewey, *Sedgwick,* p. 441; *L. & J.,* 1: 84–85, 121–126.

20. Dewey, *Sedgwick,* pp. 174, 180; *E.P.* 17 March 1827; Bryant, "A Meditation on Rhode Island Coal."

21. Dewey *Sedgwick,* pp. 183–185, 200; Charles Sedgwick, *Letters to His Family and Friends,* ed. C.M. Sedgwick (Boston, 1870), pp. 59n., 66; Henry Dwight Sedgwick, *Abolition,* and a series of forty-six articles in the Philadelphia *Banner of the Constitution,* March–Oct. 1831, signed "A Friend of the Poor."

CHAPTER 4

1. *L. & J.,* 1: 95–96, 411; *L. & J.,* 2: 31–33.

2. James Fenimore Cooper, *The Pioneers* (New York, 1958), pp. 23, 206–7, 462; Spiller, *Cooper,* 13–14, 22, 25; Marvin Meyers, *The Jacksonian Persuasion* (Stanford, Callf., 1957), 71–72.

3. Cooper, *Pioneers,* 34, 122–23; Meyers, *Persuasion,* 74, 79; *see* Cooper's letters to his family and friends in *L. & J.,* 1 and 2.

4. James Grossman, *James Fenimore Cooper* (n.p., 1949), 149; Shulenberger, 80; *L. & J.,* 2; 27, 70, 78, 187.

5. Spiller, *Cooper,* pp. 49–62; *L. & J.,* 1: 9–12, 39–40, 70; Cooper, *Correspondence,* 1; 97–998.

6. July, *Verplanck,* pp. 19–20; ed. Albert Bushnell Hart, *Commonwealth History of Massachusetts* (New York, 1927–30), 4: 357.

7. July, *Verplanck,* pp. 22–23; Gulian C. Verplanck, *An Oration Delivered July 4, 1809 . . . Before the Washington Benevolent Society* (New York, 1809), pp. 6–10, 14–15n, 20.

8. Gulian C. Verplanck, *Letter to the Hon Saml. L. Mitchell, M.D....By Abimelech Coody, esq.* (New York, 1811), pp. 3, 14, 18.
9. July, Verplanck, pp. 44–45, 70–71; Alvin Kass, *Politics in New York State, 1800–1830* (Syracuse, 1965), p. 103.
10. Murray, *Dr. Peter Bryant*, pp. 518–19; G, *B.*, I: 70–74; Bryant, *Embargo.*, ed. Mabbett, pp. 33, 37, 39, 42–43, 47.
11. G, *B.*, 1:106, 127–32; Henry Adams, *History of the United States* (New York, 1921), 8:3, 11; James Truslow Adams, *New England in the Republic, 1776–1850* (Boston, 1926), pp. 252, 259, 277, 285.
12. G, *B.*, 1:75, 185; McDowell, *Bryant*, p. xvii; Bryant, *Oration...1820*, pp. 5–8.
13. Bigelow, *Bryant*, p. 325; Shaw Livermore, Jr., *The Twilight of Federalism* (Princeton, N.J., 1962), p. 208; *E.P.*, 18, 25, 29 Oct. and 2, 17, 18, 27 November 1824; *United States Review* 1 (1826): 191.
14. *Niles' Register* 34 (1828): 258–60.
15. *E.P.*, 27 Sept., 30 October 1828.
16. July, Verplanck, pp. 19–40; *Niles' Register* 34 (1828): 188, 35 (1828–1829): 116, 178; *E.P.*, 28 October 1828.
17. G, *B.*, 1; 245; Bryant, *Embargo*, ed. Mabbott, pp. 36–37; *E.P.*, 15 Jan., 4 April, 8 April 1828.
18. *E.P.*, 14, 15, 18 January; 5, 6 August; Oct.–Nov. 1828.
19. Bryant, *Embargo*, ed. Mabbett, pp. 40–41, 45; G, *B.*, 1:242; 2: 229; *E.P.*, 1, 11, Feb. 1828; 16, Feb. 6 March 1829.
20. Livermore, *Twilight*, pp. 161–63, 221; *E.P.*, 3 October 1828; Francis Baylies, "Letters, 1827–1834," Massachusetts Historical Society, *Proceedings* 45 (1911–1912): 166.
21. G, *B.*, 1:244; *E.P.*, 5 March 1829; Bryant to R.H. Dana, 17 April 1830, G–R.

CHAPTER 5

1. *Banner of the Constitution*, 9 March 1831.
2. *Ibid.*, 9, 16, 23 March, 13, 20 April, 4, 18, 25 May, 1 June, 6 July, 21 Sept., 12 Oct., 1831.
3. *Ibid.*, 18, 25 May, 27 July, 1831.
4. *Ibid.*, 23 March, 11, 25 May, 1 June, 27 July; Sedgwick, *Abolition*, pp. 27, 30.
5. *E.P.*, 2 March, 24 Aug., 1829, 17 May, 1830.
6. *Ibid.*, Nov. 25, 1829.
7. *Ibid.*, March 4, July 26, 1828; Charles I. Glicksberg, "William Cullen Bryant and Communism," *The Modern Monthly* 8 (1934): 354–55.
8. Frank T. Carlton, "The Workingmen's Party of New York," *Political Science Quarterly*, 22 (1907), 402–5; William R. Waterman, *Frances Wright* (New York, 1924), 169–70, 205; *E.P.*, 17 Jan., 31 Oct., 1829.
9. *E.P.*, Nov. 3, 5, 14, 18, 1829; April 24, 1830.

10. *E.P.,* 27 Jan., 4 Feb., 1831.
11. *Ibid.,* 8 Dec., 1829, 1, 3 Nov., 1830; Bryant to Verplanck, Feb. 1, 1830, Berg Collection, N.Y.P.L.
12. David D. Wallace, *South Carolina: A Short History* (Chapel Hill, N.C., 1951), pp. 385, 402; Cyrus Bryant to Louisa C. Bryant, 15 April 1826,
12. David D. Wallace, *South Carolina: A Short History* (Chapel Hill, N.C., 1951), pp. 385, 402; Cyrus Bryant to Louisa C. Bryant, 15 April 1826, A. Fitch to Cyrus Bryant, 27 July 1828, Bryant Family Papers, N.Y.P.L.; D.J. McCord to Verplanck, 18 July 1828, Verplanck Papers, N.Y.H.S.
13. *E.P.,* 29, 31 Dec. 1830, 5, 8 June, 29 Aug. 1832.
14. Howard R. Floan, *The South in Northern Eyes, 1831 to 1861* (Austin, Texas, 1958), p. 155; *E.P.,* 21 April, 31 Dec. 1830, 15, 23 March, 16 May, 13 June, 29 Aug., 5 Nov. 1832; Bryant to Mrs. Bryant, 23 Jan. 1832, G–R.
15. G, B., 1: 247–48; Nevins, *Post,* p. 143; *E.P.,* 8 Jan., 10 Dec. 1830; Bryant to Verplanck, 26 Dec. 1831, Berg Collection, N.Y.P.L.
16. Verplanck, *Discourses and Addresses,* p. 236; *Knickerbocker Magazine* 3 (1834): 44, 50; Verplanck to Bryant, 7 Jan. 1830, B–G. Also see Chap. 8 of this work.
17. July, *Verplanck,* pp. 149–52; Gulian C. Verplanck, *A Letter to Col. Drayton ...in Assertion of the Constitutional Poewer of Congress to Impose Protecting Duties* (New York, 1831), pp. 7, 30–31.
18. July, *Verplanck,* pp. 162–63; Edward Stanwood, *American Tariff Controversies in the Nineteenth Century* (Boston and New York, 1903), 1:393–95; *Niles' Register* 43 (1832–1833): 305–7; Thomas Cooper to Verplanck, 15 Jan. 1833, Verplanck Papers, N.Y.H.S.; *E.P.,* 4 March 1833.

CHAPTER 6

1. Nevins, *Post,* p. 139.
2. Bray Hammond, *Banks and Politics in America from the Revolution to the Civil War* (Princeton, N.J., 1957); Arthur M. Schlesinger, Jr., *The Age of Jackson* (Boston, 1945), pp. 74–82, 115–31.
3. Henry D. Sedgwick to Theodore Sedgwick, 24 Jan. 1824, Sedgwick Papers, Mass. Hist. Sec.
4. *Ibid.; New York Review* 2 (1825–1826): 20; *Niles' Register* 29 (1825–1826): 195, 292, 324.
5. *Niles' Register,* 30 (1826), 377; *United States Review,* 1 (1826), 191; Jabez D. Hammond, *The History of Political Parties of the State of New York* (Albany, N.Y., 1842), 2: 244.
6. Charles I. Glicksberg, ed., "Letters by William Cullen Bryant," *Americana,* 33 (1939), 30; *E.P.,* 4 June 1828, 6 Jan. 1829.
7. *E.P.,* 18 Feb., 14 Nov. 1829, 9 Feb., 23 April 1830; Cooper, *Correspondence,* I, 235.

8. Hammond, *Political Parties*, 2: 300–02; *E.P.,* 24 March, 25 Nov. 1829, 13 Jan. 1830.
9. G, *B.,* 1: 249; Samuel R. Gammon, *The Presidential Campaign of 1832* (Baltimore, 1922), pp. 115, 125–26, 131; *E.P.,* 12, 15, 21, Dec. 1829, 30 March, 24 April 1830; *Niles' Register* 38 (1830): 187–88, 40 (1831): 114.
10. July, *Verplanck*, pp. 169–70; Joseph Dorfman and R.G. Tugwell, *Early American Policy: Six Columbia Contributors* (New York, 1960), pp. 222–23.
11. New York State Assembly, *Journal*, 44th sess. (1820–21), p. 528; *Niles' Register* 30 (1826): 127–32, 38 (1830): 186–88; *E.P.,* 12, 28 Feb. 1827.
12. July, *Verplanck*, pp. 215–16; Verplanck, *Discourses and Addresses*, pp. 247, 253–54.
13. *E.P.,* 24 April 1830, 3 Jan. 1831, and 9 Feb., 19 March, 16, 19, 24, 25 April 1832.
14. Nevins, *Post,* p. 136; Bryant to Verplanck, n.d., Berg Collection, N.Y.P.L.
15. *E.P.,* 4 May, 16 Aug, 10 Sept. 1832; *E.P.,* 14, 25 January 1834.
16. July, *Verplanck*, p. 178; Bryant to Verplanck, 23 May 1832, Berg Coll, N.Y.P.L.; James Watson Webb to Verplanck, 16 April 1832, Verplanck Papers, N.Y.H.S.; *E.P.,* 17, 18, 24 Oct., 3 Nov. 1832.
17. Bryant, *Oration and Addresses*, p. 227.
18. *E.P.,* 4, 5, 8, 13 November 1833, 19, 27 March, 7 June, 12, 18 September 1834; Century Club, *Proceedings...in Honor of the Memory of Gulian C. Verplanck* (New York, 1870), p. 69; R.H. Wilde to Verplanck, 27 March 1834, Verplanck Papers, N.Y.H.S.
19. Nevins, *Post,* pp. 136, 138.
20. Keith Huntress and Fred W. Lorch, eds., "Bryant and Illinois: Further Letters of the Poet's Family," *New England Quarterly* 16 (1943): 637–639; Helen L. Drew, ed., "Unpublished Letters of William Cullen Bryant," 10 (1937): 349–51; Nevins, *Post,* p. 136; Bryant to R.H. Dana, 27 April 1834, G–R. *New England Quarterly.*
21. G, *B.,* 1: 309, 311; Bryant to Thatcher L. Payne, 7 Aug. 1834, G–R; Bryant to William Ware, 11 Oct. 1834, 14 Sept. 1835, G–R.

CHAPTER 7

1. Charles I. Glicksberg, "William Leggett, Neglected Figure of American Literary History," *Journalism Quarterly* 25 (1948): 54.
2. M.J. Lamb, *History of the City of New York* (New York, 1877–1880), 1:728, 728 n.
3. Allan Westcott, "William Leggett," *Dictionary of American Biography*, 11:147–48; William Leggett, *Political Writings,* ed. Theodore Sedgwick, Jr. (New York, 1840), 1:v; Leggett told his story of the trial in *E.P.,* 21, 22, 24, 27 April 2, 21, 29 May, 11 June 1835; he published the transcript of the trial on 8 July and his defense on 24 July 1835.
4. Page S. Proctor, Jr., "William Leggett (1801–1839): Journalist and Litera-tor," *Bibliographical Society of America, Papers* 44 (1950): 241–43;

Bigelow, *Bryant*, p. 326; G, *B.*, 1: 262; Glicksberg, *Leggett*, p. 52; Frederic Hudson, *Journalism in the United States* (New York, 1873), pp. 222, 620; Leggett, *Writings*, 1:v; Hammond, *Political Parties*, 1: 514–15.

5. William Leggett, *Tales and Sketches by A Country Schoolmaster* (New York, 1829), p. 154; Richard Moody, *Edwin Forrest* (New York, 1960), p. 85.

6. Walter Hugins, *Jacksonian Democracy and the Working Class* (Stanford, Calif., 1960), pp. 51–80; *E.P.*, 2, 3, 20, 21, 24 October 1834, 10 March, 13 June 1835.

7. Leggett, *Writings*, 1:100, 102–03, 248, 274; *E.P.*, 6, 26 August 1834.

8. *Leggett, Writings* 1:154; *E.P.*, 2, 18, 20, Oct. 1834; Richard Hofstadter, "William Leggett, Spokesman of Jacksonian Democracy," *Political Science Quarterly* 58 (1943): 587–88.

9. *Ibid.*, pp. 589–90; Leggett, *Writings.* 1:66–67, 2: 164; *E.P.*, 18 June, 18 Sept. 18, 20 Oct. 1834.

10. Leggett, *Writings*, 1:78, 85, 162, 164–65; *E.P.*, 18 June, 20 Oct. 1834.

11. Leggett, *Writings*, 1:61, 107, 164, 310–11; Leggett, *Writings*, 2: 164; *E.P.*, Oct. 1, 2, 25, 1834.

12. Leggett, *Writings*, 1:128, 165, 233, 246–47, 257.

13. *Ibid.*, 104.

14. Hofstadter, *Leggett*, pp. 591–92; Joseph Dorfman, "The Jacksonian Wage-Earner Thesis," *American Historical Review* 54 (1948–1949): 298, 305; *E.P.*, 1, 3, 23 June, 20 November 1834, 1, 2 May, 5 June 1835.

15. *E.P.*, 19, 20, 24, 26, 27, 29 November 1834; 24 Jan. 1835.

16. Hugins, *Jacksonian Democracy*, 155; Hofstadter, *Leggett*, 594; Leggett, *Writings*, 1: 143; *E.P.*, 2 June, 27, 28 Nov. 1834; 10, 20, 24, 30 Jan. 1835.

17. Leggett, *Writings*, 1: 172–76, 246, 256, 262–63; *E.P.*, 10, 24 Oct. 1834 18, 23 March 1835.
Hugins, *Jacksonian Democracy*, 179, 193, 197, 200; Hofstadter, *Leggett*, 593–93.

19. *E.P.*, 5 Aug. 1829; Theodore Sedgwick, III, Notebook (1829–1830), Sedgwick Papers, Mass. Hist. Sec.

20. George Wilson Pierson, *Tocqueville and Beaumont in America* (New York, 1938), 349, 731–32; Theodore Sedgwick, III. to Theodore Sedgwick, 20 Sept. 1833, 13 Feb., 15 May 1834, to Mrs. Theodore Sedgwick, 27 Feb. 1835, Sedgwick Papers.

21. Theodore Sedgwick, III. to Martin Van Buren, Van Buren Papers, Library of Congress; Theodore Sedgwick, III to Theodore Sedgwick, 9 July 1833, 29 Jan. 1834, to Mrs. Theodore Sedgwick, 27 Feb. 1834, to Edward Livingston, 24 July 1834, Sedgwick Papers, Mass. Hist. Sec.; *E.P.*, 16, 19 Sept. 1834.

22. [Theodore Sedgwick, III], *What Is A Monopoly? or Some Considerations upon the Subject of Corporation and Currency* (New York, 1835), 18: *E.P.*, 16 Sept. 1834, 7 Jan., 3 Feb. 1836.

23. *Ibid.*, 16, 19 Sept., 14 Nov., 26, 27 Dec. 1834; Theodore Sedgwick, III. to Theodore Sedgwick, 13 Feb. 1834.

24. *Ibid.,* 5 Oct. 1835; Sedgwick, *Monopoly,* 8–9, 18–19.
26. *Ibid.,* 33–34.
26. *Ibid.,* 22–31; *E.P.,* 29 Dec. 1834; Theodore Sedgwick, III to William Leggett, 24 Aug., 15 Dec. 1834, to P. Allen, 14 Jan. 1835, Sedgwick Papers, Mass. Hist. Sec.
27. *E.P.,* 12, 13, 18 Sept., 31 Oct., 4, 12, 13 Nov. 1834, 4 April 1835.
28. Theodore Sedgwick, III. to Martin Van Buren, 29 Dec. 1834, 2 Jan. 1835, to John A. Dix, 31 Dec. 1834, Sedgwick Papers, Mass. Hist. Sec.; *E.P.,* 2, 3, 5, 21 Jan., 16, 20, 23 Feb. 1835; Leggett, *Writings,* I, 257; F. Byrdsall, *The History of the Loco-Foco or Equal Rights Party* (New York, 1842), vi, 15, 27ff.
29. *Ibid.,* 30–31; Hugins, *Jacksonian Democracy,* 36–38; *E.P.,* 18, 19 Sept. 2, 5, 19 Oct. 1835.
30. Byrdsall, *Loco-Foco,* 19, 23, 27; Nevins, *Post,* 152–53; *E.P.,* 18 May, 5 Sept., 7 Nov., 26 Dec. 1835; Michael Burnham to Bryant, 6 Nov. 1835, Henry J. Anderson to Bryant, 22 Jan. 1835 [1836], B–G.
31. Michael Burnham to Bryant, 6 Nov. 1835, B–G.; Bryant to Leggett, 15 April 1835, Bryant to Mrs. Bryant, 30 Jan. 1836, G–R; Mrs. Francis Bryant, manuscript diary, G–R.
32. Bigelow, *Bryant,* 89; Bryant to Mrs. Bryant, 1, 26 April, 23 May, 4 July 1836, G–R.
33. *E.P.,* 3 Nov. 1836.

CHAPTER 8

1. *L. & J.,* I, 396, III, 3; Cooper, *Notions,* I, 315–21, 325, 329.
2. *L. & J.,* I, xxii, 262, 263n, 287–88, 395, II, 34, 73, 84; William Dunlap, *Diary* (New York, 1929–1930), III, 606–07, 645–46; Cooper, *Notions,* I, 158–60. Grossman, *Cooper,* 76; Marius Bewley, "Fenimore Cooper and the Economic Age," *American Literature,* 26 (1954–1955), 186; James Fenimore Cooper, *A Letter to His Countrymen* (New York, 1834), 14–15.
3. William Charvat, "Cooper as Professional Author," New York Historical Assoc., *Fenimore Cooper: A Re Appraisal* (Cooperstown, N.Y., 1954), 128–43; *L. & J.,* I–II, *passim;* Cooper, *Correspondence,* I, 249.
4. *Ibid.,* 264.
5. *Ibid.,* 359; Grossman, *Cooper,* 95; Cooper, *Notions,* I, 171; James Fenimore Cooper, *The Momikins* (New York, n.d.), 327–28, 357, 360, 361, 365.
6. *Ibid.,* 326, 365; *L. & J.,* III, 233, 247, 329–30; Cooper, *Correspondence,* I, 341, 359; James Fenimore Cooper, *Homeward Bound* (New York, 1903), 243. Dorthy Waples, *The Whig Myth of James Fenimore Cooper* (New Haven, Conn., 1938), 31. *L. & J.,* II, 345–46; Cooper, *A Letter,* 14; Shulenberger, 42–43.
7. *L. & J.,* III, 213, 233, 247, 329–30; Cooper, *Correspondence,* I, 359.
8. *L. & J.,* III, 269; Meyers, *Persuasion,* 56; Cooper, *Notions,* I, 162–63; II, 315–16.

9. Bewley, 194; Edwin H. Cady, *The Gentleman in America: A Literary Study in American Culture* (Syracuse, N.Y., 1949), 106–08; Cooper, *Pioneers,* 232, 331; *Hom)ward Bound,* 10–11, 50.

10. *Ibid.,* 243–44, 413; *L. & J.,* III, 247.

11. *Ibid.,* 65–182ff; Spiller, *Cooper,* chapters XIV–XVII; Waples, *Whig Myth.*

12. *North American Review,* 35 (1832), 190, 46 (1839), 9.

13. Dewey, *Sedgwick,* 44, 47, 91, 101, 113, 237; Catherine M. Sedgwick, *The Poor Rich Man and the Rich Poor Man* (New York, 1843), 22, 39; *Home* (Boston and New York, 1837), 117, 120, 136; Birdsall, *Berkshire,* 252, 292.

14. Dewey, *Sedgwick,* 101; Catherine M. Sedgwick, *Clarence; or a tale of our own times* (Philadelphia, 1830), II, 87–88, 147, 196–97, 279–80, 285–86.

15. Dewey, *Sedgwick,* 102–03, 271; Sedgwick, *Clarence,* I, 148, 150, 240, II, 87–88, 147, 285.

16. Theedore Sedgwick (II), *Public and Private Economy* (New York, 1836–1839), I, 187–91.

17. *Ibid.,* I, 214; Sedgwick, *Home,* 40, 79–81; *The Linwoods; or "Sixty Years Since" in America* (New York, 1835), II, 286.

18. Sister Mary Michael Welsh, *Catherine Maria Sedgwick: Her Position in the Literature and Thought of Her Times*)Washington, D.C., 1937), 12, 15, 135–36, *passim;* Sedgwick, *Linwoods,* II, 286; *Home,* 13–14, 28, 117–18; *Clarence,* I, 48; *Means and Ends, or Self-Training* (Boston, 1839), 8, 17, 73, 157, 171–74, 254, 270.

19. Sedgwick, *Poor Rich Man,* 22, 39–40, 112ff, 176; *Means and Ends,* 262–66; *Linwoods,* I, 67–68.

20. Dewey, *Sedgwick,* 267; *Poor Rich Man,* 39–40, 112, 146; *Home,* 40, 117, 120; Catherine M. Sedgwick to Professor Potter, Misc. Papers, Sedgwick, N.Y.H.S.

21. *Knickerbocker Magazine,* 11 (1838), 75; Welsh, *Sedgwick,* 36; Dewey, *Sedgwick,* 252, 254, 260–61.

22. Sedgwick, *Poor Rich Man,* 178; *Means and Ends,* 15, 262–63.

23. July, *Verplanck,* 244; Julia Sands to Bryant, 23 Jan. 1836, B–G.

24. Gulian C. Verplanck, *The Advantages and Dangers of the American Scholar* (New York, 1836), 5, 7, 9–10, 11–13, 28, 44–49.

25. *Ibid.,* 21–22, 51–53; Verplanck, *Discourses and Addresses,* 226–27, 251.

CHAPTER 9

1. G, B., I, 356, 362–63, 366–67; Nevins, *Post,* 164, 166; Drew, *Letters,* 354–55.

2. *Ibid.,* 354; Nevins, *Post,* 136, 163; Bryant to J.M. Forbes, 25 Jan. 1862, Houghton Library, Harvard.

3. George V. Bohman. "A Poet's Mother: Sarah Snell Bryant in Illinois," Illinois State Historical Society, *Journal,* 33 (1940), 171n; Huntress and Lorch, 640; Drew, *Letters,* 348, 353.

4. *Niles' Register,* 48 (1835), 168, 218; [Hunt's] *Merchants Magazine and*

Commercial Review, 3 (1840), 308, 7 (1842), 187, 284–85; Bryant to Mrs. Bryant, 14 April 1836, G–R.

5. *L. & J.,* III, 208; Alfred H. Conrad and John R. Meyer, "The Economics of Slavery in the Ante-Bellum South," *Journal of Political Economy,* 66 (1958), 102; Hammond, *Political History,* II, 451–52; McMaster, VI, 341; *E.P.,* April 25, 1836.

6. Hammond, *Banks and Politics,* 158, 184–85, 577, 595; *E.P.,* 23, 25, 26, 28 April, 26 Sept. 1836, 6 Feb., 8 July 1837; Bryant to Mrs. Bryant, 4 July 1836, G–R.

7. *E.P.,* 7 April, 4 Nov. 1836, 18 March 1837.

8. G, B., I, 357; Samuel Rezneck, "The Social History of An American Depression, 1837–1843," *American Historical Review,* 40 (1934–1935), 670–74; Charles Sedgwick, *Letters,* 86, 98; Dewey, *Sedgwick,* 275, 278; Schlesinger, *Age of Jackson,* 260; *E.P.,* 21 Sept. 1837.

9. Bryant to R.H. Dana, 27 Feb. 1837, 28 June, 26 Nov. 1838, G–R.

10. *E.P.,* 7 April, 4 Nov. 1836.

11. *Ibid.,* 6 Feb., 11 May, 8 July, 4, 5 Oct. 1837, 20 March 1838, 3 June, 19 Sept. 1839; Birdsall, *Berkshire,* 31.

12. Leggett, *Writings,* II, 306, 318–19.

13. *E.P.,* 22 Sept., 31 Oct. 1837.

14. Lee Benson, *The Concept of Jacksonian Democracy: New York as A Test Case* (Princeton, N.J., 1961), 94–95, 103; [Gulian C. Verplanck, *et. al.*], *The State Triumvirate, A Political Tale* (N.Y., 1819), 67–68; *E.P.,* 1, 3, 4, Nov. 1837.

15. New York State Senate, *Journal,* 61 sess. (1838), 166, 178, 455–56, 466–68, 480; Hammond, *Banks and Politics,* 594–96.

16. Reginald C. McGrane, *The Panic of 1837* (Chicago, 1924), 100; Benson, *Concept,* 102; *United States Magazine and Democratic Review,* 5 (1839), 431; *E.P.,* 14, 15 March 1838.

17. *Ibid.,* 13, 15, 17, 19, 20 March, 21 April 1838, 19 Sept. 1839.

18. *Ibid.,* 19 Aug., 6 Oct. 1837, 20 March 1838.

19. *Ibid.,* 26 July 1837, 8 Nov. 1838, 5, 6 June, 27 July, 31 Dec. 1839.

20. Ralph Waldo Emerson, *The Heart of Emerson's Journal,* Bliss Perry, ed. (Boston and New York, 1926), 192.

21. *United States Magazine and Democratic Review,* 6 (1839), 140–42.

22. Hammond, *Banks and Politics,* 562, 571, 573–74, 584, 594–96, 599; Don C. Sowers, *The Financial History of New York from 1789 to 1912* (New York, 1914), 57–58; Dorfman and Tugwell, 235–36n.

24. Hammond, *Banks and Politics,* 329, 574, 594; G, B., I, 325n.

24. *Ibid.,* I, 356, II, 35.

CHAPTER 10

1. See Chapters IV, V, VIII.

2. Leggett, *Writings,* II, 172, 274–75, 323.

3. *E.P.,* 9 Oct., 18 Dec. 1828, 9 Oct. 1829, 7 Sept. 1838, 30 May, 6, 9 Nov. 1840.
4. Verplanck, *Influence of Moral Causes,* 26, 31–32; *Advantages and Dangers,* 57–59; Hone, *Diary,* 569–70; July, *Verplanck,* 218, 235–36, 240–42.
5. Frank L. Mott, *American Journalism* (New York, 1950), 168, 233, 310; *United States Magazine and Democratic Review,* 6 (1839), 18–19; *E.P.,* 15 May 1830, 17 March 1831.
6. Bryant, "Medfield," *Tales of Glauber-Spa; E.P.,* 23 Feb. 1829; *Democratic Review,* 6 (1839), 19.
7. Waples, *Whig Myth,* 92–109; Cooper, *Notions,* II, 102–03; Robert E. Spiller, ed., "Fenimore Cooper: Critic of His Times, New Letters from Rome and Paris," *American Literature,* 1 (1929–1930), 136; *L. & J.,* I, 243–44, 431–32, II, 76, 351, 377, IV, 106.
8. Charles I. Glicksberg, "Cooper and Bryant , A Literary Friendship," *The Colophon,* pt. 20 (1935), n.p.; Cooper, *A Letter,* 3, 5, 50, 87; *E.P.,* 13 June 1834.
9. Bryant, *Orations and Addresses,* 75; Grossman, *Cooper,* 106–13; Ethel R. Outland, *The "Effingham" Liberals on Cooper* (Madison, Wisc., 1929), 14–17, 33, *passim; L. & J.,* III, 271–284.
10. *Ibid.,* 126–28; Cooper, *Notions,* II, 102.
11. James Fenimore Cooper, *The American Democrat* (New York, 1956), 113–32.
12. James Grossman, "Cooper and the Responsibility of the Press," New York Historical Association, *James Fenimore Cooper: A Re-Appraisal* (Cooperstown, N.Y., 1954), 149; Meyers, *Persuasion,* Chap. V; Cooper, *Homeward Bound,* 37–39, 78–88, 155, 189; *Home as Found* (New York, 1903), 4, 210–11, 349; *American Democrat,* 114, 127–28; *L. & J.,* III, 269, 271, 351.
13. *Ibid.,* IV, 213; Glicksberg, *Cooper and Bryant,* n.p.,; *E.P.,* June 24, 1834, 17 June 1835, 13 April 1838, 11 Jan. 1839.
14. Waples, 14–15, 172, 218–19, 231; Grossman, *Cooper,* 131; Outland, 72–73; *Knickerbocker Magazine,* 12 (1838), 267; *L. & J.,* IV, 146.
15. Outland, 14–17; *L. & J.,* IV, 218.
16. Waples, *Whig Myth,* 294; *L. & J.,* IV, 44–46, 58, 221; Cooper, *Corres:-pondence,* II, 415–18.
17. Outland, 181, 199–200; Spiller, *Cooper,* 253; Bryant, *Orations and Addresses,* 75–76; James G. Wilson, *Bryant and His Friends* (New York, 1886), 236, 243; *E.P.,* 28 June 1839; Bryant to R.H. Dana, 27 Feb. 1837, 16 Jan. 1844, G–R.
18. Outland, 181, 199–200, 258; *L. & J.,* IV, 3, 85, 144, 195–96; *American Democrat,* 144–47.

CHAPTER 11

1. Byrdsall, *Loco-Foco,* 46, 98–99; Schlesinger, *Age of Jackson,* 234, 260; *E.P.,* 29-31 May 1839; Leggett to Bryant, 11 Oct. 1838, G–R.

2. William Trimble, "Diverging Tendencies in New York Democracy in the Period of the Locofocos," *American Historical, Review,* 24 (1918–1919), 416; David Dudley Field, *Speeches, Arguments, and Miscellaneous Papers* (New York, 1884–1890), II, 215–15; Leggett, *Writings,* I, viii; Parke Godwin, *Out of the Past* (New York, 1870), 82.

3. Charles H. Haswell, *Reminiscences of An Octogenarian of ... New York (1816 to 1860)* (New York, 1896), 381, 390–91; Birdsall, *Berkshire,* 13–14; *Hunt's Merchant's Magazine,* 10 (1844), 462; *Knickerbocker Magazine,* 24 (1844), 181–84; William C. Bryant, J. Todd, *et. al.,* ed., *Berkshire Jubilee* (Albany, 1845), 8; William Gilmore Simms, *Letters* (Columbia, S.C., 1952), I, 426; *United States Magazine and Democratic Review,* 6 (1939), 501–02; *E.P.,* 25 July 1843, 5 Sept. 1844.

4. Herbert D. Donovan, *The Barnburners* (New York, 1925), 20–21, 32–33, 41; Trimble, *Diverging Tendencies,* 409 ff; *E.P.,* 28 Nov. 1842, 16, 23 Jan., 3 Feb., 17 July 1843; Bryant to A.C. Flagg, 24 Jan. 1843, Flagg Papers, N.Y.P.L.; Lorenzo Sherwood to Bryant, 24 Jan. 1843, H.H. Vandyck, 13 Feb. 1843, B–G.

5. Donovan, *Barnburners,* 22; July, *Verplanck,* 225–26; Gulian C. Verplanck, "Report of Mr. Verplanck, from the Committee of Finance...19 April 1839," in [John Duer], *Vindication of the Public Faith of New York & Pennsylvania* (London, 1840), 47–48.

6. *E.P.,* 4, 5 Nov. 1842, 4 April, 17 July 1843, 22 May 1844.

7. McGrane, *Panic of 1837,* 143; Sowers, *Financial History,* 85–86; *E.P.,* 24 April 1843, 21 Jan., 29 June 1844, 29 Oct., 11 Nov. 1846; *Hunt's Merchant's Magazine,* 10 (1844), 74, 77, 366, 477, 12 (1845), 559, 13 (1845), 182–84.

8. John A. Garraty, *Silas Wright* (New York, 1959), 353; Margaret Clapp, *Forgotten First Citizen: John Bigelow* (Boston, 1947), 52, 57, 70; *E.P.,* 3 April, 22 May, 14 July, 17 Nov. 1843, 29 June 1844, 23 Sept., 17 Oct., 1845, 16 Feb., 14 March, 4 May, 1846.

9. Stewart Mitchell, *Horatio Seymour of New York* (Cambridge, Mass., 1938), 87–88; Donovan, *Barnburners,* 43ff; Hammond, *Political History,* III, 642, 653; John S. Jenkins, *The Life of Silas Wright* (Auburn, N.Y., 1847), 203–04; New York State, *Constitution of ... 1846* (n.p., 1847), 3–5, 21–26.

19. New York State, *Constitution,* 4–5, 15–18; Joseph S. Auerbach, *The Bar of Other Days* (New York, 1940), 208–09, 211–12; Henry W. Scott, *Distinguished American Lawyers* (New York, 1891), 359–60, 363–69; Miller, *Legal Mind,* 289–295; *E.P.,* 3 April, 1848, 3 Jan. 1850.

11. Benson, *Concept,* 102–07; *E.P.,* 6 March 1841, 23 Jan. 1845, 14 March, 4 May, 1 June 1846, 21 Feb., 21 April 1848.

12. Robert G. Albion, "Commercial Fortunes in New York," *New York History,* 16 (1935), 158–61; Sidney D. Brummer., *Political History of New York State during the Period of the Civil War* (New York, 1911), 40; *E.P.,* 8, 18, 23, Sept. 1846, 30 April 1857. *Harper's Weekly,* 17 Jan. 1857, p. 33.

13. Hammond, *Political History,* III, 694–95; *E.P.,* 19 Dec. 1845, 14 April 1846.

CHAPTER 12

1. Nevins, *Post,* 190; G, *B.,* II, 31–32; Simms, *Letters,* I, 426; *E.P.,* 29 Dec. 1843.
2. William H. Seward, *Autobiographty,* F.W. Seward, ed. (New York, 1891), I, 466; Century Club, *Proceedings ... in Honor ... of Gulian C. Verplanck* (New York, 1870), 24, 26, 63–64; John H. Gourlie, *The Origin and History of "The Century"* (New York, 1856), 10, 24; Bryant, *et. al.* to Verplanck, n.d., Verplanck Papers, N.Y.H.S.
3. Charvat, *Cooper,* 129, 134–35; L.H. Butterfield, "Cooper's Inheritance: The Otsego Country and Its Founders," New York Historical Assoc., *Fenimore Cooper: A Re-Appraisal* (Cooperstown, N.Y.), 37–38; *L. & J.,* IV, 436; Cooper, *Correspondence,* II, 568.
4. Spiller, *Cooper,* 260; Cooper, *Home as Found,* 45, 52, 295, 379–80, *passim; The Chainbearer* (Boston and New York, n.d. "Edition de Luxe," Brainard Publishing Co.), 107, 398.
5. David M. Ellis, "The Coopers and New York State Landholding Systems," New York State Historical Assoc., *James Fenimore Cooper: A Re-Appraisal* (Cooperstown, N.Y., 1954), 44–45; *Landlords and Farmers in the Hudson-Mohawk Region, 1790–1850* (Ithaca, 1946); Bewley, 190; John F. Ross, *The Social Criticism of Feminore Cooper* (Berkeley, Cal., 1933), 32–33; Cooper, *Chainbearer,* 123, 172–73, 189, 219–20, 221m, 343, 426, 472; James Fenimore Cooper, *Satanstoe* (New York and Boston, n,d., "Edition de Luxe," Brainard Publishing Co.), 13, 71, 341, 504–05; *Notions,* I, 264, II, 97–98.
6. Cady, *Gentleman,* 114ff; *L. & J.,* I, xxxi, II, 448, IV, 477–78; Cooper, *Chainbearer,* 191, 199, 432; *Satanstos,* 6; *Home as Found,* 194.
7. Jenkins, *Wright,* 179–87, 197–98; Spiller, *Cooper,* 307; New York State, *Constitution ... 1846,* 4; James Fenimore Cooper, *The Ways of the Hour* (New York, 1903), 3, 4, 10, 13–14, 23; *E.P.,* 18, 23 Dec. 1844.
8. James Fenimore Cooper, *The Crater* (Cambridge, Mass., 1962), 442–43; *American Democrat,* 69.
9. James Fenimore Cooper, *Autobiography of A Pocket-Handkerchief* (Chapel Hill, N.C., 1949), 33, 37, 55–56, 63, 67, 78–79, 88–89, 94–95; *Crater,* 354–55; *L. & J.,* III, 441.
10. James Fenimore Cooper, *The Spy* (New York, 1849), xii; Cooper, *Correspondence,* II, 732; *Crater,* 355.
11. *Ibid.,* xxiv, xxviii, 327, 430–56; Cooper, *Correspondence,* II, 574; *Ways of the Hour,* 67, 188, 202, 221, 351, 355, 359; *North American Review,* 71 (1850), 134.
12. *L. & J.,* I. xxxii, IV, 98, 116, 277; Cooper, *Correspondence,* II, 403–04, 601, 749; *Home as Found,* 154–57; *Crater,* 6.
13. *Satanstoe,* 47, 153, 173n, 320.
14. Cooper, *Correspondence,* II, 666ff, 691; *E.P.,* 25, 26 Feb. 1852 (Bryant's address can also be found in *Orations and Addresses* and in *Prose Writings,* I); Cooper, *Ways of the Hour,* 107–08.

CHAPTER 13

1. Bryant to Mrs. Bryant, 14 Sept. 1846, G–R; Ralph Waldo Emerson, *Letters,* Ralph L. Rusk, ed. (New York, 1939), III, 29; *E.P.,* 6 Feb., 13 April 1844, 4 Feb. 1846.
3. *Ibid.,* 4 May 1854.
3. Clapp, *Bigelow,* 40; Dewey, *Sedgwick,* 293, 307, 322, 420–22.
4. *Ibid.,* 307–08, 335–36, 346, 420–21.
5. *Ibid.,* 368–70; Catherine M. Sedgwick, *Married or Single?* (New York, 1857), I, v–vi.
6. *Ibid.,* I, 133, 159–60, II, 36; Parke Godwin, *Democracy, Constructive and Pacific* (New York, [1844], t,p,
7. Carlos Baker, "Parke Godwin, Pathfinder in Politics and Journalism," in *The Lives of Eighteen from Princeton,* Willard Thorp, ed. (Princeton, N.J., 1946), 212–16; G, B., I, 334–39; Parke Godwin to Mrs. Bryant, 23 Feb. 1840, B–G.
8. Godwin, *Out of the Past,* 41–44; *The Pathfinder,* 1 (1843), 33, 129.
9. Baker, *Godwin,* 216; *Pathfinder,* 1 (1843), 2, 52, 81, 129, 195.
10. *Ibid.,* 49, 97; Godwin, *Democracy,* 16, 21, 24, 55; Parke Godwin, *Vala, A Mythological Tale* (New York, 1851), 24; Charles Sotheran, *Horace Greeley and Other Pioneers of American Socialism* (New York, 1915), 137; Baker, *Godwin,* 217ff.
11. *Pathfinder,* 1 (1843), 49; Godwin , *Democracy,* 9, 12, 16, 22, 24; Parke Godwin, *A Popular View of the Doctrines of Charles Fourier* (New York, 1844), 69.
12. *Pathfinder,* 1 (1843), 66, 81; Godwin, *Out of the Past,* 87–88; *Democracy,* 25, 27; *Popular View,* 31, 47, 49; "Notes for Speech on the Organization of Labor," B–G.
13. Godwin, *Popular View,* 27–28, 51–69; *Democracy,* 32–36.
14. Lee Marx, "The Machine in the Garden," *New England Quarterly,* 29 (1956), 27–52; *The Harbinger,* 6 (1847–1848), 203.
15. Arthur A. Ekirch, Jr., *The Idea of Progress in America, 1815–1860* (New York, 1944), 143; *Hunt's Merchant's Magazine,* 11 (1844), 198; Godwin, *Out of the Past,* 48, 69, 251–52; Godwin to Charles A. Dana, 17 May, 17 Sept., 8 Nov., 1844, 14 Feb., 12 May 1845, B–G.
16. G, B., I, 370–71; Baker, *Godwin,* 217; Godwin to Charles A. Dana, 1 Aug. 1845, 5 Dec. 1846, B–G.
17. Godwin to Dana, Monday, 17 [1844?], Feb. 14, 1845, May 1846, B–G; Dana to Godwin, 18 April 1846, G–R; *Harbinger,* 6 (1847–1848), 12.
18. John Humphrey Noyes, *History of American Socialisms* (New York, 1961 [reprint of 1870 ed.], 212, 218; Clarence L.F. Gohdes, *The Periodicals of American Transcendentalism* (Durham, N.C., 1931), 103–06, 111–12; Octavius Brooks Frothingham, *George Ripley* (Boston, 1882), 178–80; *Harbinger,* 8 (1848–1849), 116.
19. Horace Greeley, *Recollections of A Busy Life* (New York, 1868), 151–52; Emerson, *Letters,* III, 21; *Works* (1911), X, 349, 352–53; Ekirch, *Progress,*

144; Parke Godwin, *Commemorative Addresses* (New York, 1895), 7–9; Godwin to Charles A. Dana, 12 Aug. 1846, B–G.

20. Merle Curti, "Young America," *American Historical Review,* 32 (1926–1927), 34–35, 38–39, 47–48; Godwin to the Editors of the Harbinger (n.d., 1846?), B–G.

21. Parke Godwin, *Political Essays* (New York, 1856), 115–21, 125–27, 156–70.

22. *Ibid.,* 71–72, 82–83, 105, 204–05, 271–72; 276–77; *Out of the Past,* 149–50, 169, 174–75, 269, 286, 314, 317–18, 323.

CHAPTER 14

1. Welsh, *Sedgwick,* 106; Sedgwick, *Abolition,* 16–17.

2. *Ibid.,* 10–18, 30–33, 38–48.

3. *Ibid.,* 32–33; Theodore Sedgwick, III. to Theodore Sedgwick, Oct. 8, 1833, Sedgwick Papers, Mass. Hist. Sec.

4. Robert E. Spiller "Fenimore Cooper's Defense of Slave-Owning America," *American Historical Review,* 35 (1930), 580–82; Cooper, *Notions,* I, 269–71, 285; Sedgwick, *Abolition,* 32–33; *E.P.,* July 8, 1834.

5. Theodore Sedgwick, III to Theodore Sedgwick, 8 Oct. 1833, Sedgwick Papers; Theodore Sedgwick, III., *A Memoir of the Life of William Livingston* (New York, 1833), 399; Theodore Sedgwick, *Public and Private Economy,* I, 248–60; Bryant, *Oration ... 1820,* 10.

6. *E.P.,* 8, 11, 19 July 1834, 10 Feb., 9 Sept. 1835, 22 Oct. 1838; Leggett, *Writings,* I, 208, II, 34–35, 53–55, 64–65, 149–50, 230, 298, 328–30.

7. G, *B.,* I, 333; *E.P.,* 21 April, 20 May, 8 Aug. 1836, 7 Feb. 1837.

8. Theodore Sedgwick, III., manscript diary, 1841, Sedgwick Papers, Mass. Hist. Soc.

9. Floan, *South,* 15–53; Simms, *Letters,* I, 350n, xciv; Bryant, *Prose Writings,* II, 34.

10. Bryant, *Oration...1820,* 5–6; *New York Review,* 2 (1825–1826), 285; *E.P.,* 23, 30 Sept. 1829, 17 June 1836, 4 Aug. 1837; James K. Paulding, *Letters of James Kirke Paulding,* Ralph M. Aderman, ed. (Madison, Wisc., 1962), 201–02.

11. *E.P.,* 14, 15 Nov., 15 Dec. 1843; A.C. Flagg to O. Hungerford, 9 May 1844, A.C. Flagg Papers, N.Y.P.L.

12. James C.N. Paul, *Rift in the Democracy* (Philadelphia, 1951), 63, 100, 120, 127, 165; G, *B.,* I, 414, 420; *E.P.,* 25 Sept. 1843, 18, 20, 25, 30 April, 9, 24, 29, 31 May, 8 June 1844.

13. G, *B.,* I, 416–20; *E.P.,* 24, 25, 27, 29 July, 8, 9, 19, 20 Aug. 1844; A.C. Flagg, draft addressed to "Gentlemen," 29 July 1844, Printed circular, A.C. Flagg Papers, N.Y.P.L.

14. Benson, *Concept,* 219–34, 256, 268–69; *E.P.,* 22 June, 21 Aug., 6, 8 Sept., 15 Oct., 8, 13, 28 Nov. 1844, 13, 15, 18, 20, 27 Jan., 10 March, 29 Nov. 1845; Bryant to C.E. Anderson, 1 Oct. 1845, G–R.

CHAPTER 15

1. Nevins, *Post*, 178–79; *E.P.*, 11, 13, 15, 20 May, 9, 18, Feb. 1848; Dewey, *Sedgwick*, 302.
2. *E.P.*, 5, 11 Feb., 4 April 1848, 13 March 1850.
3. Donovan, *Barnburners*, 80–95; Hammond, *Political History*, III, 694–95; Henry B. Stanton, *Random Recollections* (New York, 1886), 79; *E.P.*, 5, 7 Nov. 1846.
4. Donovan, *Barnburners*, 77; Joseph G. Rayback, "Martin Van Buren's Break with James K. Polk: The Record," *New York History*, 36 (1955), 54–60; Garraty, *Wright*, 363–64, 375; Bryant to George Bancroft, 14 March 1845, Bancroft Papers, Mass. Hist. Soc.; Parke Godwin to William L. Marcy, 3 Oct. 1845, B–G; John A. Dix to A.C. Flagg, 22 Nov. 1844, A.C. Flagg Papers, N.Y.P.L.
5. Donovan, *Barnburners*, 85–86, 93–97; Walter L. Ferre, "The New York Democracy: Division and Reunion, 1847–1852," Ph. D. Dissertation, University of Pennsylvania, 1953, 79–82, 99–102; *E.P.*, 2 Feb. 1847, 5 Feb. 1848.
6. Donovan, *Barnburners*, 97; G, B., II, 40–41; John H. Bryant to Bryant, Jan. and 5 Jan. 1848, B–G.
7. Theodore Sedgwick, III., *The American Citizen: His True Position, Character and Duties* (New York, 1847), 18, 26–27; *E.P.*, 2 Dec. 1847; Sedgwick to Martin Van Buren, 3 Dec. 1847, Van Buren Papers, Library of Congress.
8. Donovan, *Barnburners*, 99–103; John Bigelow, *Retrospections of An Active Life* (Garden City, N.Y., 1913), I, 71; *E.P.*, 15, 16, 19, 25 Feb., 11 March, 15 April, 6, 26 May, 1 June 1848.
9. *E.P.*, 1, 13, 15, 21, 23 June, 4 July 1848.
10. Allan Nevins, *Ordeal of the Union* (New York, 1947), I, 206; Theodore Clark, *The Liberty and Free Soil Parties in the Northwest* (New York, 1897), 140, 178; *E.P.*, 2, 10, 11, 15, Aug. 1848; Kirk H. Porter, compil., *National Party Platforms* (New York, 1924), 22–25.
11. Nevins, *Post*, 244; *E.P.*, 21 July, 28 Oct., 3, 7, 8, 13, 18 Nov. 1848.
12. Donovan, *Barnburners*, 109–16; Ferree, 237 and n., 260; Mitchell, *Seymour*, 113–14, 117–18; Clapp, *Bigelow*, 67.
13. *E.P.*, 20 March 1849, 16, 27 Aug. 14 Sept. 1850; Bigelow *Retrospections*, I, 109, 120–21.
14. G, B., II, 62–63; Roy F. Nicholas, *The Democratic Machine* (New York, 1923), 229–39; Clapp, *Bigelow*, 75, 79, 81; *E.P.*, 24 April, 2 July, 24 Sept., 5 Nov. 1850.
15. *E.P.*, 20 April, 13 June ,12 July, 21 Sept. 1848, 12 Jan., 11, 19 May, 13 July, 24 Dec. 1850; William Cullen Bryant, *Letters of A Traveller* (New York, 1871), 347–49; Bryant to Mrs. Bryant, 31 March 1849, G–R.
16. *E.P.*, 16, 20, Jan. 1849, 20 Feb., 9, 20 March, 14 June 1850.
17. *Ibid.*, 5 March 1850; Clapp, *Bigelow*, 83.

CHAPTER 16

1. *E.P.,* 1 Jan. 1851.
2. *Pathfinder,* 1 (1843), 65, 145; *Harbinger,* 6 (1847–1848), 6; Godwin to Charles A. Dana, 8 Sept. 1845, B–G.
3. *Pathfinder,* 1 (1843), 65, 146' 163; Godwin to Charles A. Dana, 24 Oct. 1845, 12 Aug. 1846, B–G.
4. Frank L. Mott, *A History of American Magazines, 1850–1865* (Cambridge, Mass., 1957), 420ff; Godwin, *Commemorative Addresses,* 31.
5. Godwin, *Political Essays,* 15–17, 32, 43–44, 51, 264–68.
6. *Ibid.,* 17–19, 29, 31, 55, 269, 271.
7. G, B., II, 56, 74; William D. Hoyt, Jr., ed., "Some Unpublished Bryant Correspondence," *New York History,* 21 (1940), 65, 67–68.
8. G, B, II, 63; Nevins, *Post,* 244–47; *E.P.,* 7, 15, 23, 24 June, 20 Sept., 26 Oct., 5, 11, Nov. 1852, 14 July 1853, 19 Jan. 1854.
9. *Ibid.,* 17, 23, 24, 25, 31 Jan., 11, 15, 17, 27, 30 March, 11, 23 May, 31 July, 4 Aug. 1854.
10. Bigelow, *Retrospections,* I, 135; *E.P.,* 8 June, 4, 8, 21 Sept. 1854.
11. *Ibid.,* 27, 30 Sept., 23, 30 Oct., 6, 11, Nov. 1854.
12. *Ibid.,* 9, 11 Oct., 9, 18, Nov. 1854; Cyrus Bryant to Bryant, 16 July 1854, G–R.
13. Editors of the *Evening Post* to Samuel J. Tilden, 3 Sept. 1855, Henry D. Rich to John Van Buren, 21 Nov. 1855, Tilden Papers, N.Y.P.L.
14. G, B., II, 89; Bigelow, *Retrospections,* I, 141–43; Andrew W. Crandall, *The Early History of the Republican Party* (Boston, 1930), 97–98; Porter, *Platforms,* 48–50.
15. Baker, *Godwin,* 223; Godwin, *Political Essays,* 313, 317, 319–20; Edward G. Bernard, "New Light on Lowell as Editor," *New England Quarterly,* 10 (1937), 337–38; Godwin to Mr. Underwood, 26 March 1858, B–G.; Francis Curtis, *The Republican Party, 1854–1904,* II, 504–05.
16. Mott, *Magazines,* 469–73; Theodore Sedgwick [Jr.], *A Treatise on the... Interpretation and Construction of Statutory and Constitutional Law,* 2nd ed. (New York, 1874), 606–07; *Address Before the Alumni Association of Columbia College* (New York, 1858), 29, 32, 33–34; *Harper's Weekly,* 1 (1857), 1, 145, 193, 241; Theodore Sedgwick, Jr., diary , Dec,. 1857, Sedgwick Papers, Mass. Hist. Sec.
17. George Templeton Strong, *Diary,* Allan Nevins, ed. (New York, 1952), 377; Sedgwick, diary, Dec. 1857, Sedgwick Papers, Mass. Hist. Sec.; Obituary of Theodore Sedgwick, *Harper's Weekly,* 31 Dec. 1859.
18. Floan, *South,* 157, 162; *E.P.,* 11 June, 24 Sept., 4 Nov. 1856.
19. John W. Higham, "The Changing Loyalties of William Gilmore Simms," *Journal of Southern History,* 9 (1943), 216–20; Nevins, *Post,* 235–36, 251; *E.P.,* 23, 27 May 1856, 18, 19, 31 Oct. 7 Nov., 1 Dec. 1859.
20. G, B., II, 127; Bigelow, *Retrospections,* I, 252–53; Nevins, *Post,* 259–60; *E.P.,* 25 April, 18, 23 May 1860; Bryant to John Bigelow, 13 April 1860, G–R.

21. James A. Briggs, *An Authentic Account of Hon. Abraham Lincoln Being Invited to give an Address in Cooper Institute* (Putnam, Conn., 1915), n.p.; *E.P.,* 28 Feb. 1860; Clapp, *Bigelow,* 137; Nevins, *Post,* 268.
22. *E.P.,* 2 May. 7 Nov. 1860; Sidney D. Brummer, *Political History of New York State during the Period of the Civil War* (New York, 1911), 88; G, *B.,* II, 145–46.
23. Brummer, *Political History,* 129–30; Harry J. Carman and Richard H. Luthin, *Lincoln and the Patronage* (New York, 1943), 14, 37, 62–63, 102; Bigelow, *Retrospections,* I, 319–20, 365.
24. G, *B.,* II, 128; Alexander C. Flick, *Samuel Jones Tilden* (New York, 1939), 119–22; Bigelow, *Bryant,* 111; *Retrospections,* I, 292–93, 423–24; *E,P.,* 15, 19, 20, 30, 31 Oct., 7, 8, Nov. 1860.

CHAPTER 17

1. Bryant, *Prose Writings,* I, 367.
2. *E.P.,* 20, Dec. 1860, 2, 5, 7 Jan., 5, 12, 15, 16, 18, 25 Feb. 1861.
3. McDowell, *Bryant,* xxi; G, *B.,* II, 158, 161; *E.P.,* 13, 16 April 1861.
4. *Ibid.,* 7 Jan. 1861, 20 Jan., 24, 25 Feb., 4 March 1862; William Cullen Bryant and Sydney H. Gay, *A Popular History of the United States* (New York, 1876), I, x; Brown, *Bryant,* 32.
5. Brummer, *Political History,* 225, 252.
6. *Ibid.,* 205–06, 225; G, *B.,* II, 201; *E.P.,* 23 Sept., 1, 2 Oct. 1862, 2, 3 Jan. 1863.
7. Brummer, *Political History,* 303, 317–18; Brother Basil Lee, *Discontent in New York City, 1861–1865* (Washington, D.C., 1943), 270; *E.P.,* 10, 19 Feb. 1863.
8. July, *Verplanck,* 223–24ff; Verplanck, draft letter to the New York Anti-Slavery Society, 24 Oct. 1837, Verplanck Papers, N.Y.H.S.; Strong, *Diary,* III, 302.
9. The Century Association, *The Century, 1847–1946* (New York, 1947), 19–20; July, *Verplanck,* 264; Bryant, *Orations and Addresses,* 243; Lee, *Discontent,* 251–53.
10. Century Association, *The Century,* 20; *Harper's Monthly Magazine,* 28 (1860), 708–09; George Haven Putnam, *A Memoir of George Palmer Putnam* (New York, 1903), II, 112; Strong, *Diary,* III, 392, IV, 279.
11. Frederick S. Cozzens to Verplanck, Verplanck Papers, N.Y.H.S.; The Century Association, *The Bryant Festival* (New York, 1865); Rev. H.N. Powers, "To William Cullen Bryant...1864," Bancroft Papers, Mass. Hist. Sed.
12. Dewey, *Sedgwick,* 389–92; John W. Clark and Thomas W. Hughes, *The Life and Letters of the Reverend Adam Sedgwick* (Cambridge, England, 1890), II, 370 and n.; Bryant to Mrs. Bryant, 10 Aug. 1864, G–R.
13. *Ibid.,;* Brummer, *Political History,* 377; William E. Smith, *The Francis Preston Blair Family in Politics* (New York, 1933), 262.

14. Gideon Welles, *Diary*, H. K. Beale, ed. (New York, 1960), 186–87; Smith, *Blair*, 280, 286; Edward L. Pierce, *Memoir and Letters of Charles Sumner* (Boston, 1893), IV, 196–97 and n.
15. Brummer, *Political History*, 427, 439; Nevins, *Post*, 313; G, *B.*, II, 223.
16. *E.P.*, 25 July 1863, 17 Nov. 1864, 6 March 1865.
17. Bryant, *Prose Writings*, I, 266–67; *E.P.*, 4, 11, 19, 25, 30 Aug., 25 Oct. 1853, 14 April 1857.
18. G, *B.*, II, 177, 201, 241; *E.P.*, 24 Jan. 1862, 2 Jan., 20 Feb., 2 Dec. 1862, 13 May 1865.
19. *Ibid.*, 19 Oct., 7 Nov., 4 Dec. 1866; Homer A. Stebbins, *A Political History of the State of New York, 1865–1869* (New York, 1913), 42.
20. *Ibid.*, 256 and n.; Pierce, *Summer*, IV, 251–52; Nevins, *Post*, 328–30; *E.P.*, 7 Feb. 1837, 19 Oct. 1860; 2 , 17 May 1865, 18 Oct., 7, 25 Nov. 1866; Bryant to Mrs. Waterson, n.d., G–R.
21. G, *B.*, II, 245–319; Theodore Hornberger, ed., *William Cullen Bryant and Isaac Henderson* (Austin, Texas, 1950), 27; Emerson, *Letters*, V, 453; Bryant to William Dean Howells, 9 Oct. 1873, Houghton Library, Harvard; Bryant to Samuel D. Chase, 13, 23 June 1868, to Christiana Gibson, Sept. 1868, G–R.
22. G, *B.*, II, 357, 374; *E.P.*, 13 Jan. 1875.
23. Simms, *Letters*, I, xciv; Nevins, *Post*, 407–09; Charles I. Glicksberg, "Letters of William Cullen Bryant from Florida," *Florida Historical Society Quarterly*, 13 (1934), 264–65; G, *B.*, II, 360; Bryant to Hamilton Fish, 19 Nov. 1873, Fish Papers, Library of Congress.
24. *E.P.*, 6, 12 Feb., 1, 6 March 1875.
25. Parke Godwin, *The Movement of Public Opinion and Its Relation to Existing Controversy* (New York, 1877), 5–6, 16, 18; *Commemorative Essays*, 41; *E.P.*, 22 Feb., 22 Oct., 1875, 12 , 21 March 1877, 24 April 1879.
26. *E.P.*, 10 March 1857, 17 Nov. 1864, 21 March 1877; Parke Godwin, "Our Political Degeneracy—Its Cause and Remedy," *Putnam's Magazine*, n.s., 6 (1870), 599; Charles Nordhoff, *The Cotton States in the Spring and Summer of 1875* (New York, 1876), 9–25.
27. Godwin, *Commemorative Essays*, 223; *E.P.*, 22 Oct., 24 Nov., 1875, 21 March 1877.

CHAPTER 18

1. *E.P.*, 1 July 1875; George Cary Eggleston, *Recollections of A Varied Life* (New York, 1910), 187–88.
2. Bryant, *Prose Writings*, II, 226; Rufus Peet to Bryant, 4 Dec. 1870, Bryant to Peet, 14 Dec. 1870, G–R.
3. Hornberger, *Bryant and Henderson*, iii–v, 29ff; Nevins, *Post*, 353, 426–30; Godwin to Bryant, 31 July 1865, Jan.–Feb. 1870 (draft), 26 Jan. 1870, B–G.
4. Hornberger, *Bryant and Henderson*, iii–iv; Dennis Tilden Lynch, *The Wild*

Seventies (New York, 1941), 32, 36; Nevins., *Post,* 385, 432; Godwin, *Political Degeneracy,* 600.

5. Earle D. Ross, *The Liberal Republican Movement* (New York, 1919), 89–90, 95, 109, 112–13 and n., 126; D.S. Alexander, *A Political History of New York, 1774–1882* (New York, 1906–1909), III, 282, 286; Nevins, *Post,* 344–45; Bryant to Charles Nordhoff, 6 June 1870, David A. Welles Papers, Library of Congress.

6. Lynch, *Wild Seventies,* 220; Ross, *Liberal Republicans,* 123.

7. Carl Schurz, *Speeches, Correspondence, and Political Papers,* Frederic Bancroft, ed. (New York, 1913), III, 228, 231, 307, 313; Parke Godwin, *Reform and Better Times* (New York, 1876), 16–17, 20–21; "The Result at Cincinnati," letter to the *Evening Post, Godwiniana,* N.Y.P.L.; *Political Degeneracy,* 598–600; *Movement of Public Opinion,* 5, 8.

8. Flick, *Tilden,* 320; Bigelow, *Restrospections,* IV, 280.

9. G., B., II, 359–60, 374–77; Bryant to John Bigelow, 12 Aug. 1876, to Christiana Gibson, 25 Nov., 1876; G–R; *E.P.,* 1 Nov. 1880.

10. Bigelow, *Retrospections,* IV, 281; Nevins, *Post,* 403.

11. G., B., II, 212, 365; Bryant, *Prose Writings,* II, 243, 246, 249, 294, 329, 333; *E.P.,* 2 , 4 Jan. 1875.

12. *E.P.,* 1 July, 1875; *Prose Writings,* II, 253; Chester M. Destler, *American Radicalism, 1865–1901* (New London, Conn., 1946), 5.

13. Bryant, *Prose Writings,* II, 248–51; Bryant to Rowland Johnson, 19 Jan. 1868, G–R; *E.P.,* 27 March 1877.

14. Godwin, *Out of the Past,* 229–31 and n., 250; *E.P.,* 7 Jan., 11 March, 15, 24 April 1879, 1, 18 Nov. 2, 16, Dec. 1880; Parke Godwin, "Commercial Diplomacy," in M. Menier, *et. al., France and the United States* (New York, 1878), 8–9, 11.

15. Nevins, *Post,* 439–40; Bigelow, *Retrospections,* V, 315–16, 368, 370; Godwin, memorandum, June 1881, B–G; Sidney Fine, *Laissez Faire and the General-Welfare State* (Ann Arbor, Mich., 1956), 51.

CHAPTER 19

1. Bryant, *Prose Writings,* I, 423.

2. *Ibid.,* 416–22; New York *World,* 5 July, 1867.

3. Bryant, *Prose Writings,* I, 430; G, B, II, 135, 137, 290–91.

4. *Ibid.,* II, 216–17, 388, 391; C.S. Johnson, *Politics and A Bellyfull, the Journalistic Career of William Cullen Bryant* (New York, 1962), 144; McDowell, *Ancestry,* 408; Bryant to R.H. Dana, 1 Sept. 1872, G–R.

5. Eggleston, *Recollections,* 195, 199, 214–17; Laura Stedman and George M. Gould, *Life and Letters of Edmund Clarence Stedman* (New York, 1910), II, 455–56.

6. G, B., II, 226, 395–96, 401; Brown, *Bryant,* 36n; McLean, 63; Frederick W. Conner, *Cosmic Optimism* (Gainsville, Fla., 1949), 172, 174; Charles I. Glicksberg, "William Cullen Bryant and Nineteenth Century Science,"

New England Quarterly, 23 (1950), 91–96; Bryant, *Prose Writings,* II, 291–93, 300.

7. G, B., II, 402–09.
8. Bigelow, *Restrospections,* V, 375; *In Memory of William Cullen Bryant* (New York, 1878).
9. Eggleston *Recollections,* 287–92; Baker, *Godwin,* 228.
10. *Ibid.,* 229–30; Eggleston, *Recollections,* 229–30, 281–84, 295; Eugene Benson, "Parke Godwin and the Evening Post," *The Galaxy,* 7 (1869), 230–35; *The Nation* (1900), 274; alse see *Godwiniana,* N.Y.P.L.
11. Notes for a speech on the death of President Garfield, B–G.

BIBLIOGRAPHY

BRYANT

For Bryant's unpublished correspondence I have depended chiefly on the Goddard–Roslyn Collection (microfilm), the Bryant–Godwin Papers, and the Berg Collection, all at the New York Public Library, and on scattered collections at the Houghton Library at Harvard. See H. E. Spivy, "Manuscript Resources for the Study of William Cullen Bryant," Bibliographical Society of America, *Papers* 44 (1950): 254–68; also see below, Biographical and Critical Studies.

Much of Bryant's prose is in the form of unsigned editorials in the New York *Evening Post*. A written list, prepared by Parke Godwin, of Bryant's editorials for the periods June 1829 to 13 Nov. 1844 and Jan. to April 1861, can be found in the Bryant–Godwin Papers. Allan Nevins, *The Evening Post* (New York and London, 1922), identifies other editorials on the basis of internal and external evidence. I have followed the same procedure.

I have used the following works by Bryant:

"An Autobiography." In Parke Godwin, *A Biography of William Cullen Bryant*. 2 vols. New York, 1883.

The Embargo (1808). A Facsimile Reproduction with an Introduction by Thomas O. Mabbott. Gainesville, Fla.: Scholars' Facsimiles & Reprints, 1955.

Letters of A Traveller. New York, 1871.

An Oration Delivered at Stockbridge, July 4th, 1820. Stockbridge, Mass., 1820.

Orations and Addresses. New York, 1873.

Poetical Works. Edited by Parke Godwin. 2 vols. New York, 1883.

A Popular History of the United States (with Sydney H. Gay). 4 vols. New York, 1876.

Prose Writings. Edited by Parke Godwin, 2 vols. New York, 1884.

Tales of Glauber-Spa (with C.M. Sedgwick, J.K. Paulding, et al.). New York, 1856.

BIOGRAPHICAL AND CRITICAL STUDIES:

Arms, George. *The Fields Were Green: A New View of Bryant, Whittier, Holmes, Lowell, and Longfellow*. Stanford, Calif., 1953.

Bernard, Edward G. "Northern Bryant and Southern Hayne," *The Colophon*, n.s. 1 (1936): 536–540.

Bigelow, John. *William Cullen Bryant,* Boston and New York, 1890.

Bryant, William Cullen, II. "The Genesis of Thanatopsis," *New England Quarterly* 21 (1948): 163–184.

———. "The Waterfowl in Retrospect," *New England Quarterly* 30 (1957): 181–189.

Birdsall, Richard D. "Bryant and Catherine Sedgwick—Their Debt to Berkshire," *New England Quarterly* 28 (1955): 349–371.

Drew, Helen L., ed. "Unpublished Letters of William Cullen Bryant," *New England Quarterly* 10 (1937): 346–355.

Eaten, Ernest R. "The Early Life of William Cullen Bryant," *Quarterly of Phi Alpha Gamma* (Dec. 1933).

———. "William Cullen Bryant, Hemeepathist, 1794–1878," *Quarterly of Phi Alpha Gamma* (Feb. 1934).

Feorster, Norman. "Nature in Bryant's Poetry," *South Atlantic Quarterly* 17 (1918): 10–17.

Glicksberg, Charles I. "Bryant and Fanny Wright," *American Literature* 6 (1935): 427–432.

———. "Bryant , the Poet of Humor," *Americana* 29 (1935): 364–374.

———. "Bryant and The United States Review," *New England Quarterly* 7 (1934): 687–701.

———. "Cooper & Bryant: A Literary Friendship," *The Colophon,* pt. 20 (1934).

———, ed. "Letters by William Cullen Bryant," *Americana* 33 (1939): 23–41.

———, ed. "Letters of William Cullen Bryant from Florida," *Florida Historical Society Quarterly* 13 (1934): 255–274.

———. "New Contributions in Prose by William Cullen Bryant," *Americana* 30 (1936): 573–592.

———. "William Cullen Bryant and Communism," *Modern Monthly* 7 (1934): 353–359.

———. "William Cullen Bryant and Nineteenth Century Science," *New England Quarterly* 23 (1950): 91–96.

———. "William Cullen Bryant: A Reinterpretation," *Revue Anglo-Americaine* (1934), 495–503.

Godwin, Parke. *A Biography of William Cullen Bryant.* 2 vols. New York, 1883.

Guilds, John C. "Bryant and the South: A New Letter to Simms," *Georgia Historical Quarterly* 37 (1953): 142–146.

Hornberger, Theodore, ed. *William Cullen Bryant and Isaac Henderson: New Evidence on a Strange Partnership.* Austin, Texas, 1950.

Hoyt, William D., Jr., ed. "Some Unpublished Bryant Correspondence," *New York History* 21 (1940): 63–70, 193–204.

Hudson, William P. "Archibald Alison and William Cullen Bryant." *American Literature* 12 (1940): 59–68.

Huntress, Keith, and Lorch, Fred W., eds. "Bryant and Illinois: Further Letters of the Poet's Family," *New England Quarterly* 16 (1943): 634–647.

In Memory of William Cullen Bryant. New York, 1878.

Johnson, C.S. *Politics and A Bellyfull, the Journalistic Career of William Cullen Bryant.* New York, 1962.

Leonard, William E. "Bryant and the Minor Poets," *The Cambridge History of American Literature.* 3 vols. New York, 1947.

McDowell, Tremaine. "The Ancestry of William Cullen Bryant," *Americana* 22 (1928): 408–420.

———. "Bryant and *The North American Review.*" *American Literature* 1 (1929–1930.): 14–26.

———. "Cullen Bryant at Williams College," *New England Quarterly* 1 (1928): 443–466.

———. "Cullen Bryant Prepares for College," *South Atlantic Quarterly* 30 (1931): 125–133.

———. "The Juvenile Verse of William Cullen Bryant" *Studies in Philology* 26 (1929): 96–108.

———. *William Cullen Bryant: Representative Selections.* New York, 1935.

McLean, Albert F., Jr. *William Cullen Bryant.* New York, 1964.

Murray, Donald M. "Dr. Peter Bryant: Preceptor in Poetry to William Cullen Bryant." *New England Quarterly* 33 (1960): 513–522.

Peckham, Harry H. *Gotham Yankee: A Biography of William Cullen Bryant.* New York, 1950.

Ringe, Donald A. "Kindred Spirits: Bryant and Cole," *American Quarterly* 6 (1954): 233–244.

———. "William Cullen Bryant and the Science of Geology." *American Literature* 26 (1954–55): 507–514.

Sanford, Charles L. "The Concept of the Sublime in the Works of Thomas Cole and William Cullen Bryant," *American Literature* 28 (1956–57): 434–448.

Waterston, Robert C. *Tribute to William Cullen Bryant.* Boston, 1878.

Wilson, James G. *Bryant and His Friends.* New York, 1886.

COOPER

Most of Cooper's letters have been published in:

Cooper, James Fenimore. *Correspondence.* Edited by J. F. Cooper. 2 vols. New Haven, Conn., 1922.

———. *Letters and Journals.* Edited by James Franklin Beard. 4 vols. Cambridge, Mass., 1960 and 1964.

WORKS BY COOPER:

The American Democrat. New York, 19456.

Autobiography of a Pocket-Handkerchief. Chapel Hill, N.C., 1949.

The Chainbearer. "Edition de Luxe," C.C. Brainard Publishing Co., New York and Boston, n.d.

The Crater. Cambridge, Mass., 1962.

Home as Found. New York, 1903.

Homeward Bound. New York, 1903.

A Letter to His Countrymen. New York, 1834.
The Monikins. Mohawk edition, New York, n.d.
Notions of the Americans. 2 vols., New York, 1963.
The Pioneers. New York, 1958.
Satanstoe. "Edition de Luxe," C.C. Brainard Publishing Co., New York and Boston, n.d.
The Spy: A Tale of the Neutral Ground. New York, 1849 and 1960.
The Ways of the Hour. New York, 1903.

BIOGRAPHICAL AND CRITICAL STUDIES:

Adkins, Nelson F. "James Fenimore Cooper and the Bread and Cheese Club." *Modern Language Notes* 47 (1932): 71–79.
Bewley, Marius. "Fenimore Cooper and the Economic Age," *American Literature* 26 (1954–55): 166–195.
Boynton, Henry Walcott. *James Fenimore Cooper.* New York, 1931.
Grossman, James. *James Fenimore Cooper.* n.p., 1949.
Memorial of James Fenimore Cooper. New York, 1852.
Meyers, Marvin. *The Jacksonian Persuasion.* Stanford, Calif., 1957: Chapter 4.
New York Historical Association *James Fenimore Cooper: A Re-Appraisal.* Cooperstown, N.Y., 1954.
Outland, Ethel R. *The "Effingham" Libels on Cooper.* Madison, Wis., 1929.
Ross, John F. *The Social Criticism of Fenimore Cooper.* Berkeley, Calif., 1933.
Shulenberger, Arvid. *Cooper's Theory of Fiction: His Prefaces and Their Relation to His Novels.* Lawrence, Kansas, 1955.
Spiller, Robert E. "Fenimore Cooper's Defense of Slave-Owning America." *American Historical Review* 35 (1930): 575-582.
———. *Fenimore Cooper: Critic of His Times.* New York, 1931.
———, ed. "Fenimore Cooper: Critic of His Times, New Letters from Rome and Paris, 1830–31." *American Literature* 1 (1929–30): 131–148.
———. "Fenimore Cooper and Lafayette: Friends of Polish Freedom, 1830–1832." *American Literature* 7 (1935–36): 56–75.
Waples, Dorothy. *The Whig Myth of James Fenimore Cooper.* New Haven, Conn., 1938.

GODWIN

For Godwin's unpublished correspondence I depended on the Goddard-Roslyn Collection (microfilm) and the Bryant–Godwin Papers, New York Public Library.

Godwin's editorials in the *Evening Post* prior to 1878 can be identified tentatively by their style and content; he was chief editor between 1878 and 1881. He wrote the editorials for *The Pathfinder* 1 (1843) and the articles initialled "P.G." for *The Harbinger* 2–8 (1845–49); he became editor of *The Harbinger* in 1847.

WORKS BY GODWIN:

Commemorative Addresses. New York, 1895.
"Commercial Diplomacy," in M. Menier, et al., *France and the United States.*
New York, 1878.
Democracy, Constructive and Pacific,. New York, 1844.
The Movement of Political Opinion and Its Relations to Existing Controversy.
New York, 1877.
"Our Political Degeneracy—Its Cause and Remedy." *Putnam's Magazine*
n.s., 6 (1870): 596–605.
Out of the Past. New York, 1870.
Political Essays. New York, 1856.
A Popular View of the Doctrines of Charles Fourier,. New York, 1844.
"Parke Godwin's Letter" 18 July 1876), *Reform and Better Times,* Democratic
party, Doc. no. 2, 1876: 15–32.
Vala, A Mythological Tale. New York, 1851.

BIOGRAPHICAL AND CRITICAL STUDIES:

Baker, Carlos. "Parke Godwin, Pathfinder in Politics and Journalism,."
Willard Thorp, ed., *The Lives of Eighteen from Princeton.* Princeton, N.J.,
1946.
Benson, Eugene. "Parke Godwin, of the Evening Post." *The Galaxy*
7 (1869): 230–236.
Godwiniana, scrapbook, New York Public Library.
Hoskins, John P. "Parke Godwin and the Translation of Zschokke's Tales,"
PMLA 20 (1905): 265–295.

LEGGETT

For a list of Leggett's writings and editorials see Page S. Proctor, Jr., "William
Leggett (1801–1839): Journalist and Literator," Bibliographical Society of
America, *Papers* 44 (1950): 239–253.

WORKS BY LEGGETT:

Naval Stories. New York, 1834.
Political Writings. Edited by Theodore Sedgwick, Jr. 2 vols. New York,
1840.
Tales and Sketches by a Country Schoolmaster. New York, 1829.

BIOGRAPHICAL AND CRITICAL STUDIES:

Bryant, William Cullen. "William Leggett," *United States Magazine and
Democratic Review* 6 (1839): 17–28.
Glicksberg, Charles I. "William Leggett, Neglected Figure of American
Literary History," *Journalism Quarterly* 25 (1948): 52–58.

Hofstadter, Richard. "William Leggett, Spokesman of Jacksonian Democracy," *Political Science Quarterly* 58 (1943): 581–594.

Meyers, Marvin. *The Jacksonian Persuasion.* Stanford, Calif., 1957: Chapter 9.

Sedgwick, Theodore, Jr. "William Leggett." *The Biographical Annual.* New York, 1841: 150–155.

Westcott, Allan. "William Leggett," *Dictionary of American Biography,* XI, 147–148.

THE SEDGWICKS

For Sedgwick letters, I have used the Sedgwick Papers at the Massachusetts Historical Society; there is also some miscellaneous manuscript material at the New York Historical Society.

Printed letters can be found in Charles Sedgwick, *Letters to His Family and Friends,* edited by Catherine M. Sedgwick (Boston, 1870) and especially Mary E. Dewey, *Life and Letters of Catherine M. Sedgwick* (New York, 1871). Theodore Sedgwick, Jr., was editor of *Harper's Weekly* I (1857).

WORKS BY THE SEDGWICKS:

Sedgwick, Catherine M. *Clarence; or a Tale of Our Own Times.* 2 vols. Philadelphia, 1830.

———. *Home.* Boston and New York, 1837.

———. *The Linwoods; or, "Sixty Years Since" in America.* 2 vols. New York, 1835.

———. *Married or Single?* 2 vols. New York, 1857.

———. *Means and Ends, or Self-Training.* Boston, 1839.

———. *The Poor Rich Man and the Rich Poor Man.* New York, 1843.

———. *Redwood; A Tale.* New York, 1824.

[Sedgwick, Henry Dwight]. "An Appeal for Justice to the Poor," by "A Friend of the Poor," Philadelphia *Banner of the Constitution,* 1830–31. 46 articles.

———. *English Practice: A Statement Showing Some of the Evils and Absurdities of the Practice of English Common Law.* New York, 1822.

———. *The Practicability of the Abolition of Slavery.* New York, 1831.

———. "On an Anniversary Discourse ... By William Sampson," *North American Review* 19 (1824): 411–439.

———. *A Vindication of the Conduct and Character of Henry D. Sedgwick.* New York, 1826.

Sedgwick, Robert and Duer John. *An Examination of the Controversy between the Greek Deputies and Two Mercantile Houses of New-York.* New York, 1826.

Sedgwick, Robert. *An Oration Delivered before the Washington Benevolent Society.* New York, 1811.

Sedgwick, Theodore [II]. *Hints to My Countrymen.* New York, 1826.

———. *Public and Private Economy.* 3 vols. New York, 1836–39.

Sedgwick, Theodore, Jr. [III]. *Address before the Alumni Association of Columbia College.* New York, 1858.

———. *The American Citizen: His True Position, Character and Duties.* New York, 1847.

———. *How Shall the Lawyers Be Paid?* New York, 1840.

———. *A Memoir of the Life of William Livingston.* New York, 1833.

———. *A Statement of Facts in Relation to the Delays and Arrears of Business in the Court of Chancery of the State of New-York.* New York, 1838.

———. *A Treatise on the Rules Which Govern the Interpretation and Application of Statutory and Constitutional Law.* New York, 1857; 2nd ed., 1874.

———. "Veto." Articles for the New York *Evening Post,* 1834–35, 1838, and 1843–44.

———. *What Is a Monopoly? or Some Considerations upon the subject of Corporations and Currency.* New York, 1835.

BIOGRAPHICAL STUDIES:

Brooks, Gladys. *Three Wise Virgins.* New York, 1957.

[Bryant, William Cullen]. An article on Henry Dwight Sedgwick, *United States Magazine and Democratic Review* 7 (1840): 148–149.

———. "Theodore Sedgwick." *The Biographical Annual.* New York, 1841.

Obituary of Theodore Sedgwick, Jr. *Harper's Weekly* 31 December 1859, 834.

Sedgwick, Henry D. "The Sedgwicks of Berkshire," *Collections of the Berkshire Historical and Scientific Society* (1900). 91–106.

Welsh, Sister Mary Michael. *Catherine Maria Sedgwick: Her Position in the Literature and Thought of Her Time up to 1860.* Washington, D.C., 1937.

VERPLANCK

The only sizable collection of Verplanck correspondence is at the New-York Historical Society. Some of his letters can also be found in the Berg Collections, New York Public Library.

WORKS BY VERPLANCK:

An Address Delivered at the Opening of the Tenth Exhibition of the American Academy of Fine Arts. New York, 1825.

The Advantages and Dangers of the American Scholar. New York, 1836.

Discourses and Addresses on Subjects of American History, Arts, and Literature. New York, 1833.

An Essay on the Doctrine of Contracts. New York, 1826.

The Influence of Moral Causes upon Opinion, Science, and Literature. New Yor, 1834.

A Letter to Col. Drayton...in Assertion of the Constitutional Power of Congress to Impose Protecting Duties. New York, 1831.

Letter to the Hon. Saml. L. Mitchell, M.D....On the Danger of Putting Money into the U. States' and Manhattan Banks ... By Abimelech Coody, esq. New York, 1811.

An Oration Delivered July 4, 1809...before the Washington Benevolent Society. New York, 1809.

"Report of Mr.Verplanck from the Committee of Finance," in [John Duer], *Vindication of the Public Faith of New York & Pennsylvania.* London, 1840.

The Right Moral Influence and Use of Liberal Studies. New York, 1833.

Speech...on the Several Bills and Resolutions for the...Reform of the Judiciary System. New York, 1839.

The State Triumvirate, A Political Tale. New York, 1819.

BIOGRAPHICAL STUDIES:

Bryant, William Cullen. "Gulian Crommelin Verplanck." *Prose Writings* I: 394–431.

Century Club. *Proceedings...in Honor of the Memory of Gulian C. Verplanck.* New York, 1870.

Hart, Charles H. *A Discourse on the Life and Services of the Late Gulian Crommelin Verplanck.* New York, 1870.

Harvey, Sara King. *Gulian Crommelin Verplanck.* Chicago, 1936.

July, Robert W. *The Essential New Yorker: Gulian Crommelin Verplanck.* Durham, N.C., 1951.

GENERAL WORKS

I have depended for manuscript material on scattered collections at the Massachusetts Historical Society, the New-York Historical Society, the New York Public Library, and the Library of Congress.

NEWSPAPERS, PERIODICALS, AND GOVERNMENT DOCUMENTS:

The American Quarterly Review (Philadelphia).
The Atlantic Magazine (1824–25).
The Atlantic Monthly.
Harper's Monthly.
[Hunt's] *Merchants Magazine and Commercial Review.*
The Nation.
New York *Commercial Advertiser.*
New York *Morning Courier.*
The New-York Review, and Atheneum Magazine.
Constitution of the State of New York Adopted November 3, 1847. Albany, 1847.
New York State Senate. *Documents,* 61 sess. (1838). 2 vols.
———. *Journal,* 61–63 sess. (1838–40).
New York State Assembly. *Journal,* 44–45 sess. (1820–22).
Niles' Register.

United States Magazine and Democratic Review.
United States Review and Literary Gazette (1826–27).

BOOKS AND ARTICLES:

Adams, Henry. *History of the United States.* 9 vols. New York, 1921.

Adams, James Truslow. *New England in the Republic, 1776–1850.* Boston, 1926.

Albion, Robert G. "Commercial Fortunes in New York," *New York History* 16 (1935): 158–168.

―――. *The Rise of New York Port.* New York, 1939.

Alexander, D.S. *A Political History of New York, 1774–1882.* 3 vols. New York, 1906–09.

Anderson, J.M. "Romantic Democracy," *American Quarterly* 2 (1950): 251–258.

Auerbach, Joseph S. *The Bar of Other Days.* New York, 1940.

Ballard, Harlan H. "A Forgotten Fraternity," *Collections of the Berkshire Historical and Scientific Society* (1913): 279–298.

Barrus, Clara. *The Life and Letters of John Burroughs.* 2 vols. Boston and New York, 1925.

Bartlett, David W. *Modern Agitators.* New York and Auburn, N.Y., 1855.

Baylies, Francis. "Letters, 1827–1834." Massachusetts Historical Society, *Proceedings* 45 (1911–1912): 166–184.

Benson, Lee. *The Concept of Jacksonian Democracy.* Princeton, N.J., 1961.

Bernard, Edward G. "New Light on Lowell as Editor." *New England Quarterly* 10 (1937): 337–341.

Bigelow, John. *Retrospections of an Active Life.* 5 vols. Garden City, N.Y., 1913.

Birdsall, Richard D. *Berkshire County: A Cultural History.* New Haven, Conn., 1959.

Boas, George. *Romanticism in America.* Baltimore, 1940.

Bohman, George V. "A Poet's Mother: Sarah Snell Bryant in Illinois." Illinois State Historical Society *Journal* 33 (1940): 166–189.

Booth, Mary L. *History of the City of New York.* New York, 1866.

Branch, E. Douglas. *The Sentimental Years, 1836–1860.* New York, 1934.

Brevoort, Henry. *Letters...to Washington Irving.* Edited by G.S. Hellman. New York, 1918.

Briggs, James A. *An Authentic Account of Hon. Abraham Lincoln Being Invited to give an Address in Cooper Union.* Putnam, Conn., 1915.

Brooks, Van Wyck. *The Times of Melville and Whitman.* New York, 1947.

―――. *The World of Washington Irving.* Philadelphia, 1944.

Brown, E.R., ed. *Life and Poems of John Howard Bryant.* N.P., 1894.

Browne, Junius H. *The Great Metropolis, A Mirror of New York.* Hartford, Conn., 1869.

Brummer, Sidney D. *Political History of New York State during the Period of the Civil War.* New York, 1911.

Bryant, William Cullen; Todd, Rev. J., et al. *The Berkshire Jubilee*. Albany, 1845.

Burroughs, John. *The Heart of Burroughs's Journals*. Edited by Clara Barrus, ed. Boston and New York, 1928.

Byrdsall, F. *The History of the Loco-Foco or Equal Rights Party*. New York, 1842.

Cady, Edwin H. *The Gentleman in America: A Literary Study in American Culture*. Syracuse, N.Y., 1949.

Carlton, Frank T. "The Workingmen's Party of New York," *Political Science Quarterly* 22 (1907): 401–415.

Carman, Harry J., and Reinhard H. Luthin. *Lincoln and the Patronage*. New York, 1943.

Century Association. *The Bryant Festival*. New York, 1865.

——. *The Century, 1847–1946*. New York, 1957.

Charvat, William. *The Origins of American Critical Thought, 1810–1835*. Philadelphia, 1936.

Chase, Salmon P. "Diary and Correspondence," American Historical Association, *Annual Report* (1903).

Clapp, Margaret. *Forgotten First Citizen: John Bigelow*. Boston, 1947.

Clark, John W. and Thomas W. Hughes. *The Life and Letters of the Reverend Adam Sedgwick*. 2 vols. Cambridge, England, 1890.

Conner, Frederick W. *Cosmic Optimism*. Gainesville, Fla., 1949.

Conrad, Alfred H., and John R. Meyer. "The Economics of Slavery in the Ante-Bellum South." *Journal of Political Economy* 66 (1958): 93–130.

Crandall, Andrew W. *The Early History of the Republican Party*. Boston, 1930.

Crowe, Charles R. "This Unnatural Union of Philansteries and Transcendentalists," *Journal of the History of Ideas* 20 (1959): 495–502.

Curti, Merle E. "Young America," *American Historical Review* 32 (1926–27): 34–55.

Curtis, Francis. *The Republican Party . . . 1854–1904*. 2 vols. New York, 1904.

Destler, Chester M. *American Radicalism, 1865–1901*. New London, Conn., 1946.

Donald, David. *Charles Sumner and the Coming of the Civil War*. New York, 1960.

Donovan, Herbert D.A. *The Barnburners*. New York, 1925.

Dorfman, Joseph. *The Economic Mind in American Civilization, 1606–1865*. 2 vols. New York, 1946.

——. "The Jackson Wage-Earner Thesis." *American Historical Review* 54 (1948–49): 296–306.

—— and R.G. Tugwell. *Early American Policy: Six Columbia Contributors*. New York, 1960.

Dunalp, William. *Diary*. 3 vols. New York, 1929–30.

Eggleston, George Cary. *Recollections of a Varied Life*. New York, 1910.

Ekirch, Arthur A., Jr. *The Idea of Progress in America, 1815–1860*. New York, 1944.

Ellis, David M. *Landlords and Farmers in the Hudson-Mohawk Region, 1790-1850*. Ithaca, N.Y., 1946.

———. "The Yankee Invasion of New York, 1783-1850." *New York History* 32 (1951): 3-17.

Emerson, Ralph Waldo. *The Heart of Emerson's Journal*. Edited by Bliss Perry, Boston and New York, 1926.

———. *Letters*. Edited by Ralph L. Rusk, 6 vols. New York, 1939.

Federal Writers Project. *The Berkshire Hills*. New York and London, 1939.

Ferre, Walter L. "The New York Democracy: Division and Reunion, 1847-1852." Ph.D. dissertation, University of Pennsylvania, 1953.

Field, Rev. David Dudley, ed. *A History of the County of Berkshire*. Pittsfield, Mass., 1829.

Field, David Dudley. *Speeches, Arguments, and Miscellaneous Papers*. Edited by A.P. Sprague. 3 vols. New York, 1884-90.

Field, Henry M. *The Life of David Dudley Field*. New York, 1898.

Fine, Sidney. *Laissez Faire and the General-Welfare State*. Ann Arbor, Mich., 1956.

Flick, Alexander C. *Samuel Jones Tilden*. New York, 1939.

Floan, Howard R. *The South in Northern Eyes, 1831 to 1861*. Austin, Texas, 1958.

Flory, Claude R. *Economic Criticism in American Fiction, 1792-1900*. Philadelphia, 1936.

Foerster, Norman. *Nature in American Literature*. New York. 1923.

Foner, Philip S. *Business and Slavery*. Chapel Hill, H.C., 1941.

Foster, Frank H. *A Genetic History of the New England Theology*. Chicago, 1907.

Fox, Dixon Ryan. *The Decline of Aristocracy in the Politics of New York*. New York, 1919.

———. *Yankees and Yorkers*. New York, 1940.

Francis, John W. *Old New York*. New York, 1848.

Frederick, John T. "American Literary Nationalism: The Process of Definition, 1825-1850." *The Review of Politics* 21 (1959): 224-238.

Frothingham, Octavius B. *George Ripley*. Boston, 1882.

Gammon, Samuel R. *The Presidential Campaign of 1832*. Baltimore, 1922.

Garraty, John A. *Silas Wright*. New York, 1949.

Ghodes, Clarence L.F. *The Periodicals of American Transcendentalism*. Durham, N.C., 1931.

Gourlie, John H. *The Origin and History of "The Century"*. New York, 1856.

Greeley, Horace. *Recollections of a Busy Life*. New York, 1868.

Hamilton, Thomas. *Men and Manners in America*. 2 vols. London, 1833.

Hammond, Bray. "Free Banks and Corporations: The New York Free Banking Act of 1838." *Journal of Political Economy* 44 (1936): 184-209.

Hammond, Bray. *Banks and Politics in America, from the Revolutions to the Civil War*. Princeton, N.J., 1957.

Hammond, Jabez D. *The History of Political Parties in the State of New-York.* 3 vols. Albany and Syracuse, 1842, 1848.

Harper, J. Henry. *The House of Harper.* New York, 1912.

Harris, Sheldon H. "John Louis O'Sullivan and the Election of 1844 in New York." *New York History* 41 (1960): 278–298.

Hart, Albert Bushnell, ed. *Commonwealth History of Massachusetts.* 5 vols. New York, 1927–30.

Haswell, Charles H. *Reminiscences of an Octogenarian.* New York, 1896.

Higham, John W. "The Changing Loyalties of William Gilmore Simms." *Journal of Southern History* 9 (1943): 210–233.

Hone, Philip. *Diary... 1828-1851.* Edited by Allan Nevins, 2 vols. New York, 1927.

Hudson, Frederic. *Journalism in the United States, from 1690-1872.* New York, 1873.

Hugins, Walter. *Jacksonian Democracy and the Working Class.* Stanford, Calif., 1960.

Hussey, Christopher. *The Picturesque: Studies in a Point of View.* London and New York, 1927.

Huth, Hans. *Nature and the Americans: Three Centuries of Changing Attitudes.* Berkeley, Calif., 1957.

Jenkins, John S. *The Life of Silas Wright.* Auburn, N.Y., 1847.

Jones, Howard Munford. *Ideas in America.* Cambridge, Mass., 1944.

Kass, Alvin. *Politics in New York, 1800-1830.* Syracuse, N.Y., 1965.

King, Charles. *Progress of the City of New-York during the Last Fifty Years.* New York, 1852.

LaBudde, K.J. "The Rural Earth: Sylvan Bliss." *American Quarterly* 10 (1958): 142–153.

Lee, Brother Basil. *Discontent in New York City., 1861-1865.* Washington, D.C., 1943.

Levermore, Charles H. "The Rise of Metropolitan Journalism, 1800–1840." *American Historical Review* 6 (1900–01): 446–465.

Lewis, R.W.B. *The American Adam: Innocence, Tragedy and Tradition in the Nineteenth Century,* Chicago, 1955.

Livermore, Shaw, Jr. *The Twilight of Federalism.* Princeton, N.J., 1962.

Lynch, Dennis Tilden. *The Wild Seventies.* New York, 1941.

Mabee, Carleton. *The American Leonardo: A Life of Samuel F.B. Morse.* New York, 1943.

Mabie, Hamilton W. *The Writers of Knickerbocker New York.* New York, 1912.

Mackenzie, William L. *The Life and Times of Martin Van Buren.* Boston, 1846.

Marckwardt, A. H. "The Chronology and Personel of the Bread and Cheese Club." *American Literature* 6 (1934–35): 389–399.

Marx, Lee. "The Machine in the Garden." *New England Quarterly* 29 (1956) 24–42.

McGrane, Reginald C. *The Panic of 1837*. Chicago, 1924.

McMaster, John Bach. *A History of the United States from the Revolution to the Civil War*. 8 vols. New York, 1918–19.

Merrian, John C. *The Garment of God: Influence of Nature in Human Experience*. New York, 1943.

Miller, H. Elmer. *Sketches and Directory of the Town of Cummington*. West Cummington, Mass., 1881.

Miller, Perry, ed. *The Legal Mind in America*. Garden City, N.Y., 1962.

Mitchell, Stewart. *Horatio Seymour of New York*. Cambridge, Mass., 1938.

Moody, Richard. *Edwin Forrest*. New York, 1960.

Morse, Samuel F.B. *Letters and Journals*. Edited by Edward L. Morse, 2 vols. Boston and New York, 1914.

Mott, Frank L. *A History of American Magazines, 1741-1850*. New York and London, 1930.

————. *A History of American Magazines, 1850-1865*. Cambridge, Maas., 1957.

————. *American Journalism...1690 to 1950*. New York, 1950.

Nevins, Allan. *The Emergence of Lincoln*. 2 vols. New York, 1950.

————. *The Evening Post*. New York, 1922.

————. *Hamilton Fish: The Inner History of the Grant Administration*. New York, 1936.

————. *Ordeal of the Union*. 2 vols. New York, 1947.

Nichols, Roy F. *The Democratic Machine, 1850-1854*. New York, 1923.

Nordhoff, Charles. *The Communistic Societies of the United States*. New York, 1875.

————. *The Cotton States in the Spring and Summer of 1875*. New York, 1876.

Noyes, John Humphrey. *History of American Socialisms*. New York, 1961.

Osgood, Rev. Samuel. *New York in the Nineteenth Century*. New York, 1867.

Pattee, Fred L. *The Feminine Fifties*. New York, 1940.

Paul, James C.N. *Rift in the Democracy*. Philadelphia, 1951.

Paulding, James K. *Letters*. Edited by Ralph M. Aderman, Madison, Wis., 1962.

Peckham, Morse. "Toward a Theory of Romanticism," *PMLA* 66 (1951): 5–23.

Pessen, Edward. *Jacksonian America*. Homewood, Ill., 1969.

————. ed. *New Perspectives on Jacksonian Parties and Politics*. Boston, 1969.

Pierce, Edward L. *Memoir and Letters of Charles Summer*. 4 vols. Boston, 1893.

Pierson, George W. *Tocqueville and Beaumont in America*. New York, 1938.

Porter, Kenneth W. *John Jacob Astor: Business Man*. 2 vols. Cambridge, Mass., 1931.

Porter, Kirk, compil. *National Party Platforms*. New York, 1924.

Pratt, Julius W. "The Origin of Manifest Destiny," *Americans Historical Review* 32 (1926–27): 795–798.

Proctor, L.B. *Lives of Eminent Lawyers and Statesmen of the State of New York.* 2 vols. New York, 1882.

Putnam, George Haven. *A Memoir of George Palmer Putnam.* 2 vols. New York, 1903.

Rawley, James A. *Edwin D. Morgan, 1811-1883.* New York, 1955.

Rayback, Joseph G. "Martin Van Buren's Break with James K. Polk: The Record," *New York History,* 36 (1955), 51-62.

Rezneck, Samuel. "The Influence of Depression upon American Opinion, 1857-1859." *Journal of Economic History* 2 (1942): 1-23.

———. "The Social History of an American Depression, 1837-1843." *American Historical Review* 40 (1934-35): 662-687.

Richardson, E.P. *Painting in America: The Story of 450 Years.* New York, 1956.

Ross, Earle D. *The Liberal Republican Movement.* New York, 1919.

Sands, Robert C. *Writings...in Prose and Verse.* 2 vols. New York, 1834.

Schlesinger, Arthur M., Jr. *The Age of Jackson.* Boston, 1945.

Schurz, Carl. *Speeches, Correspondence and Political Papers.* Edited by Frederic Bancroft. 6 vols. New York, 1913.

Scott, Henry W. *Distinguished American Lawyers.* New York, 1891.

Sedgwick, Sarah Cabot, and Marquand, Christina S. *Stockbridge, 1739-1939.* Great Barrington, Mass., 1939.

Sedgwick, William Ellery. "The Materials for an American Literature: A Critical Problem of the Early Nineteenth Century." *Harvard Studies and Notes in Philology and Literature* 17 (1935): 141-167.

Seward, William H. *Autobiography...from 1801 to 1834. With a Memoir of His Life and Selections from His Letters, 1831-1846.* Edited by F.W. Seward, 2 vols. New York, 1891.

Simms, William Gilmore. *Letters.* 5 vols. Columbia, S.C., 1952.

Smith, Alfred G. *Economic Readjustment of an Old Cotton State: South Carolina, 1820-1860.* Columbia, S.C., 1958.

Smith, Henry Nash. *Virgin Land: The American West as Symbol and Myth* New York, 1959.

Smith, Theodore C. *The Liberty and Free Soil Parties in the Northwest.* New York, 1897.

Smith, William E. *The Francis Preston Blair Family in Politics.* New York, 1933.

Sotheran, Charles. *Horace Greeley and Other Pioneers of American Socialism.* New York, 1915.

Sowers, Don C. *The Financial History of New York State from 1789 to 1912.* New York, 1914.

Spencer, Benjamin T. *The Quest for Nationality: An American Literary Campaign.* Syracuse, N.Y., 1957.

Stafford, John. *The Literary Criticism of "Young America": A Study in the Relationship of Politics and Literature, 1837-1850.* Berkeley and Los Angles, 1952.

Stanton, Henry B. *Random Recollections*. New York, 1886.

Stanwood, Edward. *American Tariff Controversies in the Nineteenth Century*. 2 vols. Boston and New York, 1903.

Stebbins, Homer A. *A Political History of the State of New York, 1865-1869*. New York, 1913.

Stedman, Laura, and Gould, George M. *Life and Letters of Edmund Clarence Stedman*. 2 vols. New York, 1910.

Still, Bayrd. *Mirror for Gotham*. New York, 1956.

State, William L. *History of New York City*. New York, 1872.

Streeter, Robert E. "Association Psychology and Literary Nationalism in the *North American Review*, 1815-1825." *American Literature* 17 (1945–46): 242–254.

Strong, Augustus H. *American Poets and Their Theology*. Philadelphia, 1916.

Strong, George Templeton. *Diary*. Edited by Allan Nevins, 4 vols. New York, 1952.

Taylor, Charles J. *History of Great Barrington*. Great Barrington, Mass., 1882.

Trent, William P. *William Gilmore Simms*. Boston and New York, 1892.

Trimble, William. "Diverging Tendencies in New York Democracy in the Period of the Locofocos," *American Historical Review* 24 (1918-19): 396–421.

———. "The Social Philosophy of Loco-Foco Democracy." *American Journal of Sociology* 26 (1920–21): 705–715.

Trollope, Frances. *Domestic Manners of the Americans*. New York, 1949.

Turner, Lorenzo Dow. "Anti-Slavery Sentiment in American Literature." *Journal of Negro History* 14 (1929): 371–492.

Van Deusen, Glyndon G. *Horace Greeley, Nineteenth Century Crusader*. Philadelphia, 1953.

Wallace, David D. *South Carolina: A Short History, 1520-1948*. Chapel, Hill, N.C., 1951.

Ward, Julius H. *The Life and Letters of James Gates Percival*. Boston, 1886.

Waterman, William R. *Frances Wright*. New York, 1924.

Welles, Gideon. *Diary*. Edited by H.K. Beale, 2 vols. New York, 1960.

Wellman, Gordon B. "Samuel Hopkins, Rational Calvinist and Mystic," *Review of Religion* 3 (1938–39): 265–275.

Wilson, James G. *Life and Letters of Fitz-Green Halleck*. New York, 1869.

Wiltse, Charles. *John C. Calhoun: Sectionalist, 1840-1850*. Indianapolis and New York, 1951.

INDEX

Names of central characters are printed in caps and small caps

village society (real and ideal), 3–5, 23,
27–28, 101, 106–7, 109, 124
Whig party, 112, 126, 170–71, 178–79,
184–85
workingmen, 49–50
Bryant, William Cullen, referred to, 31,
32, 65–66, 68, 73, 92, 102, 121, 136, 146–
47, 181, 191, 209, 215, 217
Buchanan, James, 182–83, 191
Burmeister, Hermann, 195
Burnham, Michael, 77
Burr, Aaron, 16

C

Calhoun, John C., 51, 172, 175
Calvinism, 1, 6
Cambridge, Massachusetts, 8–9
Cambridge Law School, 73
Canals, 126–27, 171. See also Erie Canal
Capitalism (capitalist), 72, 90, 93, 102, 108
130, 137, 146–49, 154, 175, 217–18. See
also spirit of enterprise
Capital punishment, 142
Carter, James C., 21
Cass, Lewis, 168–69
Catskills, 95
Century Club, 133, 191–92, 212
Chainbearer, The, 83, 134–35
Channing, William Ellery, 5–6, 145
Chase, Salmon P., 185, 197
Chatham Street chapel, 157
Chenango Telegraph, 116
"Cherubs, The," 81
Church of All Souls, 213
City, the (urban world), 15–17, 28, 48,
82–85, 91, 123–24, 139, 143–44, 150, 213.
See also Bryant and Cooper on —
Civil rights, 199
Civil Rights Act of 1875, 198
Civil service, 128
Civil War, 22, 162, 181, 193, 195, 203, 205–
6, 211, 219
Clarence, 86, 88
Class harmony, 74, 111
Class warfare, 68, 147
Clay, Henry, 44, 51, 53, 161, 184
Clinton, De Witt, 16, 37, 39, 56
Cole, Thomas, 10, 15, 22, 95, 138, 211
Coleman, Mrs. William, 62, 78
Coleman, William, 21, 24, 41–42, 56
Colonization, 156–57
Columbia College, 15–16, 24, 42, 73
Commerce, 13–15, 42, 47–48
Commercial Advertiser, 54, 114, 213
Common Council (New York), 38, 130
Communist Manifesto, 109, 148
Community, 69, 83, 85, 106–7, 109–14,

147–49, 154. *See also* village society
Compromise of 1850, 170–72
Confederacy, 189–90, 193–94
Conkling, Roscoe, 205
"Conspiracy theory," 189
Conservatives. See Hunkers
Constitution, 47, 196
Constitution of 1846 (New York), 127–29
Constitution (Washington), 183
"Coodies," 39
Coody, Abimelech, 38–39
Cooper Club (Bread and Cheese), 18, 133
COOPER, JAMES FENIMORE:
early career, 17–18
personality, 17, 81, 116, 120
novelist, 17, 19–20, 36, 80–81, 84, 120,
133, 140
financial affairs, 32–33, 81, 97, 133
compared with:
William Cullen Bryant, 20–21, 112,
134, 137, 139
Catherine M. Sedgwick, 85, 91
Gulian C. Verplanck, 91, 134, 217
Europe and return, 21, 79, 82–83, 115–16
relationships with:
William Cullen Bryant, 17, 84, 119,
140
Sedgwick family, 32–33
social critic, 17, 20, 80–83, 115, 134–40,
217
social ideals, 35–36, 83, 110, 112, 115,
134, 139. *See also* Cooper and the
landed gentleman
isolation, 133–34, 139–40
despair, 138–39
death, 140–41
COOPER, JAMES FENIMORE and:
anti-rent war, 135
Christianity, 138
the city, 13, 82–85, 87, 133, 139
Cooperstown, 83, 116, 133, 135
the courts, 116, 119, 121, 136, 138–39
Federalist party, 35, 39, 110
free-trade liberalism, 137, 217
human nature, 36, 134
Andrew Jackson, 36–37, 84, 119
Thomas Jefferson, 35–36
the landed gentleman, 35–36, 83–85,
114, 116, 118, 121, 134–35, 139, 217
law of libel, 116, 119–21
literary nationalism, 19–21, 80
materialism, 81–84, 90, 137
Negroes, 156
newspapers, 80, 84, 115–21, 137–38
politicians, 117–18, 136–38
politics, 35–37, 84, 90, 135–36, 138
public opinion, 114, 116–21, 134–37